Gili Kugler
When God Wanted to Destroy the Chosen People

Beihefte zur Zeitschrift für die alttestamentliche Wissenschaft

Edited by
John Barton, Reinhard G. Kratz, Nathan MacDonald,
Carol A. Newsom, and Markus Witte

Volume 515

Gili Kugler

When God Wanted to Destroy the Chosen People

Biblical Traditions and Theology on the Move

DE GRUYTER

ISBN 978-3-11-060582-2
e-ISBN (PDF) 978-3-11-060990-5
e-ISBN (EPUB) 978-3-11-060950-9
ISSN 0934-2575

Library of Congress Control Number: 2019930906

Bibliographic information published by the Deutsche Nationalbibliothek
The Deutsche Nationalbibliothek lists this publication in the Deutsche Nationalbibliografie;
detailed bibliografic data are available on the Internet at http://dnb.dnb.de

© 2019 Walter de Gruyter GmbH, Berlin/Boston
Typesetting: Integra Software Services Pvt. Ltd.
Printing and binding: CPI books GmbH, Leck

www.degruyter.com

MIX
Papier aus verantwor-
tungsvollen Quellen
FSC® C083411

Acknowledgements

This book first emerged at the National Library in Jerusalem, and was completed at a university office in the southern hemisphere in Sydney. As in the ancient world, a transition of location, culture, politics, and language does not put to an end, and sometimes further accelerates, preoccupations with questions of identity in and affiliation to the broader society. Often, this engagement is shadowed by doubts about continuity and uncertainty, stemming from a recognition of the temporary quality of human nature and the fragility of national being.

While the survival of a community in the ancient world and in the present is not always guaranteed, various actions by the community's own individuals may have calmed emerging existential fears. In a similar way, epistemological challenges may be transcended through the contribution of individuals who help in mitigating difficulties swarming beneath certainty. The research presented in this book has been blessed with the help of such surrounding individuals.

My partner in life, Oren Thaler, has often alerted me to blind spots and helped me navigate intersections along the way. Our children, Omri, Tamara and Amos, who were born and dragged into this journey, patiently (mostly) and inspirationally accompanied it, crawling, hopping and long-distance running.

Many others accompanied me throughout the stages of research and writing. My thanks to my doctoral supervisor, Shimon Gesundheit, who instilled in me the appreciation of wording and articulation as an access to any great ideas. My beloved friends and teachers at the *Revivim Program* at the Hebrew University have exposed me to the colourful dimensions of textual ideologies and interests, beliefs and *realpolitik*, narrators and authors, traditions and criticism: Dodani Orstav, Ruth Kara-Ivanov Kaniel, Tzahi Weiss, Sari Shimborsky, Itamar Tas, Matan Barak, Roni Magidov, Havi Levine, Ayala Paz and others. My gratitude to Richie Cohen, for constant support and good advice at critical crossroads in the academic maze.

My thanks also to my companions from the National Library in Jerusalem and the University benches, who showed interest in the research, read, responded, and advised: David Frankel, Marc Brettler, Dalit Rom-Shiloni, Eli Assis, Yisca Zimran, Naama Cohen-Hanegbi, Noam Mizrachi, Jonathan Rubin, Misgav Har-Peled. My great gratitude to Jonathan Ben-Dov and Itamar Kislev for providing profound and careful comments on the book in its early incarnation.

My new academic base, the University of Sydney, took me in for my first steps as a researcher and lecturer. The students' enthusiasm and engagement in class and after hours have helped me further develop and articulate the book's arguments. My close colleagues at the Department have supported me in pursuing the writing: Avril Alba, Michael Abrahams-Sprod, Yona Gilead, and particularly

https://doi.org/10.1515/9783110609905-201

Ian Young, who is always willing to hold the ongoing rush to have a glimpse at an academic work in process. Rachelle Gilmour, my Aussie friend, has read, commented and advised.

I thank the School of Languages and Cultures at the University of Sydney for providing academic and financial support, on a regular basis and at a critical stage of producing the book. I thank the Editorial Board of the *BZAW* series for assessing, accepting and preparing the Manuscript for publication.

Last, dear and kind, Lucy Davey, a friend and a teacher, who has accompanied the book in every step of its English version: read, corrected and spotted any misplaced letter in English, Hebrew or Greek. This book could not have happened without her.

The book is dedicated to my parents, Ruth and Aharon Kugler, who taught me, in their gentle and non-direct way, to challenge the obvious.

Gili Kugler
Sydney, November 2018

Contents

1 Introduction

1.1 To annihilate a chosen nation

The fear of extermination has accompanied the Jewish nation from its beginning. The statement in the medieval Passover Haggadah that "in each and every generation they rise up against us to destroy us" has been resonating in the Jewish consciousness for centuries.[1] This book focuses on the earliest recorded expressions of the collective fear of national destruction, embedded in the theology of the Hebrew Bible.

Biblical stories, prophecies and historiography record crises that have threatened the existence of the people of Israel since their beginning. Whether these distresses come from political or natural circumstances, they are manifestly considered as expressions of God's will or of the legal and retributional relationship with him. This theodicial perception reflects the ancients' search for coherence and logic in life while rejecting arbitrary explanations for difficulties and sufferings. Together with that, this view reveals the belief in divine providence in the world, especially among those who are considered God's followers.

A radical expression of the retributional paradigm is found in the stories about God's plan to bring an end to the existence of Israel. The scenario of annihilating a whole nation is not impossible in the eyes of the biblical narrators, who ascribe to God a reputation as a destroyer of nations and communities. The book of Genesis describes God's extermination of humankind almost in its entirety only a few generations after creating them (Genesis 6–8), and the total destruction of the sinful inhabitants of two cities soon after the rehabilitation of humanity (Genesis 19). The book of Joshua describes God's assistance in defeating and destroying the former nations of Canaan (Joshua 6–11), and the book of Samuel presents the slaughter of the entire people of Amalek in compliance with divine instruction (1 Samuel 15). The people of Israel manage to avoid this destiny but not to escape its threat. In the first period of their life as a nation, after surviving Pharaoh's attempts to destroy them, yet prior to the beginning of their own campaign to destroy other nations, the Israelites find themselves in danger of annihilation by their own God.

The image of God as a threat to the people stands in dialectic relationship with the belief of the people as God's protégé, manifested throughout all traditions in the Pentateuch (Torah). The Priestly text in the Pentateuch presents

---

1 The phrase is part of the "Ve-He She-Amda" section, known from early Amoraic and medieval versions of the Haggadah.

https://doi.org/10.1515/9783110609905-001

God's connection with the people as a statement by God promising an "...everlasting covenant, to be God to you and to your offspring after you" (Gen 17:7). Non-Priestly material in the Pentateuch defines the people as God's "treasured possession out of all the peoples" and "a priestly kingdom and a holy nation" (Exod 19:5–6). The Deuteronomic source identifies God's choice of the people with his strong affection for them:

> 6 For you are a people holy to the LORD your God; the LORD your God has chosen you out of all the peoples on earth to be his people, his treasured possession. 7 It was not because you were more numerous than any other people that the LORD set his heart on you and chose you – for you were the fewest of all peoples. 8 It was because the LORD loved you and kept the oath that he swore to your ancestors, that the LORD has brought you out with a mighty hand, and redeemed you from the house of slavery, from the hand of Pharaoh king of Egypt (Deut 7:6–8)

The belief in the status of Israel as chosen accompanies not only traditions in the Pentateuch but also stands as fundamental to the words of the prophets. Hosea likens the relationship between God and Israel to the union of man and his wife: "And I will take you for my wife forever; I will take you for my wife in righteousness and in justice, in steadfast love, and in mercy. I will take you for my wife in faithfulness; and you shall know the LORD" (Hos 2:19–20). Jeremiah equates the closeness of God with Israel to the relationship of father and son: "Is Ephraim my dear son? Is he the child I delight in? As often as I speak against him, I still remember him. Therefore I am deeply moved for him; I will surely have mercy on him, says the LORD" (Jer 31:20). Amos speaks about God's strict supervision of the people due to the special privileges he granted to them, as a teacher who puts the burden of proof on his preferred disciple: "You only have I known of all the families of the earth; therefore I will punish you for all your iniquities" (Amos 3:2).

The idea of the chosen status of Israel which occurs constantly in the biblical traditions is bound to form part in any discussion about the fate of Israel. Alongside the idea of the people's selection by God and their being protected by him, the people do not appear to be immune to danger that derives from the same power, their divine overseer. This is an expression of a central tenet in the monotheistic belief: the power that provides the foundations of life is at the same time the source of its annihilation (cf. Isa 45:7). Thus the source of the strength of Israel is at the same time the means of their extinction.

This view about the complex situation of Israel is demonstrated in God's rebuke delivered by Ezekiel against the elders of Israel in Ezekiel 20. The rebuke begins with a reference to the moment when God had chosen the people and swore "to the offspring of the house of Jacob" to be "the Lord your God" (Ezek 20:5). It ends with a recollection of God's consistent desire to pour out his wrath upon the people to make an end of them (vv. 8, 13. 21). Similarly, Psalm 106 describes the people as God's "chosen" (Ps 106:5), who were saved on occasion thanks to that status (vv. 8, 10), but also as people who were at risk of being destroyed by their God (v. 23). Similarly, Deuteronomy 9 points to God's oath and commitment to the patriarchs (Deut 9:5), followed by a determination to kill the people and replace them (v. 14), a decision only nullified thanks to Moses' appeal on that occasion (vv. 18–19, 25–29. Cf. 2Kgs 13:23).

These passages reveal the authors' questions about the boundaries of their national existence, as well as about the nature of their relationship with God. Thus, the texts reflect thoughts about the people's accountability for their own choices, and their capability to affect their destiny. By portraying the danger in association with their own deeds the writers point out the autoimmune danger of the people and their responsibility for their fate, rather than blaming random external factors. In a paraphrase of the words of Amos cited above (Amos 3:2), being chosen does not reduce God's expectations of the people. In fact, it makes his supervision of them more stringent, and requires them to prove their eligibility for such a favored status.

The engagement with questions of existence and annihilation was part of an ongoing exploration of self-definition and self-determination among ancient Israelites over a long period of time and in changing circumstances. The theme of God's threats of destruction has not yet been discussed comprehensively in research, whether through the stories in the Pentateuch, or in regard to biblical rewritings that reflect on these narratives. An engagement with this motif, it is hoped, may provide a fresh glimpse into the intellectual and theological world of the biblical scribes.

1.2 Danger in the desert: The scope of the stories

In the liminal space of the desert, where political and international matters play a less significant role, the people's encounter with their new and mighty God is on the agenda. This encounter seems to be part of an initiation of the people before moving to and settling in a habitable land and appointing a human as sovereign. According to the stories in the Pentateuch the initiation in the desert includes moments of distress and difficulty that could consolidate the national identity, but at the same time could lead to irreversible situations that threaten the very existence of the people.

The stories in the Pentateuch relate the rescue of the nation from God's destruction to two figures, Moses and Phinehas, who address God on behalf of the people. However, while the latter manages to subdue the wrath of God only after a considerable number of the people have already been stricken, Moses deals with the threats of destruction from the moment they are initiated. He comes to the rescue before any action is taken by God, immediately when it comes to his, Moses', attention.

The broader narrative of the Pentateuch, indeed, presents Moses as constantly compelled to defend the people or groups of them in facing God's wrath. In the words of the biblical scholar Yochanan Muffs: "The whole life of Moses was one long prayer to save the people of Israel from the strike of the Lord".[2] Similarly, Midrash Tanhuma reviews the time in the desert as a sequence of Moses' engagements for the sake of the people:

> "How many times do I [Moses] bother the king?" – Here, too, Moses has done much for Israel. They sinned with the Calf, and "Moses implored the LORD" (ויחל משה, Exod 32:11); with the "complainers" (מתאוננים), "and Moses prayed" (ויתפלל משה, Num 11:2); with the "spies" – "Moses said to the LORD, 'Then the Egyptians will hear...'" (Num 14:13). In the controversy involving Korah his hands were slack (he weakened), and he said: "[H]ow much can I trouble God?" Therefore (Num 16:4): "When Moses heard it, he fell on his face (Tanhuma, Korah 4)[3]

Among the events listed above two narratives relate the people stood in danger of actual annihilation by God. The first is the Golden Calf episode. God's determination to destroy the people is referred to Moses as both a suggestion and a decision: "Now let me alone, so that my wrath may burn hot against them and I may consume them; and of you I will make a great nation" (Exod 32:10). The second episode relates to the journey of the spies, when God informs Moses: "I will strike them with pestilence and disinherit them, and I will make of you a nation greater and mightier than they" (Num 14:12). The people's behavior in the two incidents supposedly ignites the wrath of God so much that it leads to his decision to annihilate the people and start a new era with Moses.

While the epic of the wilderness mentions other expressions of God's threat of destruction, the basic character of the other incidents differs from that of the Golden Calf and the spy stories. Thus, in the story of Korah (and Datan and Abiram) we hear of God's intention to consume the congregation: "Then the LORD spoke to Moses and to Aaron, saying: Separate yourselves from this congregation, so that I may consume them in a moment" (Num 16:20–21). But, as opposed to the common use of the word "congregation" (עדה) in the Priestly literature in the sense of the broader community (cf. Exod 38:25; Lev 8:3–5, 9:5, 10:6, 17; Num 1:16, 18, 14:1, 27), the word in the context of the Korah narrative refers to Korah's

---

2 Muffs 1984, 42.
3 My translation.

specific companions who demand the shattering of Moses and Aaron's hegemony (Num 16:5, 6, 11, 16, 19a).[4] Thus, the plan for destruction in the story cannot be regarded as a threat against the Israelites as a whole.

Another occurrence that raises the possibility of destruction by God appears in the Phinehas story mentioned above, which recounts the result of the people's interaction with Midianite or Moabite women. In this context, however, the danger is learned only in retrospect, from God's approval of Phinehas' deed: "Phinehas son of Eleazar, son of Aaron the priest, has turned back my wrath from the Israelites by manifesting such zeal among them on my behalf that in my jealousy I did not consume the Israelites" (Num 25:11). Thus, rather than an intention to indicate a threat of destruction against the people, the story essentially aims at presenting the power of the priest's symbolic-cultic action, suggesting that these actions have the power to appease God's jealousy, as with the role of the Levites and the priests in restraining God's wrath (Lev 10:6; Num 1:53, 17:11–14, 18:5).

In the Golden Calf and the spy stories, in contrast, Moses manages to prevent the verdict from the beginning, and in his arguments he deals directly with the essential willingness of God to eradicate the people. Indeed, the background of the two occasions is different; one story blames the people for deviation from the proper form of worship, and the other accuses them of doubting God's ability to conquer the land. Both stories, however, record a similar response from God, with the wish to eradicate the people, addressed to Moses: "Now let me alone, so that my wrath may burn hot against them and I may consume them..." (Exod 32:10); "I will strike them with pestilence and disinherit them..." (Num 14:12). Within this similarity, several elements are common and unique to these accounts, thus requiring specific examination of the two stories:

1. God expresses an explicit purpose to annihilate the people (Exod 32:9–10; Num 14:11–12).
2. God intends to replace the people with a new nation stemming from Moses (Exod 32:10; Num 14:12).
3. Moses ignores the offer addressed to him and presents a series of arguments to prevent God from realizing his plans (Exod 32:11–13; Num 14:13–19).
4. God is reconciled, and the destruction is prevented (Exod 32:14; Num 14:20).

Moses' role in the stories is crucial. His intercession eliminates the threat against the people and enables the continuation of their existence. By protecting the people from being killed he "stands in the breach" and embodies what the prophet

---

4 And cf. the use of "the congregation of Israel" in the story (v. 9) when referring to the whole nation.

Ezekiel would define as the virtue needed for the sake of the people, but never found: "And I sought for anyone among them who would repair the wall and stand in the breach before me on behalf of the land, so that I would not destroy it; but I found no one" (Ezek 22:30). Having this virtue, according to Ezekiel, is a sign of a true prophet, who differs from "the senseless prophets who follow their own spirit, and have seen nothing" (13:3). While these latter prophets promise peace (v. 10), they apparently have never managed to "go up into the breaches, or repair a wall for the house of Israel, so that it might stand in battle on the day of the LORD" (v. 5). Unlike these "senseless prophets", Moses is depicted as the prophet who protected the people from the divine wrath in the course of actual events.

Nevertheless, God's withdrawal of the punishment comes with different consequences in each story. The Calf story ends with a renewal of the covenant (Exod 34:1, 4, 28), whereas the spy story ends with the spies' death and a promise of an eventual death for the elders of the people in the desert (Num 14:22–23, 29, 32, 37). This disparity is part of a list of differences between the stories that can be a gateway to reveal their literary and historical-literary relationship. These relationships are further reflected and resonant in biblical historiography, and in prophecies and poetic texts that keep reviving and interpreting the myth of the nation.

1.3 Methodology

The similarity between the Golden Calf story and the story of the spies led rabbinic sages, as well as modern commentators, to read the two stories within a continuum.[5] The main evidence of the continuity of the two events was Moses' reference in the spy story to a former revelation of God's attributes (Num 14:17). In the words of Talmud Bavli:

> When Moses ascended on high, he found the Holy One, blessed is He, sitting and writing, "The Lord is slow to anger." He said to Him, "Towards the righteous?" The Holy One, blessed is He, answered him, "Even toward the wicked". He [Moses] said to Him "Let the wicked perish!". He said to him, "By your life, you will have need for this [patience for the wicked]. When Israel sinned at the calf and at the spies, Moses prayed before Him "slow to anger". The Holy One, blessed is He, replied to Him, Did you not tell me "toward the righteous"? He [Moses] responded, But did You not reply to me "Even toward the wicked"? (Bavli, Sanhedrin, 111a)

Unlike this interpretation that reads the events in the order recorded in the final form of the Hebrew Bible, our study endeavors to investigate the processes that

---

5 For modern readings see: Muffs 1984, 47–54; Widmer 2004, 7–8, 254–345.

developed the fixed texts found today. While the research here deals with numerous passages from varied biblical genres, its essential aim is relatively unified – to trace stages of literary formation in the text, and thus the scribes' motives and interpretive considerations. Thus, a prominent place will be given to a diachronic-based methodology, with the aim of revealing the literary and historical process of the texts in order to gain a better understanding of the background and the world-views of their authors and audience.

This approach has been commonly used by biblical scholars in the last two centuries and has featured prominently in analyses of the stories we deal with. Though most of this scholarly work shares similar basic philological and literary tools, the results of the various studies differ greatly and create a vast variety of theories and assumptions regarding the inquiry into the formation of the Bible.[6] Despite what might be called the youthfulness of the approach,[7] multiple proposals and studies have managed to succeed and fail, offer views and counteract them, find approval and lose it. The method has consistently undergone changes and transformations creating a great number of studies, where no one common answer to questions of dating and authority has been accepted.

While this variety reflects the dynamic character of research in the modern and postmodern eras, it also manifests the enigmatic nature of the material in hand and the limited capability of the method to remove vagueness from the mysteries of the ancient world. Any examination, as deep and intensive as it may be, cannot guarantee an assured identification of the stages of a text's formation, or provide an accurate account of the ideas and goals that motivated the writing. This is the power and purpose of research – to keep searching for answers as part of the desire to trace the truth, and more specifically, to better understand human life and human society.

Scholars' continuing endeavors to reach a clearer view of the hidden past are especially applicable in the case of the Bible, which is for many a source of inspiration or even a compass for life. Indeed, the Bible with its variety of voices and layers is revealed differently to each scholar, but they share the aspiration to reach some areas of agreement and bequeath them to coming generations. This current study too, being a furtherance of generations of inquiry, seeks to

---

6 For reviews of the methods and theories suggested over the last two centuries under the prism of a diachronic approach to the Hebrew Bible and to the Pentateuch in particular see: Van Seters 1999, 15–78; Nicholson 2002, 3–92; Berlin and Brettler 2004, 2096; Ska 2006, 127–164; Baden 2009, 45–98; Boorer 2010, 95–111; Brettler 2012, 3–20; Dozeman 2017, 33–133.

7 The diachronic method is "youthful" in relation to the length of the period in which people have been reading, interpreting, studying and finding inspiration in the Bible, from the time before the text was canonized to the modern era. On the artificial distinction between the period of Bible's design and the era of its interpretation see: Zakovitch 2008, 13–14, 79–80.

reveal more about the behind the scenes of the text and its formative processes. By conducting a historical-literary analysis this study pursues an understanding of some segments of the writers' evolving world.

1.3.1 Told by an omniscient narrator: Exodus 32 and Numbers 13–14

Chronicled in a literary sequence in the Pentateuch, the stories we deal with are first found in two occurrences of a form of direct narrative, related by an impersonal voice. This form differs from the literary occurrences of the events recounted in other texts, where they are mentioned either in a first-person narrative by one of the supposed protagonists in the events, or as part of a general review acknowledging a distance from the events.

Whereas the latter stories indicate the identity of the speakers or at least imply the settings of the rewriters, the narratives in impersonal voice found in Exodus 32 and Numbers 13–14 present the plot as it has been supposedly observed by an external figure who could draw a complete and objective picture of the event while allegedly having no subjective involvement in it. This is the omniscient narrator.

Who is the omniscient narrator of these stories? Who could recount occurrences that happened in public spheres, such as gatherings, worship and journeys of the people, alongside intimate incidents of private dialogues and the inner thoughts and feelings of the protagonists and the Divine? A critical engagement with the Bible moves the focus of these questions from the narrator to the author, transforming the discourse from the story to the narrative and to the writer's literary choices, directions and views. With that, the observation moves from the text's readers to the author's audience, once it is assumed that they too played a role in the writing process. To achieve an understanding of the authors' identity, however, the boundaries of their work should be traced. An archeological literary excavation is able to follow the narrative layers inside and within the stories. What is the right way of doing that?

The "classical" documentary hypothesis that tends to find separate narrative threads in the Pentateuch does not manage to restore coherent and unequivocal narratives in all texts. This is the case in the story of the Golden Calf, when it is read as part of the wider, complex account in Exodus 32–34. Such incoherence makes it difficult to reconstruct clear threads that belong to broader sources.[8] As for the spy story in Numbers 13–14, while researchers individually agree that

---

8 On the difficulty in tracing separate literary sources in the text see: Driver 1911, 346; Noth 1972, 31.

there are separate narrative threads and some patching in the text, there is major controversy about the time and stages of assembling the various components.[9]

As a reaction to the numerous suggestions of scholars regarding the Pentateuch, including the texts which we analyze, the research in the field has recently moved through trends to renounce the documentary hypothesis, while looking for other models to solve the riddle of the growth of the Pentateuch.[10] The background of this crisis may be understandable, but there is no necessity to throw the baby out with the bathwater by declaring that the defined textual distinctions have lost their validity. Thus, for example, in the material with which this current study deals, there is considerable validity in the distinction between "Priestly" and "Non-Priestly" sources in the stories of the Pentateuch.

The stories of our study will be examined separately from each other as well as in comparison to one another in an attempt to pin down linguistic, contextual and ideological considerations of the textual procedure. Such examinations may help to reveal a variety of beliefs and worldviews that are not apparent at first sight in the final form of the text. Nevertheless, the investigation will not be committed to one theory or another, but will rather consider them case by case. Thus, a philological and conceptual exploration of material might equally lead to an identification of textual units as belonging to specific literary sources, or to a classification of a bulk of independent fragments as later patches added to a primary core text.

As for the dating of these texts: as opposed to later biblical literature where their dating can be discussed with some historical evidence and thus with some confidence, the attempt to date texts from the Pentateuch involves many hypotheses and assumptions.[11] We will generally suggest a relative dating for passages from the Pentateuch, based on their wording and ideas, and in light of their broader composition and other biblical writings.

---

9 See for example: Gressmann 1913, 295–297; Coats 1968, 250–251; Noth 1972, 130; Budd 1984, 144; Frankel 2002, 153–154, 167; Wright 2014, 198, 200–202.

10 Such for example is Rendtorff's pioneering work that opposes the documentary hypothesis, suggesting it is preferable to work with minor identifiable units of text (Rendtorff 1990). For a summary of the attack on the documentary hypothesis and the new methods and models suggested for understanding the evolution of the Pentateuch see the work of: Levin 1993; Kratz 2000; Gertz 2002; Nicholson 2002, 95–131; Römer 2004, 289–307; Schmid 2006, 48–50.

11 For a broader discussion in this matter: Sommer 2011, 85–108; Gesundheit 2012, 6.

1.3.2 Allusive and partial narratives: Rewritings and intra-biblical exegeses

The stories of the days in the desert reappear in the Hebrew Bible in the form of restructured narratives, told from the point of view of the stories' protagonists providing reflection on the past. Such are the speeches of Moses in Numbers 32, Deuteronomy 1 and 9, the monologue of Caleb in Joshua 14 and God's rebuke in Ezekiel 20. Likewise, the stories appear within reviews addressed to later generations as a recollection of the predecessors' chronicles: the psalmists' memories in Psalms 78 and 106, the Levites' confession in Nehemiah 9 and again the divine rebuke in Ezekiel 20.

The multiple references to the events recorded in the Pentateuch indicate the centrality of the myths in various stages of the canonization of the Hebrew Bible, being part of the constant concern about the people's danger and resilience. Within this engagement, the use of images from the days in the desert changes due to the authors' requirements, reflecting the social and political context in which they worked.[12]

A critical reading of these texts will demonstrate the extent of the authors' influence on the process of rewriting and restructuring the known stories. The ways texts present interpretations and evaluations of the past, intentionally or unintentionally, help to uncover the setting, identity and needs of their writers.[13]

The writers' contributions can be first and foremost learned from the details that were chosen for recall as opposed to details that were only implied or not even mentioned. Among the texts that will be discussed here, some elaborate essential parts of the stories of the desert (Numbers 32; Deuteronomy 1, 9; Joshua 14), some only allude to the wrongdoing of the people (Psalm 106; Nehemiah 9), and the rest make no mention of the specific events that supposedly provided the background for the threat of destruction (Ezekiel 20; Psalm 78). Similarly, the motif of annihilation does not feature equally in the texts. While some of the reviews emphasize the danger that the people faced (Deuteronomy 9; Ezekiel 20;

---

12 For ways inner-biblical references indicate concerns with possible interests and motivations see: Fishbane 1985, 380–407; Zakovitch 1992, 9–10, 126–130; Idem. 1995, 11–15; Sommer 1998, 6–31; Idem. 2004, 1829–1835.

13 In this regard, see Brettler's study of the factors that influence the way historiography and Biblical historiography in particular has been shaped, thus the argument for the need to define notions such as "history", "ideology" and "literature" (Brettler 1995, 10–19). A "traditional" manifestation of the recognition of the contribution of later authors of the biblical texts is found in the statement in Midrash Shemot Rabbah: "Moses wrote hidden [things] in the Torah, David stood up and interpreted them" (15:22). It should be noted though that the statement does not describe David as a free interpreter, but rather as someone who discloses and explains the original intentions of the Scriptures, which were unknown.

Psalms 106), others allude to the risk that threatened the people by mentioning what did not happen (Psalm 78; Nehemiah 9), and others keep silent about the threat itself (Numbers 32; Deuteronomy 1, Joshua 14).

The extent of evolution of those images, however, depends on the sources with which the rewriters worked. In order to investigate the writers' unique touch on the myths and their motives in literary innovations, an identification of the raw material with which they worked is required. It is conceivable that the narratives conveyed from an omniscient perspective in the Pentateuch (Exodus 32 and Numbers 13–14) were not known in all their detail to all rewriters, and that the "rewritings" were not necessarily based on them. Moreover, it is possible that among the allusive and partial references of the rewritten texts one can trace earlier stages of the accounts, some of which preceded the compositional form of the current narratives in the Pentateuch.

1.4 Fear of destruction

This study delves into one of the strongest components in Jewish myth and Jewish identity: the consciousness of the danger of annihilation. The Hebrew Bible teaches that the question of existence and annihilation accompanied the process of forming the people's self-determination over a long period of time and in changing historical and cultural circumstances. These issues related to questions about the characterization of the people's relationship with God whether as a patron or as a source of threat. Moreover, the engagement with the matter of the potential destruction derived from questions about the people's ability and responsibility to influence their own destiny. Tracing the engagement with fears of extermination will not only help to better understand the ancient biblical society, but may also contribute to the development of today's humanity to replace the fear of annihilation with more vital moral action.

1.4 Fear of destruction

2 A superfluous threat of annihilation – God's reaction to the building of the Golden Calf: Exodus 32

The tradition that God threatens to annihilate the people of Israel appears in the Pentateuch's chronological sequence first in Exodus 32, in the narrative of the Golden Calf. We will examine the tradition in this context through a historical-literary prism which will assist in tracing the goals and functions of the tradition.

2.1 The Golden Calf episode: Not such a terrible sin after all

The narrative framework of the law-giving account in the book of Exodus indicates that three months after leaving the land of Egypt and forty-one days after the arrival at Mount Sinai the Israelites were threatened with destruction by their own God. This perilous moment was the result of the people's making a Golden Calf and worshiping it, violating by that the commandments that were supposedly introduced to them earlier in the journey. This blatant violation led to God's radical decision to annihilate the people.

Nevertheless, while this event is portrayed as a serious crisis in the relationship between the people and God, it plays no significant role in the broader account of the people's wandering in the desert. The event seems to have no effect either on the people's fate or on the destination of the journey and its route (cf. Num 14:22–23, 29–35). Apart from the sentence of death passed on a section of the people by the Levites (Exod 32:26–29) and a mention of God's plague sent upon the people (32:35), the crisis results in no consequences for the future of the nation and its leaders.

Moreover, the story contains no clarification of the essential sin of the people. While God's condemnation of the action accuses the people of being "quick to turn aside from the way that I commanded them" (v. 8), the story does not mention what the way was or what exact laws were violated by the people's actions.

When the 8th century prophet, Hosea, condemns the calf worship of the northern kingdom he criticizes it by confronting it with the principle of the sole sovereignty of God, alluding to the laws of the Decalogue: "And now they keep on sinning and make a cast image for themselves... People are kissing calves... Yet I have been the LORD your God ever since the land of Egypt; you know no God

https://doi.org/10.1515/9783110609905-002

but me, and besides me there is no savior" (Hos 13:2–4). In the story in Exodus, in contrast, even though its broader context recounts that the Decalogue had already been spoken to the people (Exod 19:25–20:1), the Golden Calf incident is not presented as a direct contravention of the commandments.

Thus, four principles of the Decalogue that seem to be violated in the story of the Calf are not pointed out explicitly. The first involves the people's request for an alternative god (Exod 32:1), a violation of the prohibition in the Decalogue to have no other god than YHWH (20:2–3).[1] The second is the making of an artificial image of God (32:4), which contradicts the prohibition against making a statue or "a form of anything" (פסל וכל תמונה, 20:4).[2] The third is the building of an altar to worship the Calf (32:5–6), which disobeys the instruction not to bow down to or worship an idol (20:5). And finally, the identification of the statue with the specific God of Israel, known through the past relationship with the people (32:4), disregards the prohibition against using the name of God לשוא (20:7), meaning, according to other biblical references, as a false identification (cf. Ezek 13:7; Ps 31:7).[3]

In fact, not only the people's behavior but also God's own words in the story violate the laws of the Decalogue. God adopts the people's proclamation about Moses bringing up the people "out of the land of Egypt" (Exod 32:7, cf. v. 1),

---

1 The Jewish medieval commentator Rashi, following Bavli, Sanhedrin 63a, refers to the peculiar plural form of the verb related to the word אלהים in the request from the people to Aaron. Whereas the noun אלהים in Hebrew is in plural form, the descriptors and verbs related to it can be in the singular, but in the people's request it is in the plural: "...make us a god/gods (אלהים) who shall go (ילכו [plural]) before us..." (Exod 32:1). Thus, Rashi deduces that the people "wished to have many gods" (Rashi on Exod 32:1; Rosenbaum and Silbermann 1965, 180).

2 According to Rabbi Judah Halevi this was the essential sin in the making of the Golden Calf. He argues that the people did intend to worship God but in a wrong way: "Their sin consisted in the manufacture of an image of a forbidden thing, and in attributing divine power to a creation of their own, something chosen by themselves without the guidance of God... This sin was not on a par with an entire lapse from all obedience to Him who had led them out of Egypt, as only one of His commands was violated by them. God had forbidden images, and in spite of this they made one" (Halevi 1927 [1139], 97). For further discussion about the distinction between a deliberate idolatry and an invalid worship of God see: Zimmerli 1950, 552–558; Breuer 1985, 233–224.

3 This opposes Rashi's interpretation, following Midrash Mekhilta and the Aramaic translation, that minimizes the commandment to a prohibition of the use of the name of God in a false oath, as if the commandment says: You shall not swear in vain by the name of the Lord, your God (Rashi on Exod 20:7; Rosenbaum and Silbermann 1930, 103). But the meaning of the commandment in its context seems to deal with wrong identifications of God, as opposed to the "true" attributes of God mentioned in the previous commandment (Exod 20:5–6). On this matter see: Childs 1974, 411; Carmichael 1985, 322–324.

contradicting by that the first declaration of the Ten Commandments that ascribes the act of the exodus to God alone (Exod 20:2).

The fact that the Golden Calf story lacks clear reference to the specific laws given in the supposed circumstances of the event makes it plausible that the Decalogue account was not taken into consideration in the first stages of the composition of the Calf story.[4] It is quite likely that the process of composition was actually reversed, namely that some of the commandments of the Decalogue were influenced by the Golden Calf episode and written in response to it.[5] This surmise can be supported by the multiple details in the Decalogue that seem redundant in light of the generic instruction of the first commandment (20:3) not to have other gods besides "the Lord your God" (v. 2). Thus, the prohibitions – not to make artificial gods (v. 4), not to bow down or worship them (v. 5) and not to make false identifications of God (v. 7) – are unnecessary in light of the first commandment that already prohibits any alternative to God (v. 3).[6]

In the literary context, however, the elaboration given in the Decalogue effectively anticipates the essential transgression of the people and Aaron in the Calf incident: not only did they seek an alternative to God (32:1; cf. 20:3) but they also replaced God with an image (32:4; cf. 20:4) and worshiped it (32:6; cf. 20:5), while falsely claiming it to be God (32:4–5; cf. 20:7). But when reading the story of the Golden Calf without the background of the specific prohibitions of the Decalogue, the severity of the incident diminishes. In fact, as we will see, traces in the story, as well as in other biblical references, reveal that in former stages of the evolution of the biblical text the idea of using a calf in worship ritual was legitimate. Moreover, in a certain phase, this legitimate ritual might have even been related to none other than the leader Moses.

---

4 This assertion can be supported by Wellhausen's suggestion about the late integration of the legal elements in the Sinaitic Covenant in Exodus 19–24 (Wellhausen 1886, 134), and by Tweig's argument that the description of the giving of the law in Exodus 19–20 was secondary in the work of composition (Tweig 1977, 102). See also the conclusions of Noth and Friedman regarding the supplementary account of the Ten Commandments within the narrative tradition of the Law-giving at Sinai: Noth 1962, 154–155; Friedman 2003, 153–154. This supposition weakens the argument that the Golden Calf story derives from the same writer of the Decalogue and the Covenant Code (Exodus 20–23), as part of the suggestion that three separate literary sources, J, E and P, have created the context of the covenant in Exodus 19–34 (cf. Driver 1911, 193–196; Kratz 1994, 217; Schwartz 2000(a), 258–259; Baden 2009, 157).
5 This idea was suggested by Carmichael, 1985, 318–324; Blum 2011, 295–296.
6 See Oswald's comment (2014, 182) that "it is difficult to understand why it is necessary to prohibit the worship of images when the very making of them is already prohibited".

2.2 Jeroboam's ancient role model: Moses

As known from Hosea's criticism mentioned above, the calf image played a prominent role in the Israelites' legacy. Amongst the several references to the image in the Bible, the Golden Calf story in Exodus 32 primarily corresponds with the account in 1 Kings 12 which describes King Jeroboam's building of two calves on behalf of the new kingdom of the north. Thus, the two accounts speak of golden statues of calves built by the people's leader, using the verb עשה (make) to describe the action (Exod 32:1, 4, 8, 35; 1Kgs 12:28, 34). In addition, both accounts mention an altar built next to the calves for sacrificial offerings, and a new festival (חג) established for the ritual (Exod 32:5–6; 1Kgs 12:32). Most significantly, the two accounts refer to the calves with almost identical wording, using a plural form, even though the Exodus account mentions only one calf: "Here/these are your gods, O Israel, who brought you up out of the land of Egypt" (אלה/ הנה אלהיך ישראל אשר העלוך מארץ מצרים, Exod 32:12; 1Kgs 12:28).[7]

What is the basis for the close relationship between the two episodes? The order of the accounts in the final form of the Bible supposedly suggests that the description of Jeroboam's actions in 1 Kings was based on the story of the Golden Calf in Exodus 32, and aimed to condemn the religious-political reform that took place in the northern kingdom. This suggestion can be indicated by the statement about the land of Egypt ("...who brought you up out of the land of Egypt", Exod 32:4; 1Kgs 12:28), which is better suited to the context of the Golden Calf episode, set in the time of the exodus, than to the context of Jeroboam's days.[8] But this assumption does not sufficiently engage with the core idea, reflected in the historiographical account, of the leader's genuine attempt to establish a legitimate alternative ritual in the northern kingdom.[9]

Another proposal would then suggest that the entire narrative of the Calf in Exodus was invented in order to stigmatize the customs performed in the northern kingdom. But it is difficult to assume that such an unfavorable description of Aaron and the people would be conceived solely for the sake of polemic. Rather, it is more probable that the calf ritual of the northern kingdom was initially a legitimate practice involving an image of a calf. Only later the image went through

---

7 See in comparison the description of the event in Neh 9:18, using a corrected singular form: זה אלוהיך אשר העלך ממצרים ("This is your God who brought you up out of Egypt"). With regard to the aim of the Golden Calf narrative in the reception of Nehemiah see below, chapter 6.

8 See Cassuto 1965, 285–286.

9 This problem arises regarding Grintz's argument (1976, 124–126) about Jeroboam's reform as a return to an ancient ritual tradition, while ignoring the problem that the reform supposedly adopts a custom that is considered wrong.

modifications until it emerged as a form of hostile criticism against the northern kingdom's rituals.

This assertion is supported by the widespread artifacts of calf images, used in both religious and cultural spheres, found in the region of ancient Israel.[10] Similarly, biblical references reflect the use of the calf image within recognized cultic practices (Gen 15:9; Jer 34:18; Ezek 1:7).[11] Scholars agree that as with the image of the flying "Cherubim", erected on the cover of the ark in the sanctuary (Exod 25:19–20) or in the innermost part of the temple (1Kgs 6:23–28), the calves were used as a pedestal for a divine revelation.[12] This suggests that the calves in the northern kingdom were erected as an attempt by the establishment to restore traditions from the people's ancient heritage, similar to the choice of Bethel and Dan as new-old worship centers (Gen 12:8, 31:13, 35:1; Josh 7:2; Judg 1:22, 18:26–29; 1Sam 7:16). The allusion to names and practices from the people's collective memory aided a smooth introduction to the new order.

Such an assumed positive version of the Calf story not only linked the custom of the northern kingdom with traditions from the past, but it might also have created a platform to associate the establisher of the northern kingdom, Jeroboam, with Moses, the mythical founder of the nation of Israel. This idea can be indicated from the broader portrayal of Jeroboam as "second Moses".[13] Thus, according to the historiographical account in 1 Kings, Jeroboam was chosen by God for the position (1Kgs 11:31) at a time when the people were required to build "storage towns" (ערי מסכנות, 1Kgs 9:15–19), similar to the circumstances of Moses' appointment in Egypt (Exod 1:11, 3:10). Furthermore, the narrative recounts that Jeroboam had to flee from a king who sought to kill him (1Kgs 11:40), as did Moses (Exod 2:15), and like Moses, Jeroboam reappeared after the king's death with demands addressed to the king's successor, expressing concern for the people

---

10 See: Fleming 1999, 23–27.
11 See also the Greek version of 1Kgs 10:19 which indicates the tradition that the throne in the Temple had a shape of a "calf in the back" (προτομαὶ μόσχων τῷ θρόνῳ), rather than "rounded shape in the back" (וראש עָגֹל [לכסה מאחריו) according to the MT version. While the two versions are based on the same Hebrew consonants עגל (עֵגֶל and עָגֹל), the MT, which was vocalized hundreds of years after the creation of the LXX version, seems to reflect an attempt to amend the troubling description.
12 See: Driver, 1911, 348; Eichrodt 1961, 115; Noth 1962, 247; Gray 1964, 290; Beyerlin 1965, 127; Aberbach and Smolar 1967, 135; Albright 1968, 197–98; Zakovitch 1991, 90–91; Cogan 2001, 383, 363; Shalom-Guy 1996, 25.
13 For this definition see Zakovitch 1991, 91. See Albertz's argument that the textual basis for the story of the northern tribes' revolt is inspired by the exodus narrative (Albertz 1994, 141–142). Berner opposes it with the claim that there is insufficient evidence to prove literary dependency between the texts (Berner 2017, 186).

(1Kgs 12:2–4. Cf. Exod 4:19, 5:1). Moreover, according to the story, Jeroboam's intervention at first added a heavier burden of work on the people (1Kgs 12:4), just as occurred in the narrative of Moses (Exod 5:6–9). But Jeroboam, like Moses, eventually managed to lead the people to liberation (1Kgs 11:28; Exod 14:31) and became the people's official leader (1Kgs 12:20; Exod 14:31). Within this biographical parallelism, the story of the Calf might have also played a role in connecting the two figures, as it is possible that at certain stages of the tradition it was Moses, and not Aaron, who was associated with the ritual.

This supposition can be supported by the residual detail in Judg 18:30 which mentions Moses as an ancestor of the priestly family who took on priestly ministry after setting up a carved image in Dan, one of the sites of the calf shrines.[14] This can be also deduced from the reference to Moses' role as the leader of the people's ritual of the bronze serpent in the desert (Num 21:8), which indeed, up to a certain point, was considered legitimate in Jerusalem (cf. 2Kgs 18:4).

Thus, a former manifestation of the Calf tradition might have ascribed to Moses, rather than to Aaron, a central part in the conduct of the ritual. Indeed, the Calf story in its final form presents vague and inconsistent allegations against Aaron, with no practical consequences for his part in the event. While the story mentions a clarifying exchange between Moses and Aaron (Exod 32:21–24), assigning to the latter responsibility for the event (vv. 25, 35), Aaron is exempt from both the massacre carried out by the Levites (vv. 26–29) and the verdict and punishment of the plague sent by God (v. 35).[15] Moreover, Aaron's name is missing from God's announcement to Moses about the occurrence at the foot of the mountain (vv. 7–10) as well as from the indictment of Moses in relation to the people's sin (vv. 31–32). In contrast to other stories that recount the drastic reaction to sinners who affect the whole congregation (cf. Num 25:6–15; Josh 7:11–26), Aaron is ultimately unharmed.

This blatant lacuna in the story was corrected in Deuteronomy 9 by relating Aaron's escape from punishment to Moses's intercession, stating: "The LORD was so angry with Aaron that he was ready to destroy him, but I interceded also on

---

14 Whereas in the LXX the name Moses is explicitly mentioned (and cf. modern English translations), in the MT the name Moses (Moshe) is disguised as Manasseh. The change is done by adding a small hanging letter (נ) to the name משה – מ׳שה, which reveals the endeavor of the recipients to abolish the association of Moses with the calf ritual without completely modifying the canonical work.

15 Aberbach and Smolar suggest that the narrator knew about Aaron's punishment but needed to suppress it to emphasize the people's guilt, as with the case of Aaron's complaint against Moses with Miriam (Numbers 12) where Aaron was supposedly exempted (Aberbach and Smolar 1967, 138). This suggestion, however, does not sufficiently explain the disjointed references to Aaron in Exodus 32.

behalf of Aaron at that same time" (Deut 9:20). The Deuteronomic writer explains the reason for Aaron's survival and resolves the discordant impression according to which there was no condign reaction to Aaron's deeds. This correction was indeed accepted by the scribes of 4Q paleo-Exod and the scribes of the Samaritan Torah: they added to the Exodus story a remark about God's determination to destroy Aaron followed by Moses' involvement on his behalf.[16] In the MT version of Exodus 32, however, the general inconsistency about Aaron's role reveals a stage when the tradition did not regard Aaron as the conductor of the event. This was before the stage in which the ritual was considered a violation of divine laws.

This early tradition not only preceded the creation of the Decalogue and the aforementioned criticism of Hosea (13:2–4), but also inspired the early representation of Jeroboam in the national story. Just as Moses was considered a legitimate leader of religious rituals, Jeroboam was to be remembered as a follower and reviver of an ancient tradition.

2.3 From Moses to Aaron: Denigrating Jeroboam

Jeroboam's association with Moses was changed as part of the Jerusalemite-Judaic polemic against the northern kingdom, an attack aimed to undermine Jeroboam and assert the supremacy of Jerusalem and the house of David. As part of this polemic, most northern kings were portrayed as wicked followers of Jeroboam the archetypal sinner (1Kgs 14:14, 15:30, 34, 16:2–3, 21:22; 2Kgs 3:3, 9:9, 10:29, 31, 13:2 and more). Thus, while originally the passage about the reform of Jeroboam in 1Kgs 12:25–33 was created on the basis of an acceptable northern tradition, the later polemic modified it to undermine Jeroboam, while asserting the supremacy of Jerusalem and the house of David (1Kgs 12:30, 33; cf. 13:33–34).[17]

A shift in the image of the northern ruler occurred alongside an amendment of the content and the message of the account of the Golden Calf in the desert. The account was changed from a description of an old legitimate cult conducted by the esteemed leader, Moses, to a sinful event led by a person of lesser importance, Aaron (Exod 32:1–6, 15–20, 21–24, 30–34), in such a way that his actions reflected negatively on Jeroboam.[18] Thus, a proclamation that identified the

---

16 See: Skehan 1955, 184; Tov 1985, 14.

17 See in this regard Gray 1964, 312; Cogan, 2001, 361–363. However, it is possible that the objection to the calf cult was due to a concern about an increasing identification of the calf with the abstract Divinity. See: Shalom-Guy 2006, 25.

18 Noth (1962, 245–244) suggests that Aaron already had a role in the original story in conducting the legitimate ritual, and that only later in the transmission of the story, he turned into a

Golden Calf with the Divine was ascribed to both Aaron (Exod 32:4) and Jeroboam (1Kgs 12:28).[19] Furthermore, the broader contexts of the stories provided shared details in the two men's biographies. The narrative about Jeroboam affirmed that both his sons, Nadab and Abijah (1Kgs 14:1, 15:25), died prematurely (1Kgs 14:17, 15:25–28), establishing a corresponding element with Aaron's sons, with the almost identical names, Nadab and Abihu (Exod 6:23, 24:1), who died a mysterious death while offering "alien fire" on the altar (Lev 10:2; Num 3:4).[20] In both cases, seemingly, the sons paid for the unpunished sins of the fathers.

Three other points relate to Jeroboam's stigmatized legacy. The first is the unique status of the Levites. Supposedly established by Moses in the Calf incident in the desert (Exod 32:26–29), they were rejected by Jeroboam (1Kgs 12:31). Secondly the name מסכה ("molten image") is judgementally used in the context of both events (Exod 32:4, 8; 1Kgs 14:9; 2Kgs 17:16), and finally the burning of the Calf and its altar occurs in both related accounts (Exod 32:20; 2Kgs 23:15).[21]

2.4 Back to the main question: The threat of annihilation

The assumptions about the compositional process of the Golden Calf episode can contribute to the investigation of the tradition in the story about the divine threat to destroy the people. This tradition, as we saw, had a minor impact on the broader narrative of the wandering in the desert. The understanding that the

---

sinner by remarks such as in 32:21–24, 35. Noth argues that this change occurred before Aaron was considered a Levite ancestor (4:14, 6:25; cf. 38:21; Num 3:6, 9). This suggestion may explain the silence about Aaron's Levitic roots while attributing to the Levites a significant role in the narrative (Exod 32:26–29; cf. 1Kgs 12:31).

19 See Berner's argument that the phrase stated in the Jeroboam context does not reflect "a reality beyond its literary context", but a reflection of a Deuteronomistic construct intended to express polemics against the religious policy of the north. According to his suggestion the phrase was interwoven in the current literary context with the intention "to reveal Jeroboam's outrageous political calculation", expressing "words of open revolt against the divine commandment" (Berner 2017, 187–188. See also Kratz 2005, 155). See in contrast Albertz' supposition that even though the broader narrative of 1Kgs 12:25–33 derives from an anti-northern polemic, the phrase about the calves in verse 28 reflects an actual ritual that accompanied the cultic image which "was presented to the assembled community in the temple of Bethel" (Albertz 1994, 144–145. See also Blum 2012, 43–44).

20 An indication of the puzzling nature of the death of Aaron's sons emerges through the numerous and varied suggestions of later Jewish interpretations, endeavoring to reveal the transgression of the sons. See Shenan 1979, 201–214; Kara-Ivanov Kaniel 2014, 585–653.

21 For additional similarities in the broader context of the traditions see: Aberbach and Smolar 1967, 134–129; Hayes 2004, 47; Shalom-Guy 2006, 16–19.

original story of the Golden Calf in the desert did not aim to present an act of disobedience by the people leads to a further assumption that the scene of God's threat of annihilation was not part of the narrative in the first place. And indeed, as we will see, the structural and literary discrepancies in the final form of the story indicate that the section about the near destruction was added to the text at a later stage, to ensure denigration of the incident.

2.5 A redundant dialogue

Exodus 32 opens with a brief mention of the human sphere, where the people are desperately waiting for Moses to descend from the mountain (v. 1). This exposition supposedly follows from the information about Moses' ascent to the mountain and his stay there for forty days and forty nights, as mentioned earlier in the sequence (24:12, 18; cf. 31:18).[22]

The story in Exodus 32 then moves to the heavenly sphere, recounting God's report to Moses about the earthly occurrence (vv. 7–9), followed by a proclamation of God's intention to annihilate the people and make a new nation out of Moses: "Now let me alone, so that my wrath may burn hot against them and I may consume them (ואכלם); and of you I will make a great nation" (v. 10).[23] The scene continues with Moses' plea to God to change his verdict against the people (vv. 11–13), followed by God's renunciation of his intention (v. 14).

Back in the earthly sphere, the story recounts Moses' descent to the people, carrying the two tablets of the covenant in his hands (v. 15). While not yet in the camp, Joshua, who is not mentioned earlier in the account, begins a dialogue with Moses, attempting to identify the source of the loud noise in the camp (vv. 17–18). This effort is surprising in light of the previous scene, in which God informs Moses about the people's actions (vv. 7–9). Even more surprising is Moses' furious reaction when he sees the people – dropping and breaking the tablets (v. 19). If he

---

22 Scholars who attribute Exodus 32 to the E-document (Elohistic) see the Calf story as a continuation of the remarks in chapters 24 and 31 about Moses' ascent of the mountain. See: Driver 1911, 255–256, 346–354; Beyerlin 1965, 16–18; Schwartz 1996, 114; idem. 2000(a), 258; Baden 2009, 160–163; Friedman 2003, 161, 173. See in contrast the argument that the remarks in chapters 24 and 31 were added only after finalizing the Calf story as a preparation for the later disappearance of Moses: Noth 1962, 199–200, 247; Childs 1974, 502; Aurelius 1988, 68.

23 The Hebrew root כלה (here: "consume") is commonly used as meaning "to destroy" and "to perish" in the prophetic books (Isa 1:28, 29:20, 31:3; Jer 16:4, 44:27; Ezek 5:12, 13:14). See more: Helfmeyer 1995, 160–162.

knew what was happening at the foot of the mountain, why was he surprised when he saw it and why only then did he break the tablets?

Furthermore, considering the previous dialogue with God, Moses' second appeal to God on behalf of the people later in the plot (vv. 31–32) seems unneeded. If due to Moses' intercession God has already forsaken his intention to punish the people without suggesting an alternative punishment (in v. 14), why does Moses need to ascend to God once more and beg forgiveness for the people (v. 30)?

This question was formulated by the medieval Jewish commentator, Ibn Ezra, in his exegesis to Exod 32:11: "…If God repented first, what reason was there for Moses to say, Peradventure, I shall make atonement for your sin (v. 30)?" In response, Ibn Ezra explains that the two dialogues between Moses and God are a duplicate version of one event – the appeal of Moses to God after Moses' own reaction to the people.[24] But the disparity between the two reported dialogues, and especially God's role in each one of them, makes it difficult to accept this explanation. Whereas the first dialogue is initiated by God, when he approaches Moses to tell him about the sin (vv. 7–8), the second interaction is Moses' own initiative in which he informs God about the event, as if God does not know about it: "Alas, this people has sinned a great sin; they have made for themselves gods of gold" (v. 31). This proclamation seems at odds with the earlier report given by God himself about the people's deeds (vv. 7–8).

Another medieval Jewish commentator, Nachmanides, disapproves of Ibn Ezra's suggestion, arguing that as reported, the two dialogues were part of Moses' intercession on behalf of the people before and after the descent from the mountain. At first, Moses hastens to prevent the destruction (vv. 11–13), and after attaining God's renunciation (v. 14) and punishing the people with his own efforts (vv. 20–29), he returns to God with a request to lessen the punishment planned for the people (vv. 31–32).[25] But this proposal is also difficult to reconcile

---

24 Strickman and Silver 1996, 667. Ibn Ezra's assertion stands in harmony with the information presented in Deuteronomy 9, which mentions only one appeal by Moses to God (Deut 9:25–29), after the descent from the mountain and the breaking of the tablets (vv. 13–21). On the nature of the connection between Exodus 32 and Deuteronomy 9 see below, 5.3.4.

25 "But I do not agree with this [Ibn Ezra's] opinion… if it is all one prayer which Moses said during the forty days after he returned to the mountain, why does Scripture divide it, mentioning here [in vv. 11–13] part of it, and after he had come down, mentioning the other part [in vv. 31–32]? Rather, these are two separate prayers. Therefore it appears that when God told him *Let me alone, that my wrath may wax hot against them* [v. 10], Moses immediately *besought the face of the Eternal* and did not delay at all, for he was afraid lest the wrath go out from God and the plague would begin and consume them in a moment, therefore at once he said, *Eternal, why doth Thy wrath wax hot against Thy people?*… And if you will understand what I have explained, then you will really comprehend that there were two prayers, for at first he *besought the face of the*

with the sequence in the biblical text. Each of the dialogues in the account stands independently without referring to the other. There is no indication of continuation or interdependence between them.

The lack of coherence between the scenes on the mountain together with the other aforementioned literary discrepancies in the account disappear when the first dialogue on the mountain, that is the scene of the near destruction (vv. 7–14), is removed from the account. Without this passage the hesitation of Moses (and Joshua) about the source of the noise in the camp (vv. 17–18) is clearer, as well as Moses' surprised reaction that leads him to halt the delivery of the tablets (v. 19) and punish the people (vv. 20, 27–28). Thus, without the section of the first dialogue, Moses discovers the sin himself and only then approaches God with a reflection on the behavior of the people and with a plea for atonement (vv. 30–32). This sequence, without the first dialogue with God, is more coherent and fluid.[26]

The plausibility of the secondary nature of the section on God's radical response suits the assumption that the Calf narrative was originally a tradition involving a legitimate ritual. While the original narrative is no longer accessible, we can trace some steps in the process of altering it into a defamatory manifest. The scene of God's decision to wipe out the people followed by Moses' intercession was another addition to the plot, aimed at further emphasizing the illegitimacy of the ritual. How was this unit integrated into the account?

2.6 The annihilation threat: Incorporation in the account

The section including God's threat to destroy the people contains two consecutive statements by God to Moses, each of which defines the people's behavior differently. At first the people are blamed for acting perversely (שחת, v. 7) and then for being stiff-necked (עם קשה ערף, v. 9):

> 7 The LORD said to Moses, "Go down at once! Your people, whom you brought up out of the land of Egypt, have acted perversely; 8 they have been quick to turn aside from the way that I commanded them; they have cast for themselves an image of a calf, and have worshiped it and sacrificed to it, and said, 'These are your gods, O Israel, who brought you up out of the land of Egypt!'" 9 The LORD said to Moses, "I have seen this people, how stiff-necked they are" (Exod 32:7–9)

Eternal his God, and at the end... he *fell down before the Eternal for forty days...*" (Nachmanides [Rabbi Moses ben Naḥman] on Exod 32:11; Chavel 1973, 559–561).

26 This conclusion and some of the literary analysis below were summarized in my article: Kugler 2016, 641–643.

This double charge occurs with no interjection from Moses: "The LORD said to Moses... The LORD said to Moses" (משה אל 'ה ויאמר...משה אל 'ה וידבר, vv. 7, 9). While consecutive occurrences of "saying" verbs can sometimes indicate a development in the conversation,[27] in our case the duplication presents inconsistent information.[28] In the first approach God commands Moses to return to the people, ostensibly in order to deal with their deeds in person – "Go down at once! Your people, whom you brought up out of the land of Egypt, have acted perversely" (v. 7). In the second statement God presents himself as the executor of the sentence, stating that he will deal with the people's wrongdoing directly: "Now let me alone, so that my wrath may burn hot against them" (v. 10). In Benjamin Sommer's words, God's latter announcement concerning his intention to destroy the people means that "there will be no nation for Moses to return to".[29]

Together with the contradiction in God's commands to Moses, the accusatory description of the people as "stiff-necked" (v. 9) seems odd within the context of the story. The notion "stiff-necked" usually refers to sustained disobedience to authority (cf. Deut 31:27; Jer 17:23, 19:15; Neh 9:29). This definition is less suited to the case of making a Golden Calf,[30] which derives from the people's aspiration towards God rather than a rebellion against him. The people attempt to get closer to the "God of Israel" (Exod 32:4) by actualizing him and celebrating his honor (v. 5–6).[31]

The superfluous comment from God to Moses in verse 9 is indeed missing from the Greek version of the chapter (Exod 32:8–10)

> 8 παρέβησαν ταχὺ ἐκ τῆς ὁδοῦ, ἧς ἐνετείλω αὐτοῖς· ἐποίησαν ἑαυτοῖς μόσχον καὶ προσκεκυνήκασιν αὐτῷ καὶ τεθύκασιν αὐτῷ καὶ εἶπαν Οὗτοι οἱ θεοί σου, Ισραηλ, οἵτινες ἀνεβίβασάν σε ἐκ γῆς Αἰγύπτου 9 ... 10 καὶ νῦν ἔασόν με καὶ θυμωθεὶς ὀργῇ εἰς αὐτοὺς ἐκτρίψω αὐτοὺς καὶ ποιήσω σὲ εἰς ἔθνος μέγα

The LXX offers a single introduction to God's appeal to Moses (v. 7a) followed by the charge against the people (vv. 7b–8). In this way the unrelated charge of being "stiff-necked" disappears and the description of the sin is followed directly by a proclamation of the verdict (v. 10). But the variation of the LXX does not necessarily manifest the version of the Hebrew text with which the translator worked.

---

27 As in Gen 24:24–25, 32:9–10; Exod 30:11–17, 35:1–4. See Shiloah 1964, 251–267.
28 And see Rashi on "saying" duplications in his commentary to Ezekiel: "every 'and he said... and he said' is meant to be clarified" (Rashi on Ezek 10:2; my translation).
29 Sommer 2000, 45–46.
30 Cf. Dillmann 1880, 339; Driver 1911, 351–352; Sommer 2000, 46.
31 Cf. Halevi's exegesis above, footnote 2 (p. 14).

The absence of verse 9 from the translation seems to be a result of the translator's deliberate choice to omit the redundant and complicated introduction found in the account. As John Wevers asserts: "[there are] no paleographic factors which would make such an omission accidental".[32]

The complexity in the account of God's approach to Moses in vv. 7–9, as encountered by the Greek translator, was the result of the editing work that occurred in the Hebrew text itself. Thus, the irrelevant indictment against the people as "stiff-necked" (vv. 9–14), was attached to the broader story of the Calf with the additional comment about God's accusation (vv. 7–8), referring directly to the Calf event.

While scholars have noticed the distinct quality of verses 7–14 in the Calf narrative, there was general agreement it formed an editorial, often Deuteronomistic, expansion of the story.[33] But the understanding that without vv. 7–8 the section has no link to the current narrative shows that the section existed independently and was borrowed and adjusted to the specific context. This assumption explains the contradiction and the redundancy in vv. 7–9 better than the suggestion that the whole secondary passage in vv. 7–14 was written ad hoc, as required by the current story.

2.7 Revising the compositional process

We suggested that the account of God's threat to destroy the nation should be understood in light of the compositional process of the Golden Calf story. The story stems from an early tradition about a legitimate and accepted ritual custom performed by Moses. Throughout years of reception the story was changed in a way that aimed to defame the northern kingdom's custom. This was done by invalidating the early custom and removing it from Moses' resumé. Moses instead was given the role of rebuking and condemning the custom, while the negative role of directing the practice was given to Aaron. In a later stage the criticism about the event became more severe. This was conveyed by adding a scene about God's intention to destroy the "stiff-necked" people. This scene was indeed not necessary to the plot, but it addressed a question that the account still raised – how was it that the people were not directly punished by God for such a disgraceful

---

32 Wevers 1990, 523.
33 See Driver 1911, 351–352; Von Rad 1966(a), 78–79; Childs 1974, 559; Aurelius 1988, 41–44; Blum 2002, 280, 288; Berner 2013, 403; Oswald 2014, 182.

sin? The additional scene explained that a planned divine punishment was canceled due to Moses' intercession.

This clarification however was not invented specifically for the current narrative, but rather was taken from another context that described the people as "stiff-necked".[34] The scene was patched into the Calf story by editorial "glue", namely a reference to the specific event using details given in the narrator's description: the name עגל מסכה for the Calf (v. 8, cf. v. 4), and the full citation of the people's words: "These are your gods, O Israel, who brought you up out of the land of Egypt!" (v. 8, cf. v. 4).[35]

But this addition to the narrative in itself has also increased and enriched the message of the plot, and expanded the qualities of the leading characters, Moses and God. On the basis of the final form of the incident, Moses is now regarded not only as a castigator of the people's transgressions, but also as an advocate, protecting the people from an apparently irreversible retribution. Similar tension is found in the portrayal of God in the final form of the narrative, as a deity furiously deciding to exterminate his subjects while at the same time showing moderation and restraint towards the people. If such a complex portrayal of the figures has broadened the theological message of the story, it could have occurred only because of the literary freedom the biblical scribes had in early stages of the bible composition.

Interestingly, a similar process of formation can be traced in the other account of the divine threat of destruction in the wilderness – the story of the spies. This will be discussed in the next chapter.

---

34 See the remark in Ps 95:8 about the people's hardening their hearts (rather than stiffening their necks) in the days of the desert, and the reference in Ps 78:38–39 to the threat of destruction in the desert with no mention of the Calf or the spy stories. These comments reveal the existence of traditions that relate the people's potential death to other wrongdoings. Evidence for an earlier expression of the annihilation-threat motif will be discussed in chapter 4.

35 A further notable demonstration is the description of the sin in the other dialogue between Moses and God (vv. 30–34), recounting the event with no commitment to the terminology used earlier in the plot: "Alas, this people has sinned a great sin; they have made for themselves gods of gold" (v. 31).

3 Punishment and threat of destruction in the story of the spies: Varied theological views in two parallel narratives

3.1 Too extreme a reaction

A second episode of God's determination to annihilate the people of Israel in the wilderness appears in Numbers 13–14, the story of the sending of representatives as spies to scout the land of Canaan.[1] The story describes God's response to the people's negative reaction to the report of the spies. His words accuse them of despising and not trusting God, who thus decides to "strike them with pestilence" in a way that will make Moses the only survivor of the people (Num 14:11–12).[2]

This scene, with the intervention of Moses on behalf of the people, shares similar lines with the episode of God's reaction to the building of the Golden Calf.[3] But while the scene of God's severe reaction might be justified within the broader final story of the Calf worship (as being a response to a violation of the laws that were supposedly already given to the people),[4] the extreme reaction of God in the spy story seems unjustifiable even within the final narrative context. Thus, whereas the radical reaction of God targets both the spies and the rest of the people, the initial wrongdoing, related to the spies, remains unclear. As the Jewish medieval commentator Nachmanides

---

1 The word "spies" will be used here as meaning messengers or scouts, translating the verb רגל, used in the rewritten story in Deuteronomy 1: ויפנו ויעלו ההרה ויבאו עד נחל אשכל וירגלו אתה ("They set out and went up into the hill country, and when they reached the Valley of Eshcol they spied it out", v. 24). The Hebrew word מרגלים is the traditional title of the sent representatives in Rabbinic references to the story (e.g., Tanhuma, Shelach; Bamidbar Rabbah 16. And see Nachmanides below). See in contrast Frankel and Widmer's preference for the expression "scouts", due to the military connotations of the word מרגלים (cf. Joshua 2:1–3, 7:2): Frankel 2002, 119; Widmer 2004, 229.
2 For uses of the word דֶּבֶר, "pestilence", to refer to a final collective massacre, see Exod 9:15 and Jer 14:12. The idea of a fatal strike is stressed in the LXX for these references, using the word θάνατος, meaning complete death.
3 For the shared elements see above, Introduction, section 1.2.
4 See above, 2.1, the argument that the account of the giving of the commandments at Sinai was composed later than the narrative of the Golden Calf and in response to it. Hence, the so-called Decalogue can be considered violated by the people's cult only within the final form of the complete story.

https://doi.org/10.1515/9783110609905-003

indicated, the spies seem to perform the precise instructions given to them prior to the mission:

> Here one may ask... what did the spies do [wrong], since Moses told them, "And see the land what it is; and the people that dwell therein, whether they are strong or weak, whether they are few or many" (v. 18), and he said to see about the cities [that they dwell in] whether in camps or in strongholds (v. 19), and at the least they had to give him an answer to [the questions] that he commanded them! And what was their trespass, and what was their sin when they told Moses, "Nevertheless the people that dwell in the Land are fierce, and the cities are fortified, and very great" (v. 28). Did he send them in order that they testify to him falsehood? (Nachmanides on Num 13:2)[5]

The disparity between the negligible wrongdoing of the spies and the destructive reaction of God according to the story necessitates an investigation of the literary sources of the account and its formation process. This kind of investigation is also required to explore the basis of the links between the current episode and the Golden Calf affair. It is notable that while the final configuration of the Pentateuch puts the threat of destruction in the spy episode after the results of the Golden Calf incident, it gives no explicit indication of a continuity between the accounts.[6] Neither God's verdict nor Moses' intercession in the spy episode refers to the supposed precedent at Sinai. Without direct references between the accounts we are left with the goal of analyzing each of the stories separately and within the broader framework of the biblical narrative.

3.2 The spy episode: Parallel narratives within one account

A review of the account of sending representatives to tour the land of Canaan in Numbers 13–14 finds dual information and thus various contradictions in the plot. The most blatant dual contradictory matter in the text is the identity of the specific spies who bring variant messages to the people. At first, we hear that Caleb alone steps forward and communicates an encouraging message about the

---

5 Chavel 1975, 118–119.
6 Muffs (1984, 47–54) suggests a connection between the stories based on the use of the list of God's characteristics (Num 14:17–18), that were supposedly revealed to Moses in the context of the Golden Calf (Exod 34:6–7). Similarly, Widmer's reading of the episodes in their final form argues for a direct interaction between them (2004, 7–8, 254–345). Nevertheless, as we will show below (chapter 4), the allusion to the divine characteristics – being a prominent element in intercession prayers – is not sufficient to prove literary or contextual affinity between the accounts.

capability of the people to gain possession of the land (13:30). But later in the plot it is Caleb together with Joshua who are pointed out as the spies who encouraged the people, advocating God's capability to help the people possess the land and deal with its current inhabitants (14:6–9). This inconsistency in the identity of the specific spy/spies continues in God's responses to the event. At first we hear that Caleb alone is rewarded for his encouragement of the people, granted with survival in the desert and inheritance of the land (v. 24). But immediately after the text recounts that both Caleb and Joshua are exempt from the death penalty, and thus are chosen by God to possess the land (vv. 30, 38). Neither of these two narratives of the actions and destiny of the specified spies acknowledges the existence of the other.

The contradiction about the identity of the spies is part of a duplication of almost every step of the plot in Numbers 13–14. Duplication can be found in the information about the spies' destination (13:21; 22–23); in the seemingly negative report of the spies on their return (13:27–28; 32–33); in the positive statements of the named spy/spies (13:30; 14:6–9); in the reactions of the people to the report (14:1a, 2–3, 10a; 14:1b, 4); in the divine response to the events (14:11–25; 26–35); and in the consequence of the people's disobedience, manifested by the death of a sizable number of them (14:37; 45).

A break up of the dual occurrences in each of the abovementioned elements in the narrative reveals two accounts of the affair of sending spies to Canaan, distinct in tone and content. The accounts begin with stating two different destinations for the mission, Lebo-hamath and Wadi-Eshcol:

13:21 So they went up and spied out the land from the wilderness of Zin to Rehob, near Lebo-hamath.	13:22–23 They went up into the Negeb, and came to Hebron... And they came to the Wadi Eshcol, and cut down from there a branch with a single cluster of grapes, and they carried it on a pole between two of them. They also brought some pomegranates and figs.

This twofold information is followed by a double report of the fulfillment of the mission, each of which reports relates respectively to terminology or information mentioned in the references to the destination. One report (in the right-hand column below) describes the spies' bringing fruit from the land (13:27), corresponding with the information in the destination section, about the importation of grapes, pomegranates and figs (v. 23). The other report (in the left-hand column below) contains the verb תור (v. 32) which resonates with the remark about the action of the spies, ויתרו (v. 21), in the reference to their destination. Each of these double reports can be respectively attached to one of the two separated introductions constructed above:

13:21 So they went up and **spied out** (ויתרו) the land from the wilderness of Zin to Rehob, near Lebo-hamath. [...] 32 So they brought to the Israelites an unfavorable report of the land that they had **spied out** (תרו) saying, "The land that we have gone **through as spies** (לתור אותה) is a land that devours its inhabitants; and all the people that we saw in it are of great size."

13:22–23 They went up into the Negeb, and came to Hebron... And they came to the Wadi Eshcol, and cut down from there a branch with a single cluster of grapes, and they carried it on a pole between two of them. **They also brought some pomegranates and figs.** [...] 27 And they told him, "We came to the land to which you sent us; it flows with milk and honey, and **this is its fruit.** 28 Yet the people who live in the land are strong, and the towns are fortified and very large; and besides, we saw the descendants of Anak there."[...]

The next noticeably double element in the plot is the statement of the specific spies. The shared statement of Caleb and Joshua contains the verb תור (both in the spies' utterance, 14:7, and in the narrator's introduction, v. 6), and thus can be connected to the account formulated in the left column, which uses the verb prominently (13:21, 32). The encouraging statement of Caleb alone in 13:30 seems to fit in the other column after the description of the intimidating inhabitants of the land (13:28):

13:21 So they went up and **spied out** (ויתרו) the land from the wilderness of Zin to Rehob, near Lebo-hamath. [...] 32 So they brought to the Israelites an unfavorable report of the land that they had **spied out** (תרו), saying, "The land that we have gone **through as spies** (לתור אותה) is a land that devours its inhabitants; and all the people that we saw in it are of great size." [...] 14:6 And Joshua son of Nun and Caleb son of Jephunneh, who were among those who had **spied out** (התרים) the land, tore their clothes 7 and said to all the congregation of the Israelites, "The land that we went through **as spies** (לתור) is an exceedingly good land...".

13:22–23 They went up into the Negeb, and came to Hebron... And they came to the Wadi Eshcol, and cut down from there a branch with a single cluster of grapes, and they carried it on a pole between two of them. **They also brought some pomegranates and figs.** [...] 27 And they told him, "We came to the land to which you sent us; it flows with milk and honey, and **this is its fruit.** 28 Yet the people who live in the land are strong, and the towns are fortified and very large; and besides, we saw the descendants of Anak there." [...] 30 But Caleb quieted **the people** before Moses, and said, "Let us go up at once and occupy it, for we are well able to overcome it."

The distinctive utterances of the specified spies are followed by double references to the people's reaction, stimulated by the stated encouragements. One reaction addresses a single representative (13:31), and therefore can be connected to the episode that mentions Caleb alone. The other reaction addresses men, in plural, (14:10), and thus continues the account of Caleb and Joshua:

13:21 So they went up and **spied out** (ויתרו) the land from the wilderness of Zin to Rehob, near Lebo-hamath. [...] 32 So they brought to the Israelites an unfavorable report of the land that they had **spied out** (תרו), saying, "The land that we have gone **through as spies** (לתור אותה) is a land that devours its inhabitants; and all the people that we saw in it are of great size." [...] 14:6 And Joshua son of Nun and Caleb son of Jephunneh, who were among those who had spied out (התרים) the land, tore their clothes 7 and said to all the congregation of the Israelites, "The land that we went through **as spies** (לתור) is an exceedingly good land". [...] 10 But the whole congregation threatened to stone **them.**

13:22–23 They went up into the Negeb, and came to Hebron... And they came to the Wadi Eshcol, and cut down from there a branch with a single cluster of grapes, and they carried it on a pole between two of them. **They also brought some pomegranates and figs.** [...] 27 And they told him, "We came to the land to which you sent us; it flows with milk and honey, and **this is its fruit.** 28 Yet the people who live in the land are strong, and the towns are fortified and very large; and besides, we saw the descendants of Anak there." [...] 30 But Caleb quieted **the people** before Moses, and said, "Let us go up at once and occupy it, for we are well able to overcome it." 31 Then the men who had gone up **with him** said, "We are not able to go up against this people, for they are stronger than we."

The last noticeable duplication is God's reaction to the event, which includes two consecutive speeches about punishing the people for their disbelief or complaint, together with a reference to the exceptional destiny of the faithful spy/spies. The latter element helps to sort the speeches between the two accounts. The reference to the two spies, Joshua and Caleb (14:30, 38), relates to the Joshua and Caleb account in the left-hand column. The reference to the one spy, Caleb (14:24), connects the speech with the account a bout Caleb, in the right-hand side.

13:21 So they went up and spied out (ויתרו) the land from the wilderness of Zin to Rehob, near Lebo-hamath. [...] 32 So they brought to the Israelites an unfavorable report of the land that they had spied out (תרו), saying, "The land that we have gone through as spies (לתור אותה) is a land that devours its inhabitants; and all the people that we saw in it are of great size." [...] 14:6 And Joshua son of Nun and Caleb son of Jephunneh, who were among those who had spied out (התרים) the land, tore their clothes 7 and said to all the congregation of the Israelites, "The land that we went through as spies (לתור) is an exceedingly good land". [...] 10 But the whole congregation threatened to stone them. [...]

13:22–23 They went up into the Negeb, and came to Hebron... And they came to the Wadi Eshcol, and cut down from there a branch with a single cluster of grapes, and they carried it on a pole between two of them. **They also brought some pomegranates and figs**. [...] 27 And they told him, "We came to the land to which you sent us; it flows with milk and honey, and **this is its fruit**. 28 Yet the people who live in the land are strong, and the towns are fortified and very large; and besides, we saw the descendants of Anak there." [...]

26 And the LORD spoke to Moses and to Aaron, saying: 27 How long shall this wicked congregation complain against me? I have heard the complaints of the Israelites, which they complain against me. 28 Say to them, "As I live," says the LORD, "I will do to you the very things I heard you say: 29 your dead bodies shall fall in this very wilderness; and of all your number, included in the census, from twenty years old and upward, who have complained against me, 30 not one of you shall come into the land in which I swore to settle you, except **Caleb son of Jephunneh and Joshua son of Nun**. [...] 33 And your children shall be shepherds in the wilderness for forty years, and shall suffer for your faithlessness, until the last of your dead bodies lies in the wilderness. 34 According to the number of the days in which you spied out the land, forty days, for every day a year, you shall bear your iniquity, forty years, and you shall know my displeasure."

30 But Caleb quieted the people before Moses, and said, "Let us go up at once and occupy it, for we are well able to overcome it." 31 Then the men who had gone up **with him** said, "We are not able to go up against this people, for they are stronger than we." [...]
14:11 And the LORD said to Moses, "How long will this people despise me? And how long will they refuse to believe in me, in spite of all the signs that I have done among them?... 22 none of the people who have seen my glory and the signs that I did in Egypt and in the wilderness, and yet have tested me these ten times and have not obeyed my voice, 23 shall see the land that I swore to give to their ancestors; none of those who despised me shall see it. 24 But my servant **Caleb**, because he has a different spirit and has followed me wholeheartedly, I will bring into the land into which he went, and his descendants shall possess it. (...).

Separating the duplicated literary occurrences reveals two narrative threads, each with a similar plot. Each of the threads tells of spies that reach a certain geographic area and bring back information about the place, including some challenging details. Alongside their report, though, an individual statement is made about the good quality of the land, encouraging the people to keep on moving towards the place. Each of the narratives contains a response to the event by God, with a verdict for the nation, while exempting the individuals who delivered alternative messages. One of the two responses contains the idea of possible extermination of the people.

In the exploration of the meanings and roots of the idea of the threat of annihilation, each of the divine verdicts needs to be examined in its wider account. We will begin with the second divine verdict in the sequence, the one that lacks a proposal of destruction.

3.3 The "second" divine response within one restored narrative thread

The divine speech that appears second in the sequence of the final form of the spy story (Num 14:26–35) does not include an idea of extermination. When separated from the verdict in the previous segment (vv. 11–25), it begins with a proclamation of a death penalty for the current generation only (v. 29), while stressing the continuity of the nation through their offspring (vv. 31, 33). Following this sentence from God, the narrator describes a first fulfillment of the punishment – the death of the people who went on the mission, with the exception of Joshua and Caleb (vv. 36–38). As shown in the restored account in the left column above, this information follows the references about the exceptional performance of the two spies.

But the connection of the verdict (14:26–35) with the abovementioned restored thread is also noticeable from the transgression linked to the remaining spies according to the verdict: they brought "an unfavorable report about the land" (דְּבַת הָאָרֶץ רָעָה, 14:37. Cf. v. 36). This accusation echoes the reference found in the restored thread about the nature of the report of the spies: "So they brought to the Israelites an unfavorable report of the land that they had spied out" (13:32).

By reading the current divine verdict together with the first restored narrative thread, more elements from the broader text in Numbers 13–14 can be related to the thread and complete it. Thus, the wrongdoing of the whole nation, expressed in the verdict as complaints against God ("How long shall this wicked congregation complain against me? I have heard the complaints of the Israelites, which they complain against me", 14:27),[7] goes back to the information in 14:2, using the same verb, לון: "And all the Israelites complained against Moses and Aaron". Whereas the plot regards the complaint as directed against Moses and Aaron, the verdict considers it as uttered against God (14:27). This fits with the content of the complaint as expressed in the plot, blaming God for the people's current situation: "Why is the LORD bringing us into this land to fall by the sword?..." (14:3). The reference in 14:2–3, thus, should be included in the traced thread.

Likewise, as mentioned in the verdict, the penalty for the congregation, namely ending their life in the desert (14:28–29, 32), corresponds with the people's death wish mentioned in their complaint: "...would that we had died in the land of Egypt! Or would that we had died in this wilderness!" (14:2). The people's fate according to the verdict is thus a consequence of their dreadful wishes and stands in opposition to the fate of their children, for whom they were specifically concerned, saying: "...Our wives and our little ones will become booty; would

---

7 The double clause "which they complain against me" (אֲשֶׁר הֵמָּה מַלִּינִים עָלַי) in the verse may be a result of dittography from the end of the verse to its beginning. Without the first clause we are left with a clear statement regarding the people: "...I have heard the complaints of the Israelites, which they complain against me". Although, as Licht shows (1991, 78), it is not impossible that the duplication was written like that in the first place, with an attempt to highlight the wrath of God in the scene.

it not be better for us to go back to Egypt?" (v. 3). The verdict thus stresses the ironic outcomes, in which only the complaining adults (and perhaps their wives as well?) will perish in the desert (v. 32. Cf. vv. 31, 33).[8]

A further significant element that should be added to the restored thread is the use of the number "forty". This is, according to the verdict, the number of years to be spent in the desert, chosen in line with the time the spies had spent in scouting the land: "According to the number of the days in which you spied out the land, forty days, for every day a year, you shall bear your iniquity, forty years..." (14:34).[9] Thus, the mention of the duration of the tour in 13:25 (containing again the verb תור) should be added to our restored thread.

Nevertheless, whereas the reference to the duration of the journey in 13:25 refers to the spies alone, the verdict uses the number as a punishment of the entire congregation. A similar move from the realm of the spies to the realm of the whole nation is found in 14:36 which by using the verb לון in *hiphil* (in the *qri* [reading] tradition), relates the unfavorable utterance of the spies to the whole congregation. Thus, the causative action וַיַּלִּינוּ implies that the spies influenced the people to complain about the land, even though they had not visited there: "And the men whom Moses sent to spy out the land, who returned and made all the congregation complain against him by bringing a bad report about the land" (14:36). This idea is missing from the LXX version of the verse, which, by using the preposition κατά ("to"), suggests that the complaint was said by the spies and only addressed to the people, as mentioned earlier in the plot: "So they brought **to** the Israelites an unfavorable report of the land that they had spied out, saying, 'The land that we have gone through as spies is a land that devours its inhabitants; and all the people that we saw in it are of great size'" (13:32). Contrarily, the MT version reflects an attempt to connect the whole congregation with the guilt of the spies, and thus to provide further justification for the punishment to be applied to the nation.

---

8 In their fear, the people differentiate between the danger of their death "by the sword", and the destiny of their wives and children to fall as "booty" (v. 3). The divine verdict corresponds only with the fear for the children's fate, when it affirms the continuation of the nation – not through the current generation, but through the offspring.

9 This verse should be added to the previous verse that conveys the realization of the forty-year punishment ("And your children shall be shepherds in the wilderness for forty years, and shall suffer for your faithlessness, until the last of your dead bodies lies in the wilderness", 14:33). Contrary to earlier suggestions that it is a supplement (Dillmann 1886, 62; Baentsch 1903, 515; Holzinger 1903, 59), the two verses together function as an etiological explanation for the punishment of the wandering. See Paran's linguistic considerations for the unity of the paragraph (1989, 85–88).

Back to the spies' "unfavorable report" mentioned in the restored narrative thread: some scholars consider the depiction of the land as "devour(ing) its inhabitants" (13:32) as a metaphor about the land's infertility.[10] This assumption is supposedly supported by the reaction of the two atypical spies, stressing that the land is "very good" and "flows with milk and honey" (14:7–8). But the rhetoric of the congregation's response to the report indicates that the fear is not of hunger but of war: "Why is the LORD bringing us into this land to fall by the sword? Our wives and our little ones will become booty" (14:3). Likewise, the encouragement from the specified spies engages directly with concern about the capability of the local inhabitants: "... and do not fear the people of the land, for they are no more than bread for us; their protection is removed from them, and the LORD is with us; do not fear them" (14:9). This idea can be evident also in the reference to the gigantic people in the land, implying that the land is good enough to enable such physical development (13:32–33).[11] Accordingly, the judgmental statement ויוציאו דבת הארץ ("So they brought [to the Israelites] an unfavorable report of the land", 13:32) about the spies' report does not necessarily depict the spies as lying to the people, but rather as demoralizing them, since no one denies the presence of threatening entities in the land.[12]

Tracking the segments that belong to the first restored thread, the shared mention of Joshua and Caleb in the verdict (14:30, 38) goes back to the segment in 14:6–9, about their intercession on God's behalf and their positive view of the land. The thread recounts that in response to the people's complaint (vv. 2–3), Moses and Aaron fall on their faces (v. 5),[13] whereas Joshua and Caleb try to calm the people, arguing for the good quality of the land (vv. 7–8) and for God's intentions to assist the people in confronting the inhabitants there (v. 9).[14] The

---

10 Gray 1903, 51; Kislev 2017, 41.

11 Note, though, that the comment in verse 33 about the "Anakites [who] come from the Nephilim" (בני ענק מן הנפילים) might be an additional detail that aimed to connect the remark about the Nephilim with information about the "descendants of Anak" found in the other account (13:28). This connecting remark is indeed missing in the LXX.

12 Cf. the term דִּבָּה ("unfavorable report") in the meaning of disgrace in Gen 37:2; Jer 20:10; Ezek 36:3. In contrast see Kislev's opinion about the negative tone of דִּבָּה, without asserting it to mean a lie (2017, 42).

13 This reference corresponds to the remark about addressing both Moses and Aaron in the divine verdict (14:26), as opposed to the exclusive approach to Moses in the other divine verdict (v. 11).

14 Knierim and Coats (2005, 187–188) suggest that the reference to the prostration of Moses and Aaron (14:5) was removed from its original place in the context of the appearance of the presence of the Lord (כבוד יהוה, v. 10), based on similar scenes known from the Priestly literature (Lev 9:24, Num 16:22, 17:10, 20:6). Nevertheless, the mention of the prostration of the leaders in the spy

congregation, though, oppose the positive encouragement by attempting to stone the two spies (v. 10a), but are stopped by a dramatic appearance of God's glory (כבוד יהוה, v. 10b). This sequential description is thus part of the abovementioned restored narrative, being a further explanation for the exemption of Joshua and Caleb from the fate of the other spies and of the whole generation.

The joint mention of Joshua and Caleb in the divine verdict examined above also relates to the introductory section in the broader account, which presents the list of the leaders chosen by Moses for the mission. Thus, the list mentions Caleb son of Jephunneh as the representative of Judah (13:6), and Hoshea/Joshua son of Nun as the representative of Ephraim (v. 8). The list should thus be added to our restored narrative, likewise the instruction given to Moses by God (vv. 1–2) and the double mention of Moses' fulfilment of the instruction, framing the list of the representatives ("So Moses sent them", vv. 3, 17a).[15]

The thread formed by now contains one occurrence of each of the abovementioned duplications that occur in the final form of the account in Numbers 13–14. It mentions one reference to the area visited by the spies (13:21); one critical report from the spies in their return (v. 32); one reaction of the people to the report (14:2–3); one positive statement from the specified spies (vv. 6–9); one divine response to the events (vv. 10, 26–35), referring also to those spies (vv. 30); and one account about a partial fulfilment of the verdict (vv. 36–38).

A few more elements will be further related to this literary thread, based on a diagnosis of its affinity with the Priestly literature in the Pentateuch. This conclusion will also provide a stronger grasp of the message of the divine verdict it contains.

3.4 The Priestly account

Various elements in the narrative restored above raise the likelihood that we are dealing with the work of scribes from the Priestly school (P). One element is the prominent use of numerical information, reflecting the Priestly tendency for

---

event matches the implied message about their difficulty in dealing with the complaint directed to them (Num 14:2–3), as opposed to Joshua and Caleb (vv. 6–9. Cf. also 17:10).

15 This repeated description of Moses' obedience (vv. 3, 17) should not be viewed as a mistake or unnecessary duplication, but rather as a means to link back ("Wiederaufnahme") to the information mentioned before the list (vv. 4–16). On the phenomenon of "Wiederaufnahme" in the biblical narrative see Kuhl 1952, 1–11. In contrast, some scholars point to the repeated feature of verses 3 and 17 as a consideration for the secondary nature of the list of representatives: Noth 1968, 104; Artus 1997, 95–97; Frankel 2002, 123–124, 129; Wright 2014, 197.

accuracy and schematics.[16] This is manifest in the information about the duration of the tour in the land (13:25), used as a basis for the length of the future wandering in the desert (14:33–34). A similar point concerns the age of the people punished (14:29), an age which corresponds with definitions of maturity elsewhere in the Priestly laws and accounts (Exod 30:14, 38:26; Lev 27:3; Num 1:3, 45, 26:2, 4). The tendency to order and number is manifest also in the elaborate list of the tribes' representatives (13:4–15), as known from other Priestly lists (Exod 1:1–4, 6:14–19; Num 1:5–16, 3:2–3, 17–18, 24, 30, 35).

Priestly characterization can also be detected from the content of the change of the protagonist's name, namely from Hoshea (הושע) to Joshua (יהושע). By implying that the theophoric element in the name Joshua, יהו, was not in use earlier in the timeline, the narrative corresponds with the Priestly view according to which the revelation of the Tetragrammaton occurred for the first time shortly before the departure from Egypt (Exod 6:2–3).[17] According to this view, therefore, Joshua could not be named with the theophoric element יהו in childhood, assuming he was born before the departure from Egypt.[18]

An additional Priestly indication in the account is the mention of the wilderness of Paran as the people's base (Num 13:3, 26). This stands in correspondence to data mentioned earlier in the Priestly material of the wandering in the desert (Num 10:12, 12:16). Similarly, the details of the tour destination, "from the wilderness of Zin to Rehob, near Lebo-hamath (13:21)", corresponds with the layout of Canaan's borders found in the Priestly literature: "...your south sector shall extend from the wilderness of Zin... This shall be your northern boundary: from... Mount Hor... to Lebo-hamath" (Num 34:3, 7, 8). While the outline indicates that the tour in Canaan ranged from the south end to the north (Num 13:21), its realization is supposedly indicated by the lengthy duration of the tour, forty days (v. 25). This joins the preliminary role of the forty days as a pre-justification for the people's future punishment.

A further sign of the Priestly nature of our restored thread is its vocabulary. The terms נשיא ("leader") and מטה ("tribe") in the account (Num 13:2, 4–15) are prominently used in the Priestly writings (Num 1:16–46, 2:2–31, 7:7, 10:14–27,

---

16 See: Gunkel's words: "The style of P is extremely peculiar, exceedingly detailed and aiming at legal clearness and minuteness... the author is evidently painfully exact and exemplary in his love of order" (1901, 146).

17 See: Gray 1903, 136–137; Milgrom 1990, 101; Kislev 2017, 51.

18 Priestly segments in the book of Genesis recount that the ancestors knew and used the name אל שדי rather than יהוה (Gen 17:1, 28:3, 35:11, 43:14, 48:3). Outside the Priestly tradition there is no problem with the theophoric element in Joshua's name, and he is not assumed to have had another name (cf. Exod 17:9, 13, 24:13, 32:17, 33:11; Num 11:28).

34:17–29),[19] and also the word עדה with the meaning of the whole congregation
(Num 13:26, 14:1–2, 5, 7, 10, 27, 35–36. Cf. Exod 38:25, Lev 8:3–5, Num 1:16 and
more).[20] The latter is paralleled to the term עם ("people"), and both words occur
in the reference to the people's reaction to the report of the spies: the עדה (that
"raised a loud cry", 14:1a), and the עם (that "wept that night", 14:1b). Among the
two subjects, the עדה is regarded as complaining (וילנו): "Then all the congregation raised a loud cry... And all the Israelites complained against Moses and
Aaron; the whole congregation said to them..." (14:1a, 2–3), as indeed is emphasized later in the divine accusation: "How long shall this wicked congregation
complain against me? I have heard the complaints of the Israelites, which they
complain against me" (v. 27).

Offering no proactive requirement with the criticism, the complaint of the עדה
conforms to complaints of the people described in other biblical stories, many of
which are attributed to Priestly writing (Exod 15:24, 16:2–3, 7–8, 17:3; Num 16:11,
17:6, 20; Josh 9:18). This stands in contrast to the description of the people, העם,
in their active initiative to "choose [another] captain and go back to Egypt" (נתנה
ראש ונשובה מצרימה, Num 14:4), a decision that, as we will see, belongs to the other
narrative thread.

The divine verdict that ends the current account comprises indeed a harsh
punishment for the spies and the people. Nevertheless, it does not undermine
the very existence of the people, nor their relationship with God. In this way it
matches the Priestly worldview that upholds the concept of an ongoing commitment from God, resulting from the covenants he made with the people throughout their history (Gen 9:12–17, 17:7–9; Num 25:11–12),[21] and from numerous practices of atonement offered as a means to maintain the people's life. Such is the
purification through water (Lev 14:5; Num 8:7, 19:9), fire (Num 17:11, 31:22–23. Cf.

---

19 See more in: Paran 1989, 288; Niehr 1999, 47–52. Cf. the prominent use of נשיא in the context
of Ezekiel's prophecy on the futuristic temple: Ezek 44:3, 45:7–9, 16–17, 22, 46:2, 4, 8, 10, 12, 16–18,
48:21–22.

20 On the term in the Priestly literature see: Levy and Milgrom 1999, 470–478; Baden 2009, 116.
Among the numerous occurrences of עדה in the Priestly accounts, an exception is the reference to
Korah's people, which does not concern the whole nation (Num 16:5, 6, 11, 16, 19a, 21, 22, 17:5, 10).
This peculiarity is possibly influenced by the description of Korah's group in the beginning of the
narrative as "leaders of the congregation" (נשיאי עדה, 16:2). See above, Introduction, section 1.2,
on the difference between the story of Korah and the narratives of the threat of destruction in
the wilderness.

21 In the words of Campbell and O'Brien (1993, 22): "The Priestly document is a powerful affirmation of faith in God's unconditional commitment to Israel, which, although delayed by human
fragility, will never be deflected from the ultimate goal of God's love". See also: Van Seters 1999,
183–184; Ska 2006, 157.

Isa 6:6), animal blood (Lev 14:7), scapegoats (16:21–22) and even direct killing (Num 25:8). Thus, the mention of God's willingness to destroy the people in the spy story (Num 14:13–19) seems to belong to another hand, suggesting a different view about the question of the people' resilience.

Below is the account we reconstructed and consider as a Priestly work, traced in Num 13:1–17a, 21, 25–26a, 32–33, 14:1a, 2–3, 5–10, 26–38. With some revisions, this framework follows Noth's 1968 analysis of the text,[22] which agrees with earlier analyses conducted by Bacon,[23] and Gray,[24] and is largely accepted today by scholars who use a similar methodology for tracing the text's literary sources.[25]

Num 13:1 The LORD said to Moses, 2 "Send men to spy out the land of Canaan, which I am giving to the Israelites; from each of their ancestral tribes you shall send a man, everyone a leader among them." 3 So Moses sent them from the wilderness of Paran, according to the command of the LORD, all of them leading men among the Israelites. 4 These were their names: From the tribe of Reuben, Shammua son of Zaccur; 5 from the tribe of Simeon, Shaphat son of Hori; 6 from the tribe of Judah, Caleb son of Jephunneh; 7 from the tribe of Issachar, Igal son of Joseph; 8 from the tribe of Ephraim, Hoshea son of Nun; 9 from the tribe of Benjamin, Palti son of Raphu; 10 from the tribe of Zebulun, Gaddiel son of Sodi; 11 from the tribe of Joseph (that is, from the tribe of Manasseh), Gaddi son of Susi; 12 from the tribe of Dan, Ammiel son of Gemalli; 13 from the tribe of Asher, Sethur son of Michael; 14 from the tribe of Naphtali, Nahbi son of Vophsi; 15 from the tribe of Gad, Geuel son of Machi. 16 These were the names of the men whom Moses sent to spy out the land. And Moses changed the name of Hoshea son of Nun to Joshua. 17 Moses sent them to spy out the land of Canaan [...] 21 So they went up and spied out the land from the wilderness of Zin to Rehob, near Lebo-hamath. [...] 25 At the end of forty days they returned from spying out the land. 26 And they came to Moses and Aaron and to all the congregation of the Israelites in the wilderness of Paran. [...]

32 So they brought to the Israelites an unfavorable report of the land that they had spied out, saying, "The land that we have gone through as spies is a land that devours its inhabitants; and all the people that we saw in it are of great size. 33 There we saw the Nephilim (the Anakites come from the Nephilim); and to ourselves we seemed like grasshoppers, and so we seemed to them."

Num 14:1 Then all the congregation raised a loud cry. 2 And all the Israelites complained against Moses and Aaron; the whole congregation said to them, "Would that we had died in the land of Egypt! Or would that we had died in this wilderness! 3 Why is the LORD bringing us into this land to fall by the sword? Our wives and our little ones will become

---

22 Noth, 1968, 101–102.
23 Bacon 1894, 183–89.
24 Gray 1903, 130–132.
25 Coats 1968, 138–139; Sakenfeld, 1975, 319; Boorer, 1992, 333; Levine 1993, 347–381; Campbell and O'Brien 1993, 80–82, 153–155; Frankel 2002, 120; Widmer 2004, 238–242; Baden 2009, 115–116; Schart 2013, 165; Kislev 2017, 44–47.

booty; would it not be better for us to go back to Egypt?" [...] 5 Then Moses and Aaron fell on their faces before all the assembly of the congregation of the Israelites. 6 And Joshua son of Nun and Caleb son of Jephunneh, who were among those who had spied out the land, tore their clothes 7 and said to all the congregation of the Israelites, "The land that we went through as spies is an exceedingly good land. 8 If the LORD is pleased with us, he will bring us into this land and give it to us, a land that flows with milk and honey. 9 Only, do not rebel against the LORD; and do not fear the people of the land, for they are no more than bread for us; their protection is removed from them, and the LORD is with us; do not fear them." 10 But the whole congregation threatened to stone them. Then the glory of the LORD appeared at the tent of meeting to all the Israelites. [...] 26 And the LORD spoke to Moses and to Aaron, saying: 27 How long shall this wicked congregation complain against me? I have heard the complaints of the Israelites, which they complain against me. 28 Say to them, "As I live," says the LORD, "I will do to you the very things I heard you say: 29 your dead bodies shall fall in this very wilderness; and of all your number, included in the census, from twenty years old and upward, who have complained against me, 30 not one of you shall come into the land in which I swore to settle you, except Caleb son of Jephunneh and Joshua son of Nun. 31 But your little ones, who you said would become booty, I will bring in, and they shall know the land that you have despised. 32 But as for you, your dead bodies shall fall in this wilderness. 33 And your children shall be shepherds in the wilderness for forty years, and shall suffer for your faithlessness, until the last of your dead bodies lies in the wilderness. 34 According to the number of the days in which you spied out the land, forty days, for every day a year, you shall bear your iniquity, forty years, and you shall know my displeasure." 35 I the LORD have spoken; surely I will do thus to all this wicked congregation gathered together against me: in this wilderness they shall come to a full end, and there they shall die. 36 And the men whom Moses sent to spy out the land, who returned and made all the congregation complain against him by bringing a bad report about the land – 37 the men who brought an unfavorable report about the land died by a plague before the LORD. 38 But Joshua son of Nun and Caleb son of Jephunneh alone remained alive, of those men who went to spy out the land.

As was recently suggested by Kislev, this thread itself was not formed in one attempt, and seems to reflect a process of several stages.[26] Nevertheless, the reconstruction by separating it from the other material in the chapters discloses a relatively coherent plot, that is largely sufficient for our essential goal – to examine the other account of the story, which includes the tradition of God's threat of destruction.

3.5 The Non-Priestly account

The remaining verses, found in 13:17b–20, 22–24, 26b, 27–31, 14:1b, 4, 11–25, 39–45 also reveal a separate, relatively coherent account. This account, however, unlike

---

26 Kislev 2017, 51–54. See also Frankel 2002, 129–145, 191–199.

the Priestly one, does not begin with God's instruction for the mission, but opens with the words of Moses to the spies: "…and [Moses] said to them, 'Go up there into the Negeb, and go up into the hill country'" (13:17b). In an attempt to complete the narrative, scholars point to the spy story recounted in Deuteronomy 1 as preserving the lost beginning of the second thread in Numbers 13–14.[27] The Deuteronomic account relates that the initiative of the spy mission came from the people themselves, as a prior condition for entering the land and possessing it (Deut 1:21–23). If such a scene had existed in the original outline traced in Numbers 13–14, it must have been removed in the editorial process of combining the narrative with the Priestly version of the story.[28]

Moses' instruction to the spies in Num 13:18–20 is followed by the narrator's description of the spies' performance of the mission, elaborating the places they visited in and the evidence they brought from the land (vv. 22–24). The sequence continues in the second half of verse 26, by recounting the spies' return to Kadesh with a report (דבר) and a sample of the land's fruit (פרי הארץ, v. 26. Cf. vv. 20, 23, 27). This stands in contrast to the first half of verse 26, which points to Paran as the people's base, corresponding to information given earlier in the abovementioned Priestly account (v. 3).[29]

Within this restored outline, it is noticeable that the spies' actions and the report they deliver adhere to the instructions given to them by Moses on their departure. As stated in Nachmanides' comment mentioned above,[30] Moses instructs them to go up into the Negev and into the hill country (v. 17b), and they indeed ascend to the Negev and reach Hebron (v. 22), and then head further to Wadi Eshcol (v. 23). Moses instructs them to examine the nature of the inhabitants in the land

---

27 See: Bacon 1894, 179; Wellhausen 1899, 101; Driver 1902, 22 ; Gray 1903, 130; Noth 1968, 104; Campbell and O'Brien 1993, 154–5.

28 See in contrast Frankel's suggestion to trace the original opening of the story to Numbers 20, with the people's protest at Kadesh that "this wretched place… is no place for grain, or figs, or vines, or pomegranates…" (Num 20:5). He argues that the scene of the spies' return with grapes, pomegranates and figs from the land (13:23) might be a response to an earlier complaint of the people about the infertility of the land (Frankel 2002, 149, 192). But this suggestion cannot be supported by the narrative(s) in Numbers 13–14. The text has no hint of a preceding complaint about the land, while the demand to examine the matter of fertility stands alongside the interest in the military aspect (13:18–20), as a general preparation before entering the land.

29 Verse 13:26 seems therefore to contain data and terminology from the two accounts, connected by editorial work: "*and they came to Moses and Aaron and to all the congregation of the Israelites in the wilderness of Paran*, at Kadesh; they brought back word to them *and to all the congregation*, and showed them the fruit of the land". The description of the return to Kadesh with information and fruits belongs to the second narrative sequence.

30 See p. 28.

and their cities (vv. 18–19), and the spies indeed report about having seen strong people and "descendants of Anak" and large fortified towns (v. 28). Moses asks about the fertility of the land (v. 20), and the spies report that the land "flows with milk and honey", demonstrating with a sample of fruit from the land (v. 27), as was indeed requested (v. 20). The fruit sample is carried and brought back still fresh to the camp, thanks to the relatively short duration of the journey (v. 23), as opposed to the forty-day tour according to the Priestly account.

The second restored narrative continues, following the report (vv. 26b–28),[31] with Caleb bursting into the conversation, intending to moderate the message to the people, stressing that the community is capable of ascending to the land and conquering it: "But Caleb quieted the people before Moses, and said, 'Let us go up at once and occupy it, for we are well able to overcome it'" (v. 30). Caleb's role as one of the spies is indicated only later; in presenting the spies' response to Caleb, the spies are referred to as "the men who had gone up with him" (v. 31). The other spies then argue for the people's incapacity, saying "We are not able to go up against this people, for they are stronger than we" (v. 31). In the wake of this conflict the people respond with a cry (14:1b), and unlike the Priestly account, here the weeping leads to a proposal for action, to appoint an alternate leader who will return the people to Egypt: "So they said to one another, 'Let us choose a captain, and go back to Egypt'" (v. 4).

The next stage in the sequence presents God's words to Moses, responding to the events with an utterance about the destruction of the people: "And the LORD said to Moses, 'How long will this people despise me? And how long will they refuse to believe in me, in spite of all the signs that I have done among them? I will strike them with pestilence and disinherit them, and I will make of you a nation greater and mightier than they'" (14:11–12). As a response, Moses approaches God to dissuade him from his intentions, using two main arguments: God's reputation

---

31 To the report in 13:28 one can add the remark in verse 29 about the location of the peoples in the land: the Amalekites in the "land of the Negeb"; the Hittites, the Jebusites, and the Amorites (in the LXX also the Hivites) "in the hill country"; and the Canaanites "by the sea, and along the Jordan." As the context of both accounts does not indicate that the spies visited all these places, the information about the nations of the land could be gathered ostensibly by learning it from people they met. But as Noth (1968, 107) suggests, it seems more likely that the remark is not put in the spies' mouth, but rather stated by the narrator, as background about the peoples mentioned by the spies (v. 28). The remark matches a tradition found in Josh 11:3 about the location of the inhabitants of the land, but it contradicts the two lists in the current account, locating the Amalekites and the Canaanites together either in the valley (Num 14:25) or in the hill country (14:45), and reflecting the various socio-geopolitical traditions known to the authors. See the change of "the Amalekites and the Canaanites", mentioned in Num 14:45 as residing in the hill country, to "the Amorites" in Deut 1:44, in accord with the information given in Num 13:29.

among the nations (vv. 13–16),[32] and God's self-image (vv. 17–19a). In consequence, God consents not to annihilate the people, relating it to Moses' efforts ("I do forgive, just as you have asked", v. 20), but establishes an alternative punishment of not seeing the land, a sentence passed on the mature and experienced generation of the people with the exception of Caleb:

> 22 (N)one of the people who have seen my glory and the signs that I did in Egypt and in the wilderness, and yet have tested me these ten times and have not obeyed my voice, 23 shall see the land that I swore to give to their ancestors; none of those who despised me shall see it. 24 But my servant Caleb, because he has a different spirit and has followed me wholeheartedly, I will bring into the land into which he went, and his descendants shall possess it (Num 14:22–24)

The lack of information in God's verdict regarding the fate of the offspring led scholars to unify the text with the verdict in 14:26–35, which we related to the Priestly work, as it explicitly mentions the survival of the descendants (14:31, 33).[33] But the survival of the people's offspring is implied also in the divine verdict discussed here, by designating the prohibition on the land to those who saw God's honor and signs (vv. 22–23), i.e. the adults. Thus, once the intention to eliminate

---

32 Note though that this argument is rather complex and uncertain, as it presents three supposedly different national entities in three sequential statements in Moses' speech. It first mentions "Egypt" (v. 13), then "the inhabitants of the land" (v. 14) and finally "the nations" (v. 15). Furthermore, the middle reference about the inhabitants of the land presents them as both an object, being informed about God's deeds (ואמרו אל יושב הארץ הזאת, "and they will tell the inhabitants of this land...", 14:14), and as a subject, hearing about God's presence among the people (שמעו כי...אתה יהוה בקרב העם הזה...), "...[They] have heard that you, O LORD, are in the midst of this people...", ibid). These problems are resolved in the Greek translation, which reads verse 14 as: ἀλλὰ καὶ πάντες οἱ κατοικοῦντες ἐπὶ τῆς γῆς εἶ κύριος ἐν τῷ λαῷ τούτῳ..., "And all the inhabitants of this land have heard that you are the Lord among this people...". According to this version, the statement about the inhabitants of the land is structured similarly to the statement about Egypt, both as a subject of "hearing" rumors about the God of Israel (ושמעו מצרים כי העלת בכחך את העם הזה מקרבו...), "... Then the Egyptians will hear of it, for in your might you brought up this people from among them", v. 13). As such, the reference in verse 14 covers the rest of the relevant nations in the area, and then together with the reference about Egypt, is summarized in verse 15, by the general notion "the nations": "...then the nations who have heard about you will say" (ואמרו הגוים אשר שמעו את שמעך לאמר). See Loewenstamm (1992[b], 66. Cf. Noth 1968, 109), who suggests that the complexity in the segment is a result of an attempt to join together a reference about God's deeds in Egypt (known supposedly by the Egyptians) and a reference about God's deeds in the desert (heard supposedly by the inhabitants of Canaan. Cf. Josh 2:10).

33 Sakenfeld 1975, 322; Milgrom 1990, 112; Widmer 2004, 254; Knierim and Coats 2005, 190. See also below, 5.2.5.

the whole people is renounced, the continuity of the nation will be through the newborn children who will not be deprived of the experience of the land.

The sequence continues with Moses' report of God's words "to all the Israelites" (v. 39). This leads to great mourning by the people (v. 39) and a decision to take action in response, this time as an atonement for their refusal, by ascending to the heights of the hill country: "...Here we are. We will go up to the place that the LORD has promised, for we have sinned" (v. 40). But as the people's initiative is too late, they receive no help in the battle against the local peoples and suffer defeat by the Amalekites and the Canaanites who live in the hill country (v. 45).[34]

Putting the traced narrative segments together, a relatively coherent story emerges, containing most of the narrative elements found in the other restored account. It presents instructions given to the spies; a fulfillment of the mission; a report delivered by the spies; a response from an individual spy; a panic response by the people; a reaction from God to the events; and a partial realization of the verdict, derived from the people's attempt to change the outcome of the verdict.

As opposed to the other restored account, however, the current one has no distinct characteristics that relate it to the Priestly circles, and seems to reflect a different literary setting. Some commentators indeed classify it as a product of J.[35] Others argue that it includes material from both J and E,[36] though it is hard to differentiate them.[37] We will title the account with the neutral term "Non-Priestly",[38]

---

34 Contradicting the data given by either the narrator or the spies' words in 13:29 (see above, footnote 31), as well as the data in God's words according to 14:25, the reference about the location of the Amalekites and the Canaanites in 14:45 reveals the secondary nature of one or two of the comments, and reflects the various geo-sociological traditions known to the authors.

35 See: Wellhausen 1899, 102. And later: Van Seters 1999, 181; Friedman 2003, 262–266; Baden 2009, 119, 129–130, 151. See in contrast: Schmid 2006, 48–50.

36 See: Dillmann 1886, 71–79; Bacon 1894, 180–89; Gray 1903, 129; Baentsch 1903, 519. And recently Haran 2004, 197–98, who argues that the Non-Priestly sections that are paralleled to Deuteronomy 1 belong to E and the rest belong to J.

37 For example, Bacon (1894, 129) attributes the instruction to go to the "Negeb" (Num 13:17bα) to J, and the instruction to "go up to the hill country" (13:17bβ) to E. In correlation, he refers the description of the fulfillment of going up the Negeb and Hebron (13:22) to J, and the information about visiting Eshcol creek (13:23–24) to E. This division, however, creates a new problem in which the demand to go up to the mountain in the seemingly E narrative is fulfilled by going to the creek. In this regard see Gray's comment about the difficulty of restoring two coherent narratives in E and J (1903, 129).

38 See: McNeile 1911, 68–79, and recently Wright 2014, 193. Likewise, McEvenue (1971, 92) talks about the "traditional text", while Sakenfeld (1985, 73) defines the text as an "Old Epic tradition".

and will examine its existence as a separate story. Here is the reconstruction of the Non-Priestly account in light of the conclusions above:

Num 13:17b [...] and said to them, "Go up there into the Negeb, and go up into the hill country, 18 and see what the land is like, and whether the people who live in it are strong or weak, whether they are few or many, 19 and whether the land they live in is good or bad, and whether the towns that they live in are unwalled or fortified, 20 and whether the land is rich or poor, and whether there are trees in it or not. Be bold, and bring some of the fruit of the land." Now it was the season of the first ripe grapes. [...] 22 They went up into the Negeb, and came to Hebron; and Ahiman, Sheshai, and Talmai, the Anakites, were there. (Hebron was built seven years before Zoan in Egypt.) 23 And they came to the Wadi Eshcol, and cut down from there a branch with a single cluster of grapes, and they carried it on a pole between two of them. They also brought some pomegranates and figs. 24 That place was called the Wadi Eshcol, because of the cluster that the Israelites cut down from there. [...]

26 they brought back word to them... and showed them the fruit of the land. 27 And they told him, "We came to the land to which you sent us; it flows with milk and honey, and this is its fruit. 28 Yet the people who live in the land are strong, and the towns are fortified and very large; and besides, we saw the descendants of Anak there. 29 The Amalekites live in the land of the Negeb; the Hittites, the Jebusites, and the Amorites live in the hill country; and the Canaanites live by the sea, and along the Jordan."

30 But Caleb quieted the people before Moses, and said, "Let us go up at once and occupy it, for we are well able to overcome it." 31 Then the men who had gone up with him said, "We are not able to go up against this people, for they are stronger than we." [...]

Num 14:1b and the people wept that night. [...] 4 So they said to one another, "Let us choose a captain, and go back to Egypt." [...]

11 And the LORD said to Moses, "How long will this people despise me? And how long will they refuse to believe in me, in spite of all the signs that I have done among them? 12 I will strike them with pestilence and disinherit them, and I will make of you a nation greater and mightier than they." 13 But Moses said to the LORD, "Then the Egyptians will hear of it, for in your might you brought up this people from among them, 14 and they will tell the inhabitants of this land. They have heard that you, O LORD, are in the midst of this people; for you, O LORD, are seen face to face, and your cloud stands over them and you go in front of them, in a pillar of cloud by day and in a pillar of fire by night. 15 Now if you kill this people all at one time, then the nations who have heard about you will say, 16 'It is because the LORD was not able to bring this people into the land he swore to give them that he has slaughtered them in the wilderness.' 17 And now, therefore, let the power of the LORD be great in the way that you promised when you spoke, saying, 18 'The LORD is slow to anger, and abounding in steadfast love, forgiving iniquity and transgression, but by no means clearing the guilty, visiting the iniquity of the parents upon the children to the third and the fourth generation.' 19 Forgive the iniquity of this people according to the greatness of your steadfast love, just as you have pardoned this people, from Egypt even until now." 20 Then the LORD said, "I do forgive, just as you have asked; 21 nevertheless – as I live, and as all the earth shall be filled with the glory of the LORD – 22 none of the people who have seen my glory and the signs that I did in Egypt and in the wilderness, and yet have tested me these ten times and

have not obeyed my voice, 23 shall see the land that I swore to give to their ancestors; none of those who despised me shall see it. 24 But my servant Caleb, because he has a different spirit and has followed me wholeheartedly, I will bring into the land into which he went, and his descendants shall possess it. 25 Now, since the Amalekites and the Canaanites live in the valleys, turn tomorrow and set out for the wilderness by the way to the Red Sea." [...]

39 When Moses told these words to all the Israelites, the people mourned greatly. 40 They rose early in the morning and went up to the heights of the hill country, saying, "Here we are. We will go up to the place that the LORD has promised, for we have sinned." 41 But Moses said, "Why do you continue to transgress the command of the LORD? That will not succeed. 42 Do not go up, for the LORD is not with you; do not let yourselves be struck down before your enemies. 43 For the Amalekites and the Canaanites will confront you there, and you shall fall by the sword; because you have turned back from following the LORD, the LORD will not be with you." 44 But they presumed to go up to the heights of the hill country, even though the ark of the covenant of the LORD, and Moses, had not left the camp. 45 Then the Amalekites and the Canaanites who lived in that hill country came down and defeated them, pursuing them as far as Hormah.

At first sight the segment relating God's threat of destruction belongs to this restored, Non-Priestly account. God refers to the people's behavior in the event, while exempting Caleb from the final punishment for his good conduct. But when focusing on the structure and content of the reconstructed narrative, a blunt discrepancy emerges between the sin and the punishment, namely between the actions of both the spies and the people, and the reaction of God. An examination of the verdict in 14:11–25 within the restored Non-Priestly account will help to reveal the authors' use of the tradition of annihilation and thus the theological views it reflects.

3.6 Divine threat of annihilation in context: A theological transplant within a secular story

When the segment of the divine threat of annihilation is read within the context of the Non-Priestly version of the spy story, the threat ostensibly responds to the behavior of the spies during the event. While, as we saw, the spies' actions and report do follow Moses' instructions,[39] one could point to the demoralizing message of their words, ending with frightening information about the inhabitants of the land.[40] This effect is achieved not necessarily by lying or adding unneeded

---

39 See above, 3.1.

40 Frankel's proposal regarding the original beginning of the Non-Priestly story (see above, footnote 28 [p. 41]) could allegedly support such a reading. By assuming that the first and foremost goal of the mission was to prove the fertility of the country (as a response to the people's complaint;

information, but by deviating from the order of Moses' requests. Thus, although they are first asked to report on the inhabitants of the land (Num 13:18–19), the spies begin their report with a reference to the agricultural aspect of the land (v. 27), and only then provide the threatening information about the inhabitants and the cities of the land (v. 28), summarizing with a negative chord. Here is a comparison of the instructions given to the spies and the order of their fulfilment in the report:

Go up there into the Negeb, and go up into the hill country (Num 13:17b)	They went up into the Negeb, and came to Hebron... (13:22)
and see what the land is like, and whether the people who live in it are strong or weak, whether they are few or many... and whether the towns that they live in are unwalled or fortified (13:18–19)	We came to the land to which you sent us; it flows with milk and honey, and this is its fruit (13:27)
and whether the land is rich or poor, and whether there are trees in it or not. Be bold, and bring some of the fruit of the land (13:20)	Yet the people who live in the land are strong, and the towns are fortified and very large; and besides, we saw the descendants of Anak there (13:28)

But the change in the report order can also be taken to stem from the spies' understanding of the goal of their mission – an assessment of the capacity to conquer the intended land – so they close with this topic. This slight interpretation, at any rate, is unlikely to be a reason for such grave a response from the Divine.

What other rationale could evoke God's dramatic response according to the account? One might suggest that the spies' offense was their assertion about being unable to advance towards the inhabitants: "...We are not able to go up against this people, for they are stronger than we" (13:31). Not only could this declaration discourage the people, but it also implies lack of faith in God's ability to prevail, as raised in God's later judgment: "...how long will they refuse to believe in me...?" (14:11).

Nevertheless, in assessing their own means, the spies do not refer to God's abilities or inabilities. Their declaration about their powerlessness comes as a response to Caleb's previous statement regarding the people's capability to seize

---

Frankel 2002, 152–151), the information brought by the spies about the military aspect of the land can be considered as an unsolicited, demoralizing initiative. But the Non-Priestly account mentions Moses' own interest in military information (13:18–19), and thus the information from the spies cannot be regarded as unwanted.

the land by themselves: "... 'Let us go up at once and occupy it, for we are well able to overcome it'" (13:30). It is thus Caleb who initiates a discussion over the capability of the people, by presenting his assessment with no reference to God.[41] If the problem was the issue of ignoring God's role in the equation, Caleb should have been admonished before the others.[42] But neither God nor the narrator seems to be concerned about that. On the contrary, Caleb's words purportedly lead him to be considered as God's faithful servant and entitled to a reward (14:24). It is therefore unlikely to consider the spies' response to Caleb in v. 31 as the ultimate cause for the dramatic decision to destroy the whole nation.

A supposed explanation for God's severe reaction is stated in God's own words in the verdict for the nation. They are accused not only of disbelief in God (14:11b), but also of despising and testing him (v. 11a, 22, 23). Could the people's deeds, then, reflect these admonitions? As we saw, the only explicit disbelief by the people is stated regarding their own ability (13:31), and no indication is given of an intention to question God's ability in the process.[43] As for the accusation of despising God, the spies' plot does not correspond to the common use of the notion "despising God" elsewhere, namely, breaking God's commandments (cf. Deut 31:20; 1Sam 2:17; Jer 23:17).

Indeed, in the narrative of Datan and Abiram in Numbers 16, the accusation of despising the Lord (v. 30) relates to a disobedience to Moses (vv. 28–29). This could be posited as similar to the case of the Non-Priestly spy narrative, which recounts the people's opposition to Moses, stating: "Let us choose a captain, and go back to Egypt" (Num 14:4). But unlike the story of Datan and Abiram (16:28–30), God's accusation in the Non-Priestly spy account makes no mention of the people's attitude to Moses, or of any other political issues. The people's wrongdoing is exclusively criticized in regard to the attitude to God: disbelief in his signs (14:11b, 22a), testing and not listening to him (v. 22b). The picture conveys a relationship in which the people fail to follow the Divine, despite his numerous actions and signs on their behalf.

---

41 Cf. the declaration from Joshua and Caleb in the Priestly account in regard to the role of God in the process of achieving control over the land (14:8).

42 Cf. the supposed wrongdoing of Moses and Aaron in the "Meribah" event at Kadesh, according to Numbers 20. By considering whether they will "... 'bring water for you out of this rock'" (v. 10), they allegedly attribute the success of producing water to themselves. Nevertheless, the ambiguity of this statement within the broader context gave rise to various suggestions regarding the original intention of the narrator about the leaders' transgression. See the diverse rabbinic interpretations in Milgrom 1983, 251, 257–258, 264. For a variety of modern readings of the story see: Mann 1979, 483; Margaliot 1983, 228; Propp 1988, 21; Niesiołowski-Spanò 2009, 26.

43 See in contrast: Exod 17:2; Deut 6:16; Ps 78:18, 41, 56, 95:9, 106:14.

Thus, the denunciation of the people's scorn for and distrust in God in the verdict in Num 14:11, 22–23 seems entirely irrelevant to the sequence of events described in the Non-Priestly version of the story. This discrepancy between the transgression and the punishment led some scholars to suggest that the unit of the divine verdict was not originally part of the narrative of the Non-Priestly sequence.

Indeed, focused on the people's military abilities rather than the relationship with God, the primary core of the story seems to be non-theological and one could even say "secular".[44] Thus, McEvenue talks about "a folk–tale about spying and raiding",[45] Beltz summarizes it as "an ideology of a nomadic military group",[46] and Budd traces a local, secular tradition which narrated a military defeat.[47]

The so-called "secular" characterization of the narrative is notable when compared to the Priestly account of the story which contains, as mentioned, relevant references to God. Such is the congregation's complaint about God (14:2–3) which leads to Joshua and Caleb's reaction referring to God's help (vv. 8–9). Consequently, God's verdict of the people (vv. 27–29) after revealing himself at the tent of meeting (v. 10) responds to the complaint against him (vv. 2–3). In the Non-Priestly account however, God's role seems irrelevant to the narrative and should be assumed as a later addition to the account, converting it into a theological lesson.

This assumption about the literary evolution of the Non-Priestly account of the spy story places the story in parallel with another rebellion narrative from the broad wandering epos, "Massah and Meriba" in Exod 17:1–7. An analysis of the text reveals a primary, coherent, tradition recounting a non-theological quarrel of the people with Moses:

> 1 [...] But there was no water for the people to drink. 2 The people quarreled with Moses, and said, "Give us water to drink". Moses said to them, "Why do you quarrel with me?" [...] 3 But the people thirsted there for water; and the people complained against Moses and said, "Why did you bring us out of Egypt, to kill us and our children and livestock with thirst?" (Exod 17:1–3)

---

44 The anachronistic term "secular" has been used by scholars in referring to texts that deal with non-theological issues. This is how Loewenstamm (1973, 22–23) defines the conversation of the tribes of Gad and Reuben with Moses in Numbers 32, and how Zakovitch (2003, 59) names stories with a "weak" religious dimension. The term can be used to indicate situations based on political considerations, power relations and other human motivations. See Brettler's definition (1996, 71): "Not all ideologies... are religious, and a substantial part of the canon has been shaped by secular ideologies from the political realm".

45 McEvenue 1971, 123.

46 Beltz 1974, 45.

47 Budd 1984, 155, 161.

The remaining verses in the broader account narrate the people's attempt to assess God's presence: "...Moses said to them... Why do you test the LORD?... because the Israelites quarreled and tested the LORD, saying 'Is the LORD among us or not?'" (vv. 2bγ, 7bβ-γ). These comments are attached loosely to the narrative of the quarrel with Moses,[48] and seem to be a later addition, made because of its similar function as an etiological tradition of a place name, i.e., Massah (מסה): "...because they tested (נסתם) the LORD, saying, Is the LORD among us or not?" (cf. Deut 6:16, 9:22). This was attached to a tradition about "Meribah" (מריבה), saying: "He called the place 'Meribah' because the Israelites quarreled (ריב)" (Exod 17:7. Cf. Num 20:13).[49]

The development process traced in the account of "Massah and Meribah" is similar to the process we restored in the Non-Priestly account of Numbers 13–14. In both episodes a political story was reshaped by adding a theological segment, recounting the people's sacrilege in questioning God's presence and ability (Exod 17:2b$_c$, 7b$_b$; Num 14:22). Thus, the final accounts portray the actions of the people within a theological framework of the relationship with God.[50]

While scholars have indeed noticed the weak affiliation of the divine verdict in the Non-Priestly account of the spies, no unanimous conclusion was reached about the literary background of the unit. Some have claimed that the unit was a later addition by scribes from the same Non-Priestly school of the broader account.[51] Others attributed the section to a Deuteronomistic writer, based on evidence typical to the book of Deuteronomy and other Deuteronomistic texts.[52]

---

48 Ibn Ezra also recognized the duplication in the story and explained it as a reflection of the behavior of two different factions among the people, those who complain about lack of water and those who wish to test God (Ibn Ezra on Exod 17:2). For the hypothesis of the two sources in the text see: Driver 1911, 155–158; Noth 1962, 138–139; Seebass 1962, 61–63; Hyatt 1971, 179–182; Childs 1974, 306. See in contrast scholars who classify the section as united and belonging to either E (Propp 1988, 603–604) or J (Baden 2009, 176–177).
49 These stages were already suggested by Noth (1962, 138–139). See also Childs 1974, 306.
50 A similar phenomenon can be traced in the story of the Gadites and Reubenites in Numbers 32. An analysis of the dialogue there reveals a "religious" layer, which defines the tribes' actions "before the Lord" (vv. 20, 21, 22, 27, 29, 32). This layer seems to be secondary to the "secular" narrative which ultimately reports the social and political background of the unique situation of the tribes (vv. 6, 17). See: Loewenstamm 1973, 22–23.
51 See: Wellhausen 1899, 102; Gray 1903, 129; Baentsch 1903, 515–516, 526–529; Holzinger 1903, 50–59; Gressmann 1913, 291; Seebass 1995, 91–93; Coats 1968, 138–39; Sakenfeld 1975, 323–325; Boorer 1992, 337.
52 This assertion relies upon the existence of words and expressions that are known in Deuteronomy and Deuteronomistic literature such as: "a pillar of cloud" and "a pillar of fire" (עמד ענן; עמוד אש, Num 14:14; Deut 1:38); "signs" of God ("אותות", Num 14:22; Deut 4:34, 6:22), and the motifs of God's forgiveness (Num 14:19–20; Deut 29:19; 1Kgs 8:30) and testing God (Num 14:22;

Either way, both views assume that the unit in Num 14:11–25 was a later expansion of the story, namely, extra lines added by an author who felt the need to rewrite the end of the primary plot. But this assumption is not easy to accept. The connection between the supplementary unit (Num 14:11–25) and the rest of the account is based on two pieces of information linked only loosely to the central plot: the statement of Caleb's fate (14:24) and the data regarding the peoples who dwell in the land (v. 25).

Starting with the latter, the reference to the peoples of the land in God's words (14:25), goes back ostensibly to the information mentioned earlier in the main narrative (13:29). However, the two pieces of information provide contradictory details; one indicates that "the Amalekites live in the land of the Negeb... and the Canaanites live by the sea, and along the Jordan" (13:29), and the other states that both "the Amalekites and the Canaanites live in the valleys" (14:25). If the comment in God's words about the peoples of the land was written as a supplement to the main account, one would expect a more careful correspondence with the information provided earlier.

The second comment in the text which is supposedly relevant to the main story is God's mention of Caleb, defining him as having a "different spirit" and as "following God wholeheartedly" (14:24a). These designations, however, do not match the behavior of the protagonist as described earlier in the plot, which, as we saw, does not convey any intentional loyalty to God (13:30).[53] Furthermore, the sentence about Caleb in God's words (14:24) fails to match its close context of the alternative penalty of not seeing the land (vv. 22–23), as Caleb is missing from God's initial plan to annihilate the entire people (vv. 11–12).[54] If God's goal was to

---

Deut 6:16). See: Noth 1968, 108; Budd 1984, 152–153; Balentine 1985, 66–71; Aurelius 1988, 132–134; Blum 1990, 134; Vervenne 1994, 265; Ska 2006, 93. Alongside the vocabulary argument this claim also depends on the centrality of the story of the spies in the book of Deuteronomy (chapters 1, 9). But this argument works equally well in both directions, i.e. that the story was available to the Deuteronomistic writers and influenced them.

53 The "secular" character of Caleb's encouragement of the people is further recognized in light of the speech of both Caleb and Joshua in the Priestly version, which demonstrates their eagerness to protect God's reputation (14:6–9) in response to the people's complaint (vv. 2–3).

54 Note that Moses' exemption is not stated explicitly in the transition to the punishment of not entering the land. Nevertheless, it is implied by pointing to the people as third-person subject, and designating their wrongdoing with the verb נאץ (despise): "...none of those who despised me shall see it'" (v. 23). This goes back to the first accusation of the people that contained a threat to destroy them: "...'How long will this people despise me?...'" (v. 11). Thus, Moses' exemption from the people's punishment is a continuation of the initial immunity he was granted (14:12). In fact, the idea of Moses' death in the desert alongside the whole generation seems to be unknown to the writers. Indeed, the narratives that refer to Moses' death in the desert (e.g., Num 20:12; Deut 1:37, 3:26, 4:21, 31:2, 34:4–8) contain residues of a tradition according to which Moses was destined to complete his duty and therefore to die in the desert, while the generation itself managed to enter the land. See Kugler 2018, 199–204.

treat Caleb differently because of his unique behavior, it would have been mentioned earlier as part of the initial threat of destruction. Without it, the reference to Caleb in the unit seems not to match the prior intentions of the verdict.[55]

The loose connection of God's verdict in 14:11–25 with the broader Non-Priestly account undermines the view that the verdict was an expansion of the main story. Instead, it seems to preserve an independent tradition about a potential fatal punishment for the people's unfaithful behavior to God.[56] This tradition was attached to a non-religious story about a revolt rising during the preparation for settling in the land, bound together by a reference to one of the protagonists in the story, Caleb (14:24),[57] without updating the rest of the verdict in regard to the protagonist's role (cf. 14:11–12).

Thus, while the original ending of the non-religious story was not preserved,[58] stages in the process of the story composition can be traced, revealing a pattern similar to the one we found in the Golden Calf episode. The two accounts share not only the scene of the threat of destruction, but also the literary process in which a unit with God's deathly threat was a secondary addition to the main plot.

What are the connections between the two units of the threat of destruction found here and in the Calf episode, and where did they stem from? We deal with these questions in the next chapter.

---

55 Frankel (2002, 153–154, 167) argues for the secondary nature of Caleb in the broader Non-Priestly account, based on his sudden appearance without an introduction (Num 13:30), and on his absence from the scene of the people's disobedience in going up the hill (14:44). This argument deviates from the commonly held view that the reference to Caleb was rooted in the ancient account, providing justification for the Calebites' connection to Hebron. See: Gressmann 1913, 295–297; Coats 1968, 250–251; Noth 1972, 130; Budd 1984, 144.

56 The unit seems not to include the idea of forty years of wandering in the desert, in contrast to the information given in the Priestly account (Num 14:34).

57 This conclusion was briefly implied, without explanations, in McEvenue's analysis of the text (1971, 91): "It is clear that v. 24, which deals with Caleb, belongs to the JE account... But surely the idea of seeing glory and signs, Egypt and the desert, the 'ten occasions'... of vv. 21–23a belong rather to the context of Sinai and Exodus 32 than to the context of the original spy-story...".

58 The continuation of the editorial work can be found in Num 14:39–45, describing the efforts of the people to change the divine decision.

4 The annihilation-threat tradition

4.1 Two occurrences of one proto-tradition in the Pentateuch

Due to the similar structure and related themes in the units of the threat of destruction embedded in the Golden Calf and the spy episodes, scholars tend to suggest a literary reliance of one text on the other. The common view is that the shorter unit, found in Exod 32:7–14, was the foundation of the more complex one in Num 14:11–25.[1] Thus, Moses' arguments in Num 14:13–19 are assumed to be an expansion of the appeal in Exod 32:11–13, and God's final sentence in Num 14:20–24 is considered an amplification of the brief decision in Exod 32:14.

Nonetheless, numerous linguistic and textual differences between the units weaken the plausibility of a direct literary reliance of one upon the other. A notable difference between the units lies in the accusations against the people. While in Exodus 32 the people are blamed for being "stiff-necked" (v. 9), in Numbers 14 they are accused of disbelief, despising God and testing him (14:11, 22). Another point of difference is the concern about the image of God, according to Exod 32:12, as a killer of his own people, as opposed to the concern according to Num 14:13–16, about his being viewed as powerless by the Egyptians and the peoples of the land. A further noticeable distinction is the different terminology for similar matters in the units. The notion of annihilation is stated in Exodus 32 with the root כלה (ואכלם, v.10), while in Numbers 14 it is expressed with the noun דֶּבֶר (pestilence, v. 12). Additionally, the reference to the proven quality of the God-Israel relationship in the past, manifested by the rescue from Egypt, is expressed in Exodus 32 with the root יצא (הוצאת מארץ מצרים, v. 11), and in Numbers with the root עלה (העלית בכחך, Num 14:13).

To this record of mismatches, one should add the different nature of the list of God's attributes,[2] found in the spy episode (Num 14:18) and in the broader context of the Golden Calf story (Exod 34:6–7). While the latter does not appear in the immediate narrative of the people's deeds at Sinai, but rather in the context of the second giving of the law, some claim that the list is a continuation of the event

---

1 See: Sakenfeld 1985, 73–74; Boorer 1992, 331–63; Levine 1993, 380–381; Nicholson 2002, 191–192.

2 The sages use the name *Middot* ("attributes") to indicate the list of divine features, and reckon a total of thirteen (Bavli, Rosh Hashana 17:2). However, the text does not include this number, as demonstrated by Shadal (Samuel David Luzzatto, 1800–1865) who provides thirteen (!) different ways of counting the listed divine characteristics (Klein 2015, 447–450).

https://doi.org/10.1515/9783110609905-004

of the Golden Calf.[3] Based on this assumption they argue that Exod 34:6–7 influenced the list cited by Moses in Num 14:17–18. The key argument for this derives from Moses' words to God in Numbers 14, כאשר דברת ("as you said", v. 17), seemingly pointing to a previous moment in which God revealed his sacred characteristics to Moses.[4]

However, while the two lists contain similar terms such as ארך אפים ורב חסד ("slow to anger, and abounding in steadfast love", Exod 34:6; Num 14:18); נשא עון ופשע ("forgiving iniquity and transgression", Exod 34:7; Num 14:18), and נקה לא ינקה פקד עון אבת על בנים... ("by no means clearing the guilty, visiting the iniquity of the parents upon the children", ibid.; ibid.) – the list considered the later, in Numbers 14, omits two expressions found in Exod 34:6–7: רחום וחנן ("merciful and gracious". Cf. Exod 34:6) and נצר חסד לאלפים ("keeping steadfast love for the thousandth generation". Cf. Exod 34:7). One would expect to find the use of these expressions in Numbers 14 as a support for Moses' purpose to manifest God's gracious ways.[5]

---

3 See: Childs 1974, 612; Tweig 1977, 71; Moberly 1983, 131–128; Levine 1993, 381. See in contrast the claim that Exodus 34 does not belong to the same scribe(s) or school as in Exodus 32: Driver 1911, 350–367; Schwartz 2000(a), 256–258; Friedman 2003, 173–177. Cf. Noth (1968, 109, 261) who claims that Exod 34:6–7 is secondary in the contextual J narrative that frames it, suggesting that the list derives from an ancient ritual context and was embedded into a context that engaged with the description of God. For similar assumptions about the nature of Exod 34:6–7 see: Holzinger 1900, 115; Baentsch 1903, 281; Dentan 1963, 34–38; Beyerlin 1965, 137–138; Hyatt 1971, 323–322; Durham 1987, 454.

4 It is rather difficult, however, to determine the identity of the speaker in Exodus 34. In the statement that "The LORD passed before him, and proclaimed 'The LORD, the LORD...'" (ויעבר יהוה על פניו ויקרא יהוה יהוה, 34:6) it is unclear whether the name of God was said by God himself (cf. Exod 20:4–5) or by Moses (cf. Jonah 4:2). Ibn Ezra argues that God is the speaker: "Do not be astonished for Hashem calls 'Hashem' because he alone knows, and knowing, and is known, and this is a very deep concern..." (Ibn Ezra on Exod 34:6. My translation). Nevertheless, the commentator finds it difficult to explain the syntactic structure of the sentence: "... the Gaon [Rabbi Saadia Gaon] said that the first name ["the Lord", יהוה, v. 6] follows [the verb] "proclaimed" [i.e., ויקרא יהוה, "The Lord proclaimed"]. If this is true, why do the cantillations not adhere with that?" In this regard see Ehrlich's commentary, from the end of the 19th century, who solves the "problem" of the cantillation tradition on the basis of the reference in Num 14:17, where Moses cites God, saying "in the way that you promised when you spoke" (כאשר דברת) (Ehrlich 1969, 204). See also Jacob 1992, 982.

5 Cf. Nehemiah's use of the more compassionate attributes for his needs: ואתה אלוה סליחות חנון ורחום ארך אפים ורב חסד ולא עזבתם ("... But you are a God ready to forgive, gracious and merciful, slow to anger and abounding in steadfast love, and you did not forsake them", Neh 9:17. Cf.: Ps 103:6–9).

Their relevance is certainly much stronger than a statement such as נקה לא ינקה (Num 14:18), which proclaims a message opposed to compassion.[6]

Thus, it is difficult to agree with the supposition that the list in Exod 34:6–7 was the basis for creating the one in Num 14:17–18. It is rather more likely that the two lists reflect a widely common custom of stating divine characteristics as a mantra in a context of appeals to God, as known from various liturgical texts in the Bible, using a similar basic formula (Jer 32:18; Joel 2:13; Jonah 4:2; Nah 1:2–3; Ps 86:15, 103:8, 111:4, 112:6, 116:5, 145:8; Neh 9:17, 31).[7]

The differences of content and terminology in the accounts of God's threat of destruction in Exod 32:7–14 and Num 14:11–25, including the abovementioned disparity in the lists of divine attributes (Exod 34:6–7; Num 14:18), indicate a lack of direct influence between the two texts. Instead, we would suggest that each one of them is a different manifestation of a tradition about a moment of threat to the existence of the people of Israel. This tradition reflects a theological world-view of the fragile and uncertain nature of the people despite their connection with God, as stated in the supposed context of the aftermath of the Calf event: "... 'you are a stiff-necked people; if for a single moment I should go up among you, I would consume you...'" (Exod 33:5). The failure and potential disappearance of the community, according to this view, is regardless of their status as God's ally. This idea is known from texts outside the Priestly literature, where the scenario of a total ruin of the people is presented as a plausible method among various modes of punishment (e.g., Exod 33:3, 5; Deut 4:25–26, 8:19–20, 11:17, 28:19–22, 62–64, 30:17–18; Josh 23:16; 2Kgs 24:1–2; Jer 7:29, 9:10–12, 27:10).[8] This approach

---

6 See Muffs' discomfort with the inappropriate choice of attributes in the appeal of Moses in Numbers 14: "This quotation [Num 14:18] is unexpected. After all, a verse such as 'visiting the iniquity of the parents upon the children... and by no means clearing the guilty' [the reverse of the text order is based on Muff's citation] ought to increase the wrath of the divine, but in the story of the spies would we not expect words of conciliation?!" (Muffs 1984, 48. My translation).
7 See Gray's suggestion (Gray 1903, 155) that Num 14:17–18 uses the list from Exod 34:6–7 together with additional ancient material. See also Fishbane's comment: "... it is clear that Moses [in Num 14:17] recites the formulary to YHWH as a reminder to him of the divine attributes revealed after the people's apostasy through worship of the Golden Calf. It must be kept in mind, however, that Num 14:17 may actually reflect an interpretation of Exod 34:6a – an exegetical *traditio* – not the original text of the *traditio*" (Fishbane 1985, 335).
8 In this regard it is worth mentioning the statements in Jeremiah 4–5 that promise that a full destruction will not occur while the broader literary context envisages a complete end of the land and the people: "For thus says the LORD: The whole land shall be a desolation; yet I will not make a full end" (Jer 4:27); "Go up through her vine-rows and destroy, but do not make a full end..." (5:10. Cf. v. 18. And see in context: 4:23–28, 5:9–11, 15–19). The discrepancy indicates the secondary nature of the comments about limited destruction, implemented in texts that in the first place proclaimed a full disaster with no exceptions. See: Rofe 2014, 224–225.

differs from what is found in texts belonging to the Priestly school, that even when considering a disaster to be applied on the collective, they either portray it as restrained or partial, or suggest an escape route to ensure remnants (e.g., Lev 26:38–45; Num 17:9–15, 25, 25:10–13).[9]

As we showed, the literary units found in the Golden Calf and the spy episodes, recounting high risk moments in the people's life, are not coherent with the broader narrative in which they are embedded.[10] The particular units relate the divine threat of destruction to either rebellious behavior of the people (considered "stiff necked", Exod 32:9), or to their conduct in despising and distrusting God (by testing him repeatedly, Num 14:11, 22–23). These categories of behavior are not demonstrated, as said above, in the actual stories where the units of destruction are set, indicating that these units belong to other narratives that were not preserved in their complete form.

Whereas the "original" narratives cannot be restored, allegations similar to the abovementioned categories are found in another text in the Hebrew Bible, Psalm 78, which also mentions the potential danger of annihilation from the time of the wilderness. An examination of this narrative within the broader context of the psalm will provide further evidence for the existence of the motif of the threat of destruction as a notion separate from the two stories of the Pentateuch.

4.2 "And [he] did not destroy them": A threat of annihilation implied in Psalm 78

Within the extensive review of the story of the people of Israel in Psalm 78, a considerable portion is devoted to the period of the people's wandering in the wilderness (vv. 13–41, 52–54). This section includes an allusion to a momentary threat to destroy the people (v. 38) by stressing that being compassionate (והוא רחום) God has not fulfilled the threat of destruction (ולא ישחית),[11] while not specifying the reason that aroused the danger.

---

9 And see above, Introduction, section 1.2, and 3.4.

10 See above, 2.6 and 3.6.

11 The lethal meaning of שחת is manifest in numerous occurrences of the verb in regard to God's destruction: Gen 6:13, 13:10, 19:14, 29; Ezek 9:8, 43:3; Lam 2:5–6. Likewise, it is demonstrated in the equivalence with the root כלה in Ezek 20:17 (cf. Exod 32:10), and the lexical variation in Ps 106:23 (שמד-שחת). The combination of שחת and compassion (רחם) appears in Jeremiah's prediction of the calamity over Judah: "I will not pity or spare or have compassion (ארחם) when I destroy them (מהשחיתם)" (Jer 13:14).

The reference to God's avoidance of destruction fits the message of the historical review in the psalm. The review contrasts the people's blatant violation of the divine laws with God's good intentions on behalf of the people. It stresses that whereas the people have unceasingly transgressed and rebelled against God (vv. 17, 18–20, 32, 36–37, 40–41), God kept making positive gestures on their behalf (vv. 13–16, 23–28).[12] Thus, even when the people evoked God's wrath – "Therefore, when the LORD heard, he was full of rage; a fire was kindled against Jacob, his anger mounted against Israel" (v. 21) – God punished them using all sort of methods (vv. 22–33) but repressed his anger and forsook the intention to destroy them (v. 38). However, from the negative phrasing we grasp the tendency: God had intended to destroy the people. Moreover, this happened, apparently, repeatedly: "... often (והרבה) he restrained his anger, and did not stir up all his wrath" (v. 38).

The unbalanced relationship between God and the people is further portrayed in the psalm by a lengthy reference to the period in Egypt (v. 42–51), oddly positioned after the elaborated review of the time in the wilderness (vv. 13–41). While one could claim that an editorial error affected the psalm's chronological outline,[13] it is more likely that the peculiar placement of the spectacular events in Egypt, namely the plagues suffered by the Egyptians (vv. 42–51),[14] was chosen

---

12 Some scholars point to the expressions in verse 2, "parable" (משל), and "enigmas of the past" (חידות מני-קדם), as the psalmist's amazed diagnosis of the people's supposed lack of reciprocity during the history in regard to God's favors. See: Weiser 1962, 541; Clifford 1981, 125; Witte 2006, 33. Less convincing is Wagner's interpretation of the psalmist's "riddle" as a perplexity over the fall of Judah and Jerusalem "...even though God had elected its people, city and kingdom" (Wagner 2014, 21). More than the psalm deals with exile or destruction, it engages with God's rejection of Ephraim/Israel as an explanation for the choice and therefore the hegemony of the Davidic monarchy (vv. 68–72).
13 See: Campbell 1979, 59; Briggs and Briggs 1986, 179, 187.
14 The list of the plagues in the psalm does not correspond with the entire list known from the final form of Exodus and seems to reflect a tradition of a shorter list, of seven plagues only. This number is obtained by two alternative counts. The first separates the parallelism of the "swarms of flies" (ערב) and the "frog" (צפרדע) in verse 45 (Goulder 1995, 78; Leonard 2008, 248). The second proposes to join the "swarms of flies" together with the "frog" but to regard the second mention of the hail (ברד) in verse 48 as another affliction, as may be preserved in the Symmachus Greek manuscript (see Loewenstamm 1992[b], 80–81; Kraus 1989, 122; Zakovitch 1997, 122). As the number seven is typologically equivalent to ten, it is possible that Psalm 78 reflects an alternative tradition to the one known from Exodus 7–11. Moreover, it is plausible that the list of ten in Exodus is based on a collection of seven, as appearing in Psalm 78 and in Ps 105:27–36 (see: Loewenstamm 1992[b], 83. Cf. Kirkpatrick 1898, 473).

deliberately.[15] Thus, the section about Egypt resonates with the marvels in the time of the exodus (vv. 12–16), and frames the description of the people's ungrateful behavior (vv. 17–42).[16] This enhances the image of God's unappreciated generosity to the people in the wilderness.

As part of the portrayal of the people's ingratitude for God's generosity, the review points to them as "a stubborn and rebellious generation... whose heart was not steadfast, whose spirit was not faithful to God" (v. 8), and characterizes their transgressions as testing God (vv. 18–20, 41) and expressing their disbelief in him (vv. 22, 32, 37). These allegations allude to the accusations heard in our two units of the threat of destruction in the Pentateuch. The first describes the people as "stiff necked" (Exod 32:9), meaning disobedient to authority (cf. Deut 31:27; Jer 17:23, 19:15; Neh 9:29).[17] And the second accuses them of despising and distrusting God by testing him repeatedly (Num 14:11, 22–23). In light of these links, one would expect to find an allusion in the psalm to at least one of the two stories mentioned in the Pentateuch, as the supposed settings where God proclaimed the possible destruction. But this is not the case. Despite the reference to the danger of annihilation and the appearance of similar allegations, the psalm does not allude to either the Golden Calf story or the spy episode.

The absence of the stories of the Calf and the spies from the psalm's review can be supposedly explained as a result of the author's random choice of events. Thus, the psalm mentions the splitting of the Sea (Ps 78:13. Cf. Exod 14:21–22); the divine guidance by pillars of cloud and fire (Ps 78:14. Cf. Exod 13:21); the water for the people from rocks (Ps 78:15–16. Cf. Exod 17:6; Num 20:8–11); the people's demand for food (Ps 78:18–20. Cf. Exod 16:2–3, 17:2; Num 11:4–6, 20:5); and the rain of manna (Ps 78:24. Cf. Exod 16:4, 15), and meat (Ps 78:27–31. Cf. Exod 16:13; Num 13:31–34).[18] At the same time the psalm makes no reference to many events, mentioned both in the Pentateuch and in various other historical reviews in the Bible, such as the giving of the law at Sinai (Exodus 19; Neh 9:14), the giving of

---

15 See: Clifford 1981, 129, 133; Hoffman 1983, 98–99; Greenstein 1990, 209; Zakovitch 1997, 165. See also the definition by Gärtner (2015, 378), talking about "two rounds through the salvation history of Israel [according to the psalm] with a structural and conceptual analogy".

16 The people's rebellion (vv. 17–41) is also framed with references to God's actions at the sea. The information in verses 52–53 that "Then he led out his people like sheep, and guided them in the wilderness like a flock. **He led them** (וינחם) in safety, so that they were not afraid; but **the sea overwhelmed** (כסה הים) their enemies", echoes the description in verses 13–14: "**He divided the sea** (בקע ים) and let them pass through it, and made the waters stand like a heap. In the daytime **he led them** (וינחם) with a cloud, and all night long with a fiery light".

17 See above, 2.6.

18 On the literary affinities of the psalm to the Pentateuch see: Haglund 1984, 90–95; Briggs and Briggs 1986, 183–185; Greenstein 1990, 204–208; Leonard 2006, 129–221.

the Sabbath (Exod 16:23, 20:8–11; Neh 9:14); the incident involving Dathan and Abiram (Num 16:25–33; Ps 106:17); the fight at waters of Meribah (Num 20:13; Ps 106:32); the victory over King Sihon of Heshbon and King Og of Bashan (Num 21:23–35; Neh 9:22); and the action of Pinehas (Num 25:8; Ps 106:30). Could the absence of the Calf and the spy incidents be no more than random?

As we will see, these two central stories of the wandering narrative, the Calf and the spies, could fit well within the psalm's literary structure and didactic messages, even without the notion of near destruction. As such, the stories' absence might indicate that the author had no awareness of them in any literary form, and thus, that he was familiar with the concept of near destruction from different sources or contexts.

4.3 The affinity between the generations and the absence of the Calf and spy stories

While it is usually difficult to trace the scope and shape of a text's literary sources from what it does not say, the absence of the episodes of the Golden Calf and the spy mission in the collective memory embodied in Psalm 78 may reveal something about the author's knowledge of literary material.

The absence of the two stories from the chronological list is noticeable when considering the equivalence drawn in the psalm between the new era in the land and the days in the desert. The psalm recounts that when the people finally settled in the land they turned away and acted treacherously,[19] and in this way repeated the behavior of their ancestors who were "...twisting like a treacherous bow" (נהפכו כקשת רמיה, v. 57). This simile for the treacherous behavior of the people in the land indeed corresponds to a reference in the historical review of the conduct of the so-called "Ephraimites", who were "armed with the bow", but "turned back on the day of battle" (נושקי רומי קשת הפכו ביום קרב, v. 9).[20] Whereas the allegation conveys a vague image of the event of the withdrawal,[21] its immediate

---

19 ויסגו ויבגדו (v. 57). Cf. the NRSV's translation: "were faithless", like other uses of the word בגד in the meaning of a betrayal of God: Jer 3:20, 5:11; Hos 5:7, 6:7; Ps 73:15.

20 The warriors are described with both the words נשק and רמה, referring to the skills of archery (cf. Jer 4:29; 1Chr 12:2; 2Chr 17:17). Some suggest that the word נושקי in the verse (Ps 78:9) is a gloss that was added to explain the earlier but less familiar expression, רומי קשת. See Campbell 1979, 56; Zakovitch 1997, 128–129.

21 In an attempt to identify the event alluded to in verse 9, Weiser (1962, 540) points to the defeat against the Philistines at Gilboa and the death of Saul and his sons; Clifford (1981, 132) points to the war period in the days of the northern kingdom; Haglund (1984, 90–89) refers to the destruction of the kingdom; and Eissfeldt (1958, 33), Campbell (1979, 61) and Zakovitch

context connects the withdrawal with lack of faith in God (v. 8) and a violation of his laws (v. 10).[22] These allegations are indeed stated in regard to the treacherous people situated in the land (vv. 56b–57), who, as explicitly said, have continued the behavior pattern of their predecessors: they "turned away and were faithless like their ancestors" (v. 57).

The description of the people's pattern of behavior includes also a reference to a tendency to rebel against God and test his abilities: "Yet they tested the Most High God, and rebelled against him" (וינסו וימרו את אלהים עליון, v. 56a). This indeed resonates with the behavior in the time in the wilderness, when the people "... sinned still more against him, rebelling against the Most High in the desert. They tested God in their heart by demanding the food they craved" (ויוסיפו עוד לחטא לו למרות עליון בציה. וינסו אל בלבבם לשאל אכל לנפשם, vv. 17–18), and as is reaffirmed: "How often they rebelled against him in the wilderness and grieved him in the desert! They tested God again and again, and provoked the Holy One of Israel" (כמה ימרוהו במדבר יעציבוהו בישימון. וישובו וינסו אל וקדוש ישראל התוו, vv. 40–41).

The close affinity between the past and the present generations is implied also by the dual meanings associated with the term "Ephraimites" mentioned in the historical review. Whereas verse 11 states that the Ephraimites had seen God's "miracles that he had shown them", pointing to either the miracles in Egypt, or in the desert, verse 12 communicates that the Ephraimites were the descendants of those who had seen "marvels in the land of Egypt", thus identifying them as the offspring of the exodus generation.[23] The apparent duality of the identity of the Ephraimites as both the Egypt generation and their offspring draws a close connection between the generations, while almost losing a distinction between them.

The absence of distinction appears also in the description of the journey from Egypt to the land, portrayed as a journey of a single entity along the entire way. Thus, the psalm narrates that God:

(1997, 129) identify it with the war against the Philistines that caused the destruction of Shiloh, as mentioned later in the psalm.

22 For the affinity of verse 9 with the verses nearby see: Kirkpatrick 1898, 476; Gosling 1999, 505–506.

23 The Midrash, followed by Rashi, solves this duality by identifying the "Ephraimites" as a factional group among the Egypt generation that advanced towards the land before the rest of the people: "...the Ephraimites... who are of the seed of kingship and mighty men in war took their wives out of Egypt, and the Egyptians chased them and killed two hundred thousand, all of them mighty..." (Pirke De-Rabbi Eliezer, 48. My translation). The Midrash proposal might be based on the ambiguous reference in Chronicles that points to the Ephraimites who settled in the land before the time of the exodus: "The sons of Ephraim... Now the people of Gath, who were born in the land, killed them, because they came down to raid their cattle" (1Chr 7:20–21).

52... led out his people like sheep,
and guided them in the wilderness like a flock.
53 He led them in safety, so that they were not afraid;
but the sea overwhelmed their enemies.
54 And he brought them to his holy hill,
to the mountain that his right hand had won.
55 He drove out nations before them;
he apportioned them for a possession
and settled the tribes of Israel in their tents (Ps 78:52–55)

Whereas elsewhere in the psalm the psalmist has no difficulty in pointing to the people's numerous generations or groups (as elaborated in the prologue: "our ancestors"; "their children"; "the last generation"; "Jacob"; "Israel"; "the children yet unborn", vv. 3–8), the blurred boundaries between the generation of the desert and the people that entered the land seem deliberate.[24] This further manifests that God's generosity was granted to the people despite their ongoing ingratitude towards him, and despite their continuous misbehavior during the desert period and since then.[25]

The close affinity between the period in the wilderness and the time in the land, as portrayed in the psalm, could be strongly supported by alluding to the episodes of the Golden Calf and the spy mission. Considering first the latter incident, the spy story could be used in the psalm as a demonstration of the allegations about the people's tendency to test God and rebel against him (Ps 78:56. Cf. v. 18). Thus, the divine verdict in the Non-Priestly version of the spy story points to the people's tendency to despise God, disbelieve in him (Num 14:11), and test him (v. 22). Moreover, as the Non-Priestly version of the spy story recounts a supposed retreat of the people to Egypt (Num 14:4), the historical review of Psalm 78 could refer to the spy event to demonstrate the allegation about the withdrawal as treachery in the past (Ps 78:57. Cf. v. 9).[26] Additionally, the spy story could fit well

---

24 Cf. the review in Ezekiel 20 that distinguishes between the ancestors and the offspring in the desert (vv. 18–26), and the distinction in Nehemiah between the forefathers in the desert and the sons who inherit the land (9:23–24). The review in Ps 105, in contrast, does not mention the various generations but distinguishes between "they" of the past and "we", the speakers, who wish to be saved in the present (Ps 105:33–48).

25 The direct continuity between the generations might also reflect an older Deuteronomic tradition according to which the people who entered the land were the same people who left Egypt and walked in the desert, as they were not supposed to perish in the desert (cf. Deut 3:26, 4:21). See Kugler 2018, 201–204.

26 See Barnes' attempt to attribute to the "Ephraimites" mentioned in verse 9 the sin of the spies in the desert: "The historical reference [in v. 9] is no doubt to the refusal of Israel, when they heard the report of the spies, to advance into Canaan (Num XIV 1–10)... It is promptly punished by the

into the pro-Judaic advocacy of the psalm, presenting the superiority of Judah over the other tribes (Ps 78:67–68),[27] by pointing to the past preference for the Judean spy, Caleb, over the representatives of the other tribes (Num 14:24).[28] While the psalm contains no essential material of Priestly traditions,[29] it uses abundant Non-Priestly material known from the Pentateuch (J or E),[30] and one might then expect familiarity with the Non-Priestly version of the spy story.

The striking absence of the spy story from the psalm is stressed in Ibn Ezra's attempt to find an allusion to the event in the psalm, arguing that the expression "in spite of all this they still sinned" in verse 32 in the psalm (בכל זאת חטאו עוד) implies the accusation mentioned in the spy story in Numbers 14, stating "...and yet [they] have tested me these ten times and have not obeyed my voice"

---

sentence that Israel should remain forty years in the wilderness" (Barnes 1931, 377). Furthermore, Barnes claims that the "Ephraimites" in their new incarnation in the land also sinned in adopting and implementing the Golden Calf cult into the northern kingdom's rituals: "Ephraim went beyond Judah in rebellion by adopting the worship of the Golden Calf" (ibid.).

27 And it is not impossible (Kugler, forthcoming) that the psalm's emphasis on the Judean superiority reveals a direct familiarity with the northern tribes, as "the other entity" portrayed within the socio-political equation.

28 Cf. the superiority of both the Judean and the Ephraimite representatives, Caleb and Joshua, over the other tribes, according to the Priestly version of the spy story (Num 13:6, 8, 14:30, 38). While the identity of Caleb as a Judean is mentioned only in the Priestly account (Num 13:3), the tradition of Caleb's connections with the tribe of Judah or the Judean territory is implied also outside the Priestly account (Num 13:22; Josh 14:6, 15:14; Judg 1:10; 1Sam 25:2–3, 30:14; 1Chr 2:42), and could be in the background of the above mentioned separated Non-Priestly spy story.

29 One could claim that the psalm attests familiarity with the Priestly source through the reference to the crossing of the divided sea (v. 13), known from the Priestly thread in Exod 14:16, 21, 22–23 (see: Driver 1953, 119; Propp 1999, 480–481; Friedman 2003, 143). But the image of the sea in the psalm is closer to the terminology found in the poetic description of the event in Exodus 15, considered a Non-Priestly composition and one of the earliest works in the Pentateuch. Thus, both the psalm and the ancient poetry in Exodus 15 use the verb יצב ("stand"), and the image נד (כמו נד, "like a heap", Exod 15:8; Ps 78:13) to describe God's operation on the water. Likewise, the two texts use the verb עבר in referring to the crossing of the people (Ps 78:13; Exod 15:16). These all differ from the prosaic text in Exodus that uses the verbs בוא (14:16, 22), הלך (14:21), and the word חמה (wall, v. 22) for the water.

30 See Day (1986, 9, 11), who argues that the psalm uses mainly material from J rather than P or E (Cf. Leonard 2006, 111–115, 2008 248–250). Kraus claims a use of Non-Priestly traditions arrived orally to the psalm rather than in writing (Kraus 1989, 123. Cf. Greenstein 1990, 214). Goulder argues that the psalmist was familiar with traditions of the wandering in the wilderness without the Sinaitic traditions, some of which were E, thus reinforcing the claim about the northern origin of the psalm (Goulder 1995, 78–79). Leonard argues that the psalm relies on Non-Priestly traditions with ancient roots like the song in Exodus 15; the song in Deuteronomy 32; the story of the ark in 1 Samuel 4–6 and 2 Samuel 6, and other material from the JE traditions (Leonard 2006, 274–300, 2008, 248).

(וינסו אתי זה עשרה פעמים, Num 14:22). Ezra also tracks the consequence of the spy event in the psalm's description of God's responsibility for the abrupt death of the people: "So he made their days vanish like a breath, and their years in terror" (Ps 78:33). The word "breath" in the verse (הבל, Ps 78:33) is for Ezra a marker for the people's punishment in the spy story, an outcome caused by not fulfilling the mission "for which they have left Egypt", in Ezra's words.[31] In that way he adds to the psalm the missing tradition of the death of the generation of the desert.

As with the narrative of the spies, an allusion to the Golden Calf episode could also demonstrate the equivalence drawn in the psalm between the deeds in the wilderness and the behavior in the land. The story could be used as a precedent for the accusation stated in the psalm that the people performed idolatry in the land (v. 58), as a pattern continuing from the days of their fathers (v. 57). A reference to the Golden Calf event could also enhance the psalm's socio-political message, aimed at delegitimizing Joseph and Ephraim (Ps 78:67). Thus, as the calf worship was a central element in the propagandist discourse against the northern kingdom (cf. 1Kgs 12:32; 2Kgs 10:29, 17:16; Hos 8:5–6, 13:2), a reference to the ritual from the past could be an effective support for the psalmist's condemnation of the conduct in the north.

Scholars engaged with the noticeable absence of the Calf story from the psalm by explaining it as a result of the psalmist's reluctance to defame the northern kingdom's cult. This was suggested by Leonard together with the deduction that the psalm was written in the days of Hezekiah's reign. Leonard suggests that the psalmist avoided condemning the sacred customs of the north in order to obtain the northern refugees' trust.[32] But it is difficult to accept that the psalmist was so considerate about this custom of the northern kingdom whereas he kept recounting Israel's transgressions and failures (vv. 56–67).

Alternatively, the absence of the past narratives is explained as an attempt to relate the people's idolatrous behavior to the time after the erection of Shiloh.[33] However, not only is the episode from the wilderness entirely missing from the psalm's review, but also absent from the psalm is the calf ritual performed by the northern kingdom after the time of Shiloh, even though it could demonstrate the allegation about the later idolatry in the land (v. 58. Cf. 1Kgs 12:28–30; Hos 8:5–6). The silence about the calf ritual in the land might reflect the circumstances of the psalm's composition, when the northern kingdom's cult was not

---

31 Ibn Ezra to Ps 78:33 (my translation).
32 Leonard 2006, 338–340.
33 See Zakovitch 1997, 178.

yet a target for criticism, or was not even in existence.[34] Consequently, the Penta-teuchal tradition of the Golden Calf was at that point not yet used as an attack on the nation's cultic customs.

The absence of the Golden Calf and the spy episodes from the review in Psalm 78 is therefore noticeable in light of the chronological outline and didactic struc-ture of the text. Without the known stories, the idea of God's recurrent threat to destroy the nation is presented in the psalm (v. 38) as an outcome of generally rebellious behavior and lack of trust in God (vv. 17–18, 32, 37, 40–42). Neither the people's tendencies nor God's inclination to destroy them, are explained in the psalm as deriving from the narratives recounted in the Pentateuch.

This deduction strengthens our conclusion above that the concept of the divine threat of destruction in the desert existed in other forms before it was inte-grated into the narratives of the Golden Calf and the spy mission. Only in a later stage of their composition did those narratives adopt the motif of destruction, changing their theological and didactic message.

4.4 God's compassion

As Psalm 78 does not mention the Calf and the spy incidents from the days in the wilderness, it also lacks the scene of Moses' attempt to prevent the threat of destruction. Instead, the withdrawal of the destruction is attributed to God's own initiative, due to his compassionate nature[35]: "Yet he, being compassionate, forgave their iniquity, and did not destroy them; often he restrained his anger, and did not stir up all his wrath" (v. 38).

Whereas the Pentateuchal events are not mentioned, the reference to God's compassionate character links to the divine attributes listed in the context of the

---

34 I would argue that the psalm reflects a relatively early stage in the relationship of the two po-litical entities (Kugler, forthcoming). This stands in contrast to the claim that the psalm was writ-ten after the fall of the northern kingdom, indicated by the declaration of the rejection of Israel in verses 59 and 67 (Leonard 2006, 336–337; Clifford 1981, 138–141). But the description of David's superiority to Jacob-Israel seems to indicate Israel as still existing. Other analyses date the psalm to the post-exilic period on the basis of its supposedly anti-Samaritan inclination (Carroll 1971, 150; Gerstenberger 2001, 97; Berlin 2005, 78; Witte 2006, 39). Nevertheless, the psalm contains no references to any distress from either a preceding destruction or exile. At the earlier end of the dating range scholars relate the psalm to the Davidic reign, relying on the climactic declaration of the king's chosen status in verses 68–71 (Eissfeldt 1958, 36–37; Campbell 1979, 61, 75–76; Tate 1990, 286). However, with the mention of God's "sanctuary" in Mount Zion (v. 69) at least the Solomonic period needs to be considered.
35 Cf. 2Kgs 13:23, 14:26–27; Neh 9:17.

spy event (Num 14:18) and in the context related to the Golden Calf incident (Exod 34:6–7). Nevertheless, just as the lists in the Pentateuch do not reflect a textual interdependence,[36] so the list in Ps 78:38 seems to reflect an independent version of the formulation of God's characteristics. Thus, while the verse in the psalm uses a few words found in the lists in the Pentateuch, such as רחום ("compassionate", Exod 34:6), עון ("iniquity", Exod 34:7; Num 14:18) and אפו ("anger", Exod 34:6; Num 14:18), the differences between the texts are rather notable.

The lists in the Pentateuch speak of God's essential characteristics as being חנון ורחום ("merciful and gracious", Exod 34:6); ארך אפים ("slow to anger", ibid.; Num 14:18); רב חסד ("abounding in steadfast love", Exod 34:6; Num 14:18); נשא עון ופשע ("forgiving iniquity and transgression", Exod 34:7; Num 14:18); and לא נקה ינקה ("by no means clearing the guilty", Exod 34:7; Num 14:18). In contrast, the psalm mentions only one essential quality, רחום (compassionate), and then points to God's actual actions: "…forgave their iniquity and did not destroy them; often he restrained his anger and did not stir up all his wrath" (יכפר עון ולא ישחית והרבה להשיב אפו ולא יעיר כל חמתו, Ps 78:38).

The reference to God's character in the psalm is employed to explain God's conduct in the past as his own initiative, manifesting his role as the ultimate defender and protector of the people. This stands in contrast to the use of the divine attributes according to the story of the spies in the Pentateuch, where Moses reminds God that his divine characteristics can allow him to step back from the will to destroy (Num 14:13–19. Cf. Exod 34:8–9). According to the psalm, God himself remembers the attribute of compassion and employs it to avoid the destruction of the people.

In the absence of an external intervention on behalf of the people, what encourages God to act in this way? The answer is given in the following verse in the psalm: God's awareness of the temporary nature of his subjects: "He remembered that they were but flesh, a wind that passes and does not come again" (v. 39).[37] It seems thus that the people's human limitations prompt God to be

---

36 See above, 4.1.

37 This statement has challenged medieval commentators who maintained a belief in the resurrection from the dead, e.g., Rashi argues that the verse conveys the idea that in the world to come there will be no evil inclination in human kind: "Since He remembered THAT THEY WERE FLESH (Ps 78:39) and that the evil inclination is embedded in their hearts and that this [evil inclination] is A SPIRIT THAT DEPARTS when they [humans] die, and that that SPIRIT WILL NOT RETURN to them in the future era, [for] when they experience resurrection, the evil inclination will not have dominion over them. It is [theologically] untenable to interpret A SPIRIT THAT DEPARTS BUT DOES NOT RETURN [to mean] 'their SPIRIT OF LIFE which is in them', for if you so interpret, you deny [the dogma of] the resurrection of the dead. Thus it is pointed out in *Aggadath Tehillim* (Midrash Tehillim 78:8)" (Rashi to Ps 78:39. Gruber 1998, 365).

compassionate. But this existential argument is supposedly valid for all human beings; they are all "flesh" and "wind that passes and does not come again". How could an argument based on characteristics common to humankind help in explaining the protection of God's particular nation?[38]

Read in the broader context, the recognition of the inherent limitation of human life does not convey a concern or compassion towards humanity in general. The historical review does not indicate God's intention to protect humans, as God does not change the habit of overwhelming such beings – from his own people (vv. 63–64) or from other nations (v. 66). Thus, the statement about the people's mortal nature concerns the "national" rather than the "universal" aspect, in accordance with the prominent idea in the psalm of the exclusive relationship of God with the people of Israel (vv. 20, 37, 52, 62, 71). The divine compassion is applied to the nation thanks to the understanding that they are a collective of mortals, whose existence, even the sinners among them, is temporary and transient. The trait of the transitoriness of the people allows God to keep them alive and enables the relationship to proceed. God is considered compassionate for his avoidance of annihilation because he recognizes the actual finite existence of his chosen subjects.

The role of the divine compassion in protecting the people from annihilation is known from Deuteronomy 4. But as opposed to the psalm, the Deuteronomic speech relates the compassion towards the people to their sincere repentance[39]:

> 31 In your distress, when all these things have happened to you in time to come, you will return to the LORD your God and heed him. 31 Because the LORD your God is a merciful God (אל רחום), he will neither abandon you nor destroy you (ישחיתך); he will not forget the covenant with your ancestors that he swore to them (Deut 4:30–31)

According to this framework, God can fulfill his duty not to destroy the people, if the people do their part, i.e., "return" to him. This is not so according to the psalm, where the people's "return" is considered false and unreliable (Ps 78:34–37), and thus cannot be the basis for a promise of non-annihilation. Instead, the people's

---

38 Cf. the "national" rationale in Moses' arguments in Exodus 32:13, about God's commitment to the people's patriarchs.

39 The approach to God's compassion is not uniform in the various texts that contain a list of the divine attributes. In Exodus 34 the notion is part of the dichotomous concept of retribution (contrasting to "...yet by no means clearing the guilty...", Exod 34:7), in Jonah, the notion explains the readiness of God to "relent from punishing" (Jonah 4:2), where the entire world is related (Cf. Ps 145:8–9), and in Joel it is the quality of God that enables the return to him (Joel 2:12), as we saw in Deuteronomy 4. All references use language similar to the liturgical formula but with clearly different intentions.

survival is based on a divine recognition of the people's mortality. For this recognition God is known as compassionate. In contemporary discourse one could grant God a Nobel peace prize for not pressing the nuclear weapon button.

4.5 God's mythological personality

While the vulnerable nature of the people leads to a near destruction, the nature of their mortality is, according to the psalm, the reason for their survival. This dialectic fate, which relies on the decision of the people's patron and creator, resonates with Mesopotamian myths that recount the potentially destructive and precarious fate of humans due to the decision of their deities, their creators. The Babylonian Flood story *Atrahasis* presents this dialectic notion by ascribing to the gods both the existence of mortals and their potential destruction. Humanity is thus created for the sake of the gods, who, according to the suggestion of Ea the god of wisdom, will use the people to bear their burdens. A following divine whim, triggered by the people's increasing noise in the world, leads to the destruction of humanity. Enlil, the main deity, harries the people with exterminatory afflictions: plagues, drought and famine.[40]

Thus, due to their vulnerable state, humans have to find a means to gain divine support. According to *Atrahasis*, humans had been making offerings to the gods, and this eventually became the incentive to allow their reappearance. Even so, the people's mortal nature would mean they constantly lived their lives threatened by risks derived from the gods. As Pryke points out, the "relations between the divine and human worlds... [were] dangerous and destructive, and capable of jeopardizing the survival of humankind, animals, and the natural world".[41]

The tradition attested in Psalm 78 relates the divine inclination to destroy the people, as well as the hesitation to do so, to the nature of the people as mortals. More than any historical or political explanation, this tradition should be understood as first and foremost a reflection of the mythological portrayal of the personality of God.[42]

Returning to our stories in the Pentateuch, the evidence from Psalm 78 supports our earlier deduction that the image of the threat of destruction existed

---

40 *Atrahasis* Epic, tablets I–III. Cf. *Gilgamesh* tablet XI. See more Leick 1991, 64–65; Pryke 2016 (on line). Such are the myths about the Sumerian deity Iškur and the Akkadian deity Adad/Haddad, the gods of storm and rain, who provide life, alongside drought, storm and flood that cause destruction to the fields, and famine and death to the people. See Schwemer 2007, 134 142, 150.
41 Pryke 2016 (on line).
42 I thank Jonathan Ben-Dov for this definition.

separately from the Calf and the spy narratives. It indicates that the myth of near destruction demonstrates a general and repetitive pattern in the relationship between the people and God.

By separating the unit of the near destruction from its two familiar narrative contexts in the Pentateuch, we discover the characteristics of God as perceived at early stages of the ancient Israelite belief. The intrinsic danger in the relationship with God is inherent in the deity's tendency to be disappointed by his subjects when they do not meet his expectations. They fail and transgress repeatedly, reflecting their imperfect and inadequate human character, which undermines their definition as God's chosen ones.

God's disappointment with his subjects is nothing new. The pre-national myths offer that God despaired of all humans and so decided to destroy them by flood. Only after the destruction, when he had recognized their mortal weakness as humans, he understood the futility of destruction: "...I will never again curse the ground because of humankind, for the inclination of the human heart is evil from youth; nor will I ever again destroy every living creature as I have done" (Gen 8:21). Muffs makes an effective summary of the complex personality of God as reflected in the story of the Flood:

> The naïveté of God's original optimism and the depth of His subsequent pessimism are transmuted into what one may call divine realism. God now realizes that He cannot expect perfection from man and that human corruption is something He will have to make peace with. Man is not totally good, nor is he totally bad; he is simply human. God concludes that the appropriate reaction to man's sinfulness is not an outburst of punitive anger – His bow and arrow, which appear in nature as the rainbow, are permanently laid aside – but rather forbearance and an educational discipline in harmony with man's less-than-perfect nature.[43]

As in the case of all humanity, the chosen people find themselves under threats of annihilation due to God's expectations from them. In the moments after the flood, the Israelites' existence is made possible thanks to a decline in the expectations. Specifically, the intervention of an external mediator seeks to deter God from destruction without promising any particular change in the nature of the people. Rather than delving into the conduct of the rebellious people, the ancient tradition examines the process that God, the patron and authority, goes through: he is disappointed, becomes angry, threatens, and finally surrenders his negative judgement and consents to spare the people.

---

43 Muffs 2005, 100.

Nevertheless, the implementation of the ancient tradition within the two specific narrative settings in the Pentateuch has restricted the portrayal of the people's God as a furious mythological deity, and has limited the people's fragile nature. A general threat that accompanied the people's life in the desert is reduced to a danger that occurred only on specific occasions, when God was not only dangerous and unpredictable but also compassionate and capable of changing his expectations.

In the next chapters we will examine the way the idea of the threat of destruction was perceived by later biblical authors who received the motif through the two Pentateuchal narratives into which it was embedded.

5 Told by the protagonists: Retelling episodes of the time in the desert

The episodes of the Golden Calf and the spy mission are retold in the Pentateuch as well as in the book of Joshua through references put in the mouth of two of the stories' protagonists, Moses and Caleb. Whereas the episode of the Golden Calf is retold only once, in Moses' speech in Deuteronomy 9, the incident of the spies is recounted or mentioned several times in the so-called protagonists' retrospective comments. It is mentioned in Moses' speech to the Gadites and the Reubenites in Numbers 32, in his speech to the people of Israel before the entrance into the land in Deuteronomy 1, and in a reference embedded in his speech in Deuteronomy 9, as part of the theme of the people's rebellious character in the desert. The event of the spies is further mentioned in Joshua 14 in Caleb's appeal to Joshua regarding his rights to a portion of the land.

Among the several references to the two past events, though, only the one on the Golden Calf in Deuteronomy 9 mentions the motif of God's threat of destruction. None of the references to the incident of the spies, including the remark in Moses' speech in Deuteronomy 9, alludes to the idea of God's intention to destroy the people. This examination raises several enquiries: why was the narrative of the risk of destruction associated in the indirect speech references only with the Calf episode? Was the narrative of the near destruction threat not yet known to the authors of the accounts of the spy episode put in the protagonists' mouth? Alternatively, was it disregarded due to the authors' needs?

We will discuss the retrospective accounts of the Golden Calf and the story of the spies in comparison with the stories told by the omniscient narrators in Exodus 32 and Numbers 13–14. This will allow us to trace the process of the production of the retrospective accounts while exposing their varied socio-theological purposes. The order of the discussion will follow the order of the texts in the final form of the Bible, beginning with the speech of Moses to the Gadites and the Reubenites in the wilderness (Numbers 32), continuing with Moses' speeches to the people in Deuteronomy (chapters 1 and 9), and ending with Caleb's appeal in Joshua 14.

5.1 Numbers 32: Risk of destruction – not by God

5.1.1 The spy story in a new context

In the days before entering the land, the Reubenites and the Gadites approach Moses with a request to remain in the eastern side of the Jordan (Num 32:5), a

https://doi.org/10.1515/9783110609905-005

territory which appears to be outside the designated land.[1] Moses replies to the request with a two-section reprimand: he rebukes the tribes for intending not to take part alongside the other tribes in the coming war ("Shall your brothers go to war while you sit here?", v. 6), and he warns them against undermining the motivation of the rest of the people to enter the land ("Why will you discourage the hearts of the Israelites from going over into the land that the LORD has given them?" v. 7). The second clause is followed by a long reference to a past event (vv. 8–15) that occurred forty years earlier (v. 13): The fathers were sent to see the land (v. 8), and on their return they discouraged the rest of the people from entering the land (v. 9). This resulted in a punishment for the whole generation: to die in the wilderness instead of entering the land (vv. 11, 13).

The response of the Reubenites and the Gadites to Moses, mentioned in verses 16–19, relates to the first section of Moses' reprimand, concerning their supposed attempt to be exempt from participating in the fight alongside the rest of the tribes (v. 6). They reply that they intend to leave only their sheepfolds and children behind (vv. 16–17), while they themselves will join the battle, even serving as the war's frontline, before going back to the eastern side of the river:

> But we will take up arms (LXX προφυλακὴ [חֻמָּשִׁים]; cf. MT חֲמֻשִׁים, ready) as a vanguard before the Israelites, until we have brought them to their place... We will not return to our homes until all the Israelites have obtained their inheritance. We will not inherit with them on the other side of the Jordan and beyond, because our inheritance has come to us on this side of the Jordan to the east (Num 32:17–19)

In their reply, then, the two tribes do not refer to Moses' second indictment about the risk of demoralizing the other tribes about entering the land. Correspondingly, Moses' response to the two tribes makes no further mention of the concern about the potential damage of their request to the people' motivation (v. 7), nor to the past incident of sending "the fathers" to the land (vv. 8–13). Instead, the initiative of the

---

1 See the definition of the eastern boundaries of the inherited land according to the Priestly document in Numbers 34: "...and the boundary shall go down, and reach the eastern slope of the sea of Chinnereth; and the boundary shall go down to the Jordan, and its end shall be at the Dead Sea. This shall be your land with its boundaries all around" (vv. 11–12). Accordingly, the crossing of the Jordan by the people is considered the beginning of the conquest: Num 33:51–54, 35:11–12. Cf. the image of the land on the eastern side of the Jordan as "unclean" as opposed to "the LORD'S land" across the river (Josh 22:19). This stands in contrast to Non-Priestly writings that reflect the view that the eastern bank of the Jordan is an integral part of the promised inherited land: Gen 15:16–21; Exod 23:31; Deut 11:24. This view also emerges in the tradition of the establishment of Jacob's relationship with God at Peniel, on the eastern side of the Jordan (Gen 32:29–31), as opposed to the Priestly narrative in Gen 35:8–15, about Jacob's encounter with the Divine on the western side of the Jordan.

tribes to go up as a vanguard before the people (vv. 17–19) reassures Moses, and he gives the tribes permission to hold the specific land they requested as their own possession: "So Moses said to them, 'If you do this – if you take up arms to go before the LORD for the war, and all those of you who bear arms cross the Jordan before the LORD... and this land shall be your possession before the LORD'" (vv. 20–22).[2]

The lack of further references to the issue of morale, demonstrated by the mention of the episode from the past, leads to an assumption that the tradition in Numbers 32 dealt initially only with the question of the extent of engagement of the two tribes in the process of possessing the western part of the land. This question was related to a larger discussion about the connection of the two tribes to the people that resided west of the Jordan (cf. Joshua 22). Accordingly, the issue of demoralization with the allusion to the past event seems to have been added secondarily to the speech, with an effort to highlight the risk of the separation of the two tribes from the rest of the nation.[3]

According to this abovementioned aim, many of the elements in the story of sending representatives to the land, known from the spy narrative(s) in Numbers 13–14, as well as from the retrospective accounts in Deuteronomy and Joshua, do not seem required, and are then not mentioned in the speech. Neither the specific instructions for the operation (cf. Num 13:17–20), nor the names and origins of the spies (cf. Num 13:3–16), nor the actual report brought back from the land (cf. Num 13:25–33; Deut 1:25–28; Josh 14:8) are relevant to the speech in Numbers 32. But unlike these details, the scene of God's near destruction of the people, known from Numbers 14 (vv. 11–12), could fit into the context of Moses' rebuke to the two tribes according to Numbers 32. The rebuke ends with a warning of a potential destruc-

---

2 The realization of this promise, carried out by Moses, is mentioned in 32:33 with the verb give (נתן), in regard to Moses' action (cf. vv. 5, 29, 40). This differs from the reference to the process by which the other tribes would achieve their territories, namely by lot, and not through Moses (33:54). Thus the territory on the eastern side of the Jordan, which was gained by war (32:4), could supposedly be given as booty. In contrast, according to this account, the area on the other side of the Jordan was allocated by God in advance (cf. 34:1–13, and see footnote 1, above), and thus its fate was linked to a divine intervention (cf. Josh 18:6, 8, 10).

3 See: Bacon 1894, 241; Baentsch 1903, 659–665; Loewenstamm 1973, 20–21; Milgrom 1990, 494; Blum 1990, 112; Nicholson 2002, 192. In fact, one can rationalize Loewenstamm's suggestion (ibid., 18–20, 25) that the chapter was based on a tradition that originally described Moses' consent to the tribes' request, as can be traced in the references in Num 32:24, 33 (cf. Deut 3:3–5). A similar idea was raised by Noth (1968, 238), who relates the willingness of the two tribes to participate in the war (Num 32:16–19) to a personal initiative that came after earlier receiving a territory located east of the Jordan. Accordingly, the conversation with Moses and the reference to the episode of the spies were added at the stage when there was a need to give further endorsement for the settlements east of the Jordan.

tion of the people, due to the two tribes' behavior: "… and you will destroy all this people" (ושחתם לכל העם הזה, v. 15). This deadly risk could have been demonstrated by a reference to the threat of destruction from the past event.

What can we learn from the absence of the scene of God's threat of destruction from the retrospective reference to the spy event mentioned in Numbers 32? Was the motif not known to the rewriters, or was it ignored by them due to their literary or ideological needs? We will first examine the speech in Numbers 32 in comparison with the text in Numbers 13–14, namely their literary connections and possible dependence. In a second stage we will discuss the role of the motif of the threat of destruction in the literary context of Numbers 32.

5.1.2 Literary sources

Some of the details of the past event mentioned in Numbers 32:7–15 are consistent with the features known from the Priestly version of the spy story restored from Numbers 13–14:

1. The people punished in the event according to Numbers 32 were "the people who came up out of Egypt, from twenty years old and upward" (v. 11). This conforms to the information in the Priestly version of the spy story in Num 14:29, while differing from the Non-Priestly version that points to "[all (כל)] the people who have seen my glory and the signs that I did in Egypt and in the wilderness" (Num 14:22), as the punished group.
2. According to Numbers 32, the punishment imposed on the people was a forty-year wandering in the wilderness (v. 13). This fits the narrative of the Priestly version in Num 14:33–34, and not the Non-Priestly version of the story, where there is no reference to the intended time in the wilderness, and no explicit idea of remaining in the wilderness (Num 14:23).
3. According to Numbers 32 both Joshua and Caleb survived the collective punishment of the generation after the spy affair: "except Caleb son of Jephunneh the Kenizzite and Joshua son of Nun…" (v. 12). This data adheres to the information from the Priestly account in Num 14:6, 38, and contradicts the information about the survival of Caleb alone as appears in the Non-Priestly version in Numbers 14 (v. 24; cf. Deut 1:36).
4. The past event is described in Numbers 32 with no reference to a dialogue between God and Moses regarding the nature of the punishment. There is also no reference to Moses' mediation in the event, as known from the Non-Priestly account of the spy story (Num 14:13–19). Rather, the punishment is considered as God's own decision, as depicted in the Priestly version of the story (Num 14:26–35).

Based on these similarities, one could consider the account of the spy event in Numbers 32 as relying first and foremost on the Priestly version of Numbers 13–14.[4] But this conclusion disregards the strong affinity Num 32:8–15 also has with the Non-Priestly version of the spy story, noticeable through numerous literary elements[5]:

1. The information regarding the arrival of the spies to the Valley of Eshcol (Num 32:9) corresponds to the information in the Non-Priestly version of the story about the arrival of the spies at the place (Num 13:23–24. Cf. Deut 1:24). This differs from the information in the Priestly version about the spies walking all the way "from the wilderness of Zin to Rehob, near Lebo-hamath" (Num 13:21).

2. The expression מלאו אחרי, "unreservedly followed me [God]", mentioned in Numbers 32 in regard to Caleb and Joshua's distinctive behavior (v. 12. Cf. v. 11), is known from the argument in the Non-Priestly version in Numbers 14 about Caleb's nonconformist non-compliant behavior during the event (verse 24. Cf. Deut 1:36).

3. The uses of the root ראה in Numbers 32 in regard to the spies' performance in the land and in regard to the verdict of God resonate with the uses of the root in the Non-Priestly story:

Numbers 32	Non-Priestly version in Numbers 13–14
9 When they went up to the Wadi Eshcol **and saw the land**...	13:18 ... and **see what the land is like**...
11 'Surely **none of the people** who came up out of Egypt... **shall see the land**...	14:22 none of the people who **have seen my glory** and the signs that I did in Egypt and in the wilderness... 23 **shall see the land**... (and cf. Deut 1:35)

---

4 Cf. Baden (2009, 145–146), who defines the unit in 32:7–15 as Priestly, standing in parallel to Moses' other rebuke in verse 6, which he considers as belonging to the hand of E. HaCohen (2010, 258–260) relates the reference to the spy event (32:7–15) to an author from the Holiness school who worked with the combined text of the spy episode in Numbers 13–14.

5 Some of the elements in the list below are considered by Baden a result of a later adjustment in accordance with the combined story of Numbers 13–14, by adding details that are marginal to the plot, such as Kadesh-barnea and Valley of Eshkol (Baden 2009, 143, 276–277). But the argument that the Non-Priestly elements in Moses' rebuke in Numbers 32 are marginal to the core story weakens Baden's proposal: if the details were not central to the plot, what reason was there to add them to the text in the first place?

The second use of the verb stands in contrast to the description in the Priestly account of the way the people are prevented from reaching the land, using the verb בוא (והביאתי אתם ...אם אתם תבואו, Num 14:30–31).

4. The verdict of the people according to Numbers 32 refers to God's oath to the people's ancestors in the past: "...the land that I swore to give to Abraham, to Isaac, and to Jacob..." (v. 11). This echoes the verdict in the Non-Priestly version that refers to "...the land that I swore to give to their ancestors..." (Num 14:23. Cf. Deut 1:35).[6]

5. The place of the spies' departure for the mission, "Kadesh-barnea" (Num 32:8), matches the information found in the rewritten accounts of the spy story in Deuteronomy 1 (v. 19) and Joshua 14 (vv. 6, 7), which, as we will see, appear to be unfamiliar with the Priestly account of the story.[7] The name is also traced in the edited comment in Num 13:26 ("in the wilderness of Paran, at Kadesh" [מדבר פארן קדשה]), in contrast to the information found in the Priestly material about departing from the desert of Paran (Num 13:3. Cf. 12:16).

Budd, indeed, raises the claim that the text in Numbers 32 was written by an exilic Deuteronomistic editor who used the Non-Priestly version of the spy story known from Deuteronomy 1.[8] Details known from the Priestly version of the spy story, such as the punishment criterion of the age of twenty (Num 32:11. Cf. Num 14:29), and the duration of forty years of the generation (32:13. Cf. Num 14:33–34), are considered later supplements in the plot, added without affecting the main thread.[9]

This assumption though is difficult to accept. First, the account in Numbers 32 highlights the spies' responsibility for the fate of the community, unlike the version of Deuteronomy 1, which does not explicitly point to the blame of the

---

6 In contrast to the collective name אבות ("ancestors") in the Non-Priestly versions of the story (Num 14:23; Deut 1:35), the reference in Num 32:11 mentions the three patriarchs by names. The elaboration seems to result from the earlier use of the name אבות in the context, in regard to the representatives who went out for the mission in the land and failed (Num 32:8–9). The narrator thus makes sure not to use the same title for the righteous patriarchs.

7 See below, 5.2.2.; 5.4.2.

8 See Budd 1984, 342, 346. Bacon (1894, 241), too, mentions the contribution of a Deuteronomist editor to the text but argues that this editor knew the full story of Numbers 13–14, including the Priestly version.

9 Similarly, Friedman (2003, 301) attributes vv. 7–12 in Numbers 32 to J with the exception of the comment about Joshua in verse 12. This, he argues, was to be added at a later stage in order to match the account with the final text of Numbers 13–14.

spies in the event (Deut 1:25–28).[10] Furthermore, the information about the punishment of forty-year wandering in the desert, known from the Priestly version of the story, is significant in the reference in Numbers 32. It implies that the current request of the Reubenites and the Gadites may lead to a similar consequence: delay in and even withdrawal from the effort to reach the land (v. 15). This data thus cannot be considered secondary to the passage.

The disadvantages of the two proposals mentioned above lead to a consideration of Bacon's earlier assumption that the reference to the spy story in Numbers 32 was based on the already combined text of Numbers 13–14.[11] This suggestion is evident from the relatively coherent structure of the passage of the story in Numbers 32, containing neither contradictions nor obviously redundant information.[12] This is unlike the final text in Numbers 13–14, which reflects commitment to two separate narratives.

In light of this supposition, two terminological elements in the spy narrative in Numbers 32 require clarification, as they cannot be fully traced in the complete text of Numbers 13–14: the title "Kenizzite" for Caleb (Num 32:12), and the indication of Kadesh-barnea as the people's campsite (v. 8). The title "Kenizzite" may have surfaced in Numbers 32 from other traditions about Caleb, found outside the combined text of Numbers 13–14 (cf. Josh 14:6, 14, 15:17; Judg 1:13 and 1Chr 4:13–15). Likewise, the name Kadesh-barnea for the people's camp-site and thus for the spies' point of departure could derive from various traditions about the place, as widely known in Priestly (Num 34:3–4; Josh 15:1–3), Deuteronomic and Deuteronomistic accounts (Deut 1:2, 19, 2:14, 9:23; Josh 10:41). The name has been also partially preserved in the combined text of Numbers 13–14 in the mention of "Kadesh" as the place where the spies returned (אל מדבר פארן קדשה, Num 13:26).[13]

With this suggestion, however, a question remains regarding the choice of the name Kadesh-barnea over the name Paran, found in the framework of the text in Numbers 13–14 (Num 13:3. Cf. 12:16). Hacohen suggests the Priestly version

---

10 And thus, emphasizing the people's misbehavior in the event by detaching their rejection of the land from an "objective" report delivered to them. See the discussion below, 5.2.4.

11 Bacon 1894, 241.

12 An exception is the double use of the expression ויחר אף יהוה ("The LORD'S anger was kindled") in verses 10 and 13. Nevertheless, the two occurrences function as introductions for two stages consequent on the event: the verdict that the adults are not to see the land (v. 11), and the realization of the sentence by determining a forty-year delay in the wilderness until the death of these adults (v. 13).

13 See above, 3.5. Note, though, that some occurrences preserve the separate name "Kadesh" as a place in the desert: Gen 14:7, 16:14, 20:1; Num 20:1, 14, 16, 22, 33:36, 37; Deut 1:46; Judg 11:16; Ps 29:8.

of the story originally also contained the name "Kadesh" or "Kadesh-barnea", and only in the compilation of the combined text in Numbers 13–14 was the name changed to the wilderness of Paran, to stress that the journey began outside the borders of the land.[14] This assumption implies that the spy account embedded in Numbers 32 is itself a combination of two separate narratives before they were combined together. In other words, that the speech in Numbers 32 is another example of merging together the two alternative versions of the spy story. This possibility has no confirmation in the text. The close lexical relationship of the passage in Numbers 32 to the final form of Numbers 13–14, without noticeable mismatches, makes it unlikely to assume that it was formed from two separate sources. Instead, it is not impossible that the author was familiar with additional traditions of the story that mentioned Kadesh-barnea (Deut 1:19; Josh 14:6), and that pointed to Caleb's Kenizzite roots (Josh 14:6).[15]

5.1.3 Omission of the annihilation-threat motif

The conclusion that the story of the spies in Numbers 32 is based mainly on the combined text in Numbers 13–14 highlights the question about the absence of any scene of a threat of destruction in Numbers 32. The absence, as stated, is notable in light of Moses' critical comments to the Gadites and the Reubenites about the potentially dreadful consequence of their request – bringing calamity on all the people (Num 32:15).

But the mention of the divine threat of destruction known from Numbers 14 is irrelevant when reading the reference to the spy episode within the broader context of Numbers 32. The episode of the spies is used here because of the final outcome of the event in the past – the continuous wandering in the wilderness. The same punishment threatens the people in the current situation. But while the punishment might cause a destruction (Num 32:15b), this will not be due to God's initiative. Rather it will be the consequence of further delay in the desert: "If you turn away from following him, he will again abandon them in the wilderness, and you will destroy all this people" (v. 15).

---

14 Hacohen 2010, 165–166.
15 On the use and meaning of Caleb's title as "the Kenizzite" in the context of the spy event in Joshua 14, see below, 5.4.3.

The tribes' wrongdoing according to Moses' rebuke in Numbers 32 is their discouragement of the Israelites (Num 32:7). This is a similar offense to the spies' conduct in the past (v. 9). The transgression, whether past or present, is expressed with the same wording:

The spies in the past: ...they discouraged (ויניאו) the hearts of the Israelites from going into the land that the LORD had given them (v. 9)

The Reubenites and the Gadites now: Why will you discourage (תניאון) the hearts of the Israelites from going over into the land that the LORD has given them? (v. 7)

The verb that connects the two allegations, נוא, alludes to the uncommon noun תנואה, used in the verdict of God in the spy story in direct speech (וידעתם את תנואתי, Num 14:34).[16] But whilst the latter refers to the reaction of God to the spies' behavior, Num 32:9 recounts the impact of the spies on the congregation. Thus, rather than a rebellion against God or against the leaders (cf. Num 14:4, 9, 11, 27), the wrongdoing of the spies, according to Numbers 32, was the demoralization of the people. This characterization of the past event demonstrates the potentially destructive influence of individuals on the community – damaging the collective motivation is a risk to all. Whether the arguments of the spies in the past were justified or false is not specified and not important in the current context. The reference stresses that the spies' crime was to harm the people's morale at a crucial moment, indicating the similar effect that might occur due to the Reubenites' and the Gadites' request.

The verb נוא that connects the tribes' request with the spies' crime, resonates also with the root נוע, which refers to the punishment of the people as linked to the spies: וינעם במדבר ארבעים שנה ("...and he made them wander in the wilderness for forty years...", Num 32:13). The assonance of the verbs enhances the deterrent message to the two tribes: as the spies caused continuous wandering of the people in the desert (v. 13), the Reubenites and the Gadites may cause damage to the whole congregation by further delaying them in the wilderness: ויסף עוד

---

16 The root נוא appears only in *hiphil*, meaning prevent or violate: "The LORD brings the counsel of the nations to nothing; he frustrates (הניא) the plans of the peoples" (Ps 33:10. Also Num 30:9). The rare term תנואה (found elsewhere in Job 33:10) refers, according to Num 14:34, to an opposition or deliberate damaging. The NRSV translates: "...and you shall know my displeasure", namely the people will suffer from a change in God's attitude. The KJV concentrates on God's undertaking, stating that the people will experience what it is like when God does not keep his promise: "...and ye shall know my breach of promise", while the JPS conveys the people's perspective: they will become aware of the power they tend to disregard by disobeying: "... and ye shall know what it means to thwart me". Despite various attempts to clarify the phrase it remains relatively ambiguous.

להניחו במדבר, "he will again abandon them in the wilderness" (v. 15).[17] The consequence of holding the people in the wilderness will apparently cause great destruction, even though this is not God's intention in the first place: ושחתם לכל העם הזה, "... and you will destroy all this people" (v. 15).

The accountability of the two tribes for the threat of the people's destruction is further stressed in the LXX version of the verse, which translates the word ושחתם in the warning of destruction (Num 32:15) with the verb ἀνομέω that conveys damage and harm done by human beings (cf. Exod 32:7; Deut 4:16, 25, 9:12, 31:29; 1Kgs 8:47; Isa 43:27). This is used instead of the verb καταφθείρω that usually translates the root שחת in contexts of destruction brought by God (Gen 6:13, 17, 9:11).[18]

The focus of Moses' rebuke of the two tribe explains why the reference to the spies' event does not include the scene of the potential annihilation of the people, even though it could be known to the scribe who worked with the merged text of Numbers 13–14.[19] The past threat of extermination might have been in the back of the author's mind, but is not mentioned here explicitly. To clarify the magnitude of the danger in the present and to convey that this is not a futile threat, a reference to a so-called punishment that was decreed and fulfilled is more effective than a threat of annihilation that was not carried out. Hence, the earlier moment when the people stood at the entrance to Canaan and missed the opportunity to enter is an actual precedent for the current affair.

5.2 Deuteronomy 1: Silence about the threat of destruction: Evidence of compilation and interpretation

5.2.1 The episode of the spies mentioned in Moses' speech in Deuteronomy 1

Deuteronomy 1 opens with Moses' speech to the people on the eastern side of the Jordan. The narrator indicates the time and place of Moses' address (Deut

---

17 To express the potential consequence of the two tribes' demand on the people, the Peshitta uses: ויניעכם. This corresponds to the verb נוע in verse 13, as well as to the use of second person plural (as opposed to להניחו in the MT).

18 And see in this regard the distinction between total destruction, כלה, and a partial destruction, שחת, in the prophet's call for vengeance in Israel: עלו בשרותיה ושחתו וכלה אל תעשו ("Go up through her vine-rows and destroy, but do not make a full end", Jer 5:10).

19 See the argument below (5.2.5) that the divine verdict with the threat of destruction in Numbers 14 was added to the Non-Priestly version of the story before the stage of combination with the Priestly version.

1:1–5) and continues with Moses' words in direct speech.[20] His words begin with a reminder of God's instruction to leave Horeb and to continue the journey towards the land (vv. 6–8), and this is followed by a reference to two events from that time: the appointment of commanders and judges for the people (שפטים, שטרים, שרים, vv. 9–18) and the sending of spies to the land (vv. 19–45).[21]

A major portion of Deuteronomy 1 is thus devoted to the story of the spies. It recounts that the people reach Kadesh-barnea (v. 19), located at the border of the designated land (v. 20), and are instructed by Moses to ascend and inherit the land (עלה רש, "go up, take possession", v. 21). But the people, according to the account, are reluctant to obey the instruction immediately and request representatives be sent to examine the route and the cities that they aim to reach (v. 22). Moses agrees and chooses twelve people, one from each tribe (v. 23), who are to set out and go up into the hill country to Valley Eshcol and spy it out (ויירגלו אתה, v. 24). According to the speech, the spies return with a sample of the land's produce (מפרי הארץ, v. 25) together with a message that "it is a good land that the LORD our God is giving us" (v. 25). Nevertheless, this does not seem to reassure the people. They refuse to go up to the land (v. 26) because of a threat from the Amorites (v. 27). This threat, according to the people's complaint (רגן, v. 27), was known to them from their "brothers", who informed them of the existence of people "stronger and taller...", and cities that are "large and fortified up to heaven" and "the offspring of the Anakim" (v. 28). Besides the people's complaint, though, the account in Moses' speech does not indicate any discouraging information reported directly by the spies.

The simple positive message of the spies' words mentioned in Moses' speech differs from the narrative by the omniscient narrator in Numbers 13–14. Both the Priestly and the Non-Priestly versions in Numbers 13–14 recount that on their return from the mission the spies provide a complex portrayal of the land and thus undermine the motivation of the people to conquer the land. The testimony of Moses in Deuteronomy 1 lacks such an accusation against the spies.

This variant of the story in Deuteronomy 1 is accompanied by a lengthy sermon from Moses to the people, which is not known from the accounts in Numbers 13–14. Additionally, the retrospective text in Deuteronomy 1 lacks mention of the moment of the risk of destruction by God. Do we have here another version of the spy story? Is this an interpretation of one of the stories we know?

---

20 According to the final sequence of Deuteronomy, the speech stops at Deut 4:40 and starts again at 5:1aβ.
21 On the choice of "spy" for מרגלים see the clarification about the use of the term in the discussion of Numbers 13–14: 3.1, footnote 1 (p. 27).

We will discuss the extent of the literary relationship between the spy story in Deuteronomy 1 and the narratives by the omniscient narrator in Numbers 13–14. The discussion will provide insights into both the methods of inner-biblical interpretation and the process of the compilation of the original tradition, preserved today in Numbers 13–14.

5.2.2 Deuteronomy 1 and the two versions in Numbers 13–14

The episode of the spies in Deuteronomy 1 shares numerous details and choices of wording with the Non-Priestly version of the story in Numbers 13–14. Both accounts narrate that the spies reached as far as Valley of Eshkol (Num 13:23; Deut 1:24) and brought fruit to prove the fertility of the land (Num 13:23; Deut 1:25). And both accounts, in the words of the spies or the words of people respectively, mention the existence of strong people (עז העם, Num 13:28; עם גדול ורם ממנו, Deut 1:28), fortified and large cities (והערים בצרות גדלת מאד, Num 13:28; ערים גדלת ובצורת בשמים, Deut 1:28), and descendants of Anak/Anakim (וגם ילדי הענק ראינו שם, Num 13:28; וגם בני ענקים ראינו שם, Deut 1:28). These details stand in contrast to the information attributed to the Priestly version of the story in Numbers, such as the definition of the route of the spies as crossing the entire country "from the wilderness of Zin to Rehob, near Lebo-hamath" (Num 13:21), the reference to the spies' conclusion that the land "devours its inhabitants" (ארץ אכלת יושביה הוא, v. 32), and the description of the population in the land as people "of great size" (אנשי מדות, v. 32) and "Nephilim" (נפילים, v. 33).[22]

In addition, unlike the Priestly version, the Deuteronomic account does not mention as God's initiative the decision to send the spies on the mission (cf. Num 13:2), and most importantly, it does not recount Joshua's positive fate as a result of the spy mission alongside Caleb (cf. Num 14:30, 38). While Joshua is indeed mentioned in Deuteronomy 1, as one of those who will be exempt from the punishment of death in the desert (Deut 1:36–39), his fate is related to his role as Moses' successor (v. 38), and not to the spying event. Unlike Caleb, then, who is defined as someone who "set foot" in the land (דרך בה, v. 36), Joshua is presented

---

22 The reference to the "Nephilim" in Num 13:33 stands with an explanation "the Anakites come from the Nephilim". This seems to stem from an editorial work that integrated the information about the nature of the people in the land, the Nephilim, with the remark on the "descendants of Anak" in the Non-Priestly version in Num 13:28. See above 3.3, footnote 11 (page 35).

as standing in front of Moses (הָעֹמֵד לְפָנֶיךָ, v. 38), and his future is bound with Moses' completion of leadership (v. 37).[23]

In fact, the remark about Joshua's survival (v. 38), alongside the mention of Moses' fate (v. 37), relates to the concern with exactly who will eventually inherit the land (vv. 35–39), and distracts from the verdict on the incident of the spies. Without the reference to Moses and Joshua, the text contains a direct mention of the consequences of the incident of the spies:

> 34 When the LORD heard your words, he was wrathful and swore: 35 "Not one of these—not one of this evil generation—shall see the good land that I swore to give to your ancestors, 36 except Caleb son of Jephunneh. He shall see it, and to him and to his descendants I will give the land on which he set foot, because of his complete fidelity to the LORD." [37 Even with me the LORD was angry on your account, saying, "You also shall not enter there. 38 Joshua son of Nun, your assistant, shall enter there; encourage him, for he is the one who will secure Israel's possession of it.] 39 And as for your little ones, who you thought would become booty, your children, who today do not yet know right from wrong, they shall enter there; to them I will give it, and they shall take possession of it. 40 But as for you, journey back into the wilderness, in the direction of the Red Sea" (Deut 1:34–36, 39–40)

Indeed, the information about Moses' fate, dying in the desert like the rest of the generation, is not known from either one of the versions of the spy story in Numbers 13–14. Moreover, this information stands in contrast to the message found in the approximately complete form of the Non-Priestly version, which recounts that Moses was offered the possibility of replacing the people and inheriting their privileges in the relationship with God (Num 14:12). It is likely, thus, that the comment about Moses' death in Deuteronomy 1, followed by the remark about Joshua his successor, was added to the account after the stabilizing of a tradition about Moses' end.[24] In this regard, it is worthwhile considering Loewenstamm's

---

23 Joshua' legitimacy as a successor of Moses is mentioned elsewhere with no allusion to the spy story: Deut 3:21, 28, 31:3, 14, 23, 34:9; Josh 1:1–2. These accounts seem to be familiar neither with Joshua's role in the incident, nor with the incident itself. See Loewenstamm 1992(a), 138; Baden 2009, 120; Kislev 2017, 50.

24 Rofe suggests that the remark about Moses' fate in Deuteronomy 1 reflects the author's opposition to the idea that the leader carries out military or semi-military initiatives without God's approval, as supposedly recorded in vv. 22–23 (cf. 3:1–2; Josh 8:1) (Rofe 2006, 30). But this suggestion seems unlikely, considering the lack of reference in Deuteronomy 1 to a war that requires success. Moreover, the numerous references to Moses' coming death elsewhere in Deuteronomy indicate the continuous engagement of the writers with the topic. Thus, unlike the tradition reflected in Deuteronomy 1 about Moses' death together with the rest of the generation (v. 37), there are references in Deuteronomy suggesting that Moses died instead of the people (3:23–27, 4:21–24). This idea is consistent with the information that the generation of the desert did enter the land eventually (Deut 5:2–3, 11:2–10), and thus with the view that the period in the desert was not a

suggestion, that these remarks were the trigger for later literary attempts such as the one recorded in the Priestly version of the spy story, and the tradition about Moses' transgression in Numbers 20, that aimed to provide a broader background for the death of Moses and the survival of Joshua.[25] Thus, without the reference to Moses and Joshua (Deut 1:37–38) the spy story in Deuteronomy 1 corresponds better with the Non-Priestly version of the story.

As widely recognized in research, a literary affinity between Deuteronomy 1 and the Non-Priestly version of the spy story is highly likely.[26] It is possible, in addition, that the account in Deuteronomy 1 preserves details that stood originally in the Non-Priestly version of the spy story and did not survive through the process of combining the two versions in Numbers. One such detail is the information about Kadesh-barnea as the people's campsite (Deut 1:2, 19, 46), which was possibly removed from the narrative in the process of creating Numbers 13–14, as can be learned from the residue left in the editorial remark in Num 13:26.

Nevertheless, the text in Deuteronomy 1 contains a few expressions known specifically from the Priestly version of the spy story in Numbers 13–14. The comment about the nature of the land in the spies' words, "It is a good land" (טובה הארץ, Deut 1:25), corresponds to the report from Caleb and Joshua about the virtue of the land, as mentioned in the Priestly version (Num 14:7). Likewise, the number twelve for the people chosen by Moses (Deut 1:23) matches the list of representatives sent on the mission according to the Priestly version, even though the number twelve is not explicitly mentioned there (Num 13:3–15). In addition, the expression "and bring back a report to us" (וישיבו אלינו דבר), mentioned twice in Deuteronomy 1 in regard to the spies' task (vv. 22, 25), echoes the words of the narrator in Num 13:26, which continue the thread of the Priestly account (vv. 25–26). And finally, the reference to the "little ones" (טף) in God's verdict according to Deuteronomy 1 (וטפכם אשר אמרתם לבז יהיה, Deut 1:39), cites the exact phrase found in the Priestly account in Numbers about the destiny of the people's offspring (Num 14:3, 31).

The presence of these elements in the spy story in Deuteronomy 1 requires further clarification of the text's literary relationship with Numbers 13–14. Ostensibly,

---

result of a sin of the spies or any other iniquity (8:2–4, 29:4). See in this regard my arguments in Kugler 2018, 191–204.

25 Loewenstamm 1992(a), 138.

26 See Driver 1901, 19–29; Von Rad 1966(a), 38, 40; Noth 1972, 131; Weinfeld 1991, 144–145, 153; Nelson 2002, 25–26; Achenbach 2003, 65–77; Baden 2009, 121–130. Cf. Schart's suggestion that Deuteronomy 1 shared the same oral tradition with the "J" version of the spy story (Schart 2013, 184).

the account in Deuteronomy 1 can be assumed to be based on the complete narrative of Numbers 13–14, as in the case of Numbers 32:8–15.[27] But it is notable that apart from the abovementioned terminology, Deuteronomy 1 does not share any valuable narrative details with the Priestly sections of the final story. For the same reason it is difficult to assume that the final text in Numbers 13–14 or the Priestly version found there was written on the basis of Deuteronomy 1. Instead, each of the "Priestly" expressions in Deuteronomy 1 can be explained individually, pointing to various stages within the writing or editing process. We will examine the details each in turn.

1. טובה הארץ ("It is a good land", Deut 1:25b; cf. Num 14:7): This description of the land is ostensibly not necessary for the spies' message, as the act of bringing fruit (Deut 1:25a) is tantamount to demonstrating the quality of the land. But the verbal declaration טובה הארץ increases the gap implied in the plot between the positive report of the spies and the determined refusal of the people to go and conquer the land (v. 26). For that, the author of Deuteronomy 1 might have used the common adjective טוב from his general language rather than a specific source, similar to the use of the adjective in the following words of God: "... the good land that I swore to give to your ancestors" (Deut 1:35). The expression also resonates with Moses' instruction to the spies in the Non-Priestly version, to enquire "whether the land... is good or bad" (ומה הארץ הטובה היא אם רעה, Num 13:19); and thus, the answer of the spies in Deuteronomy 1 serves as a relevant response to it.

2. שנים עשר אנשים (Twelve men, Deut 1:23; cf. Num 13:3–15): This information also does not have to be attributed to the Priestly account. It may reflect the general knowledge of the writer about the structure of the nation, or alternatively, information that stood at the opening of the Non-Priestly version of the story, and was shortened in the process of assembling the versions in Numbers 13–14.

3. וישבו אתנו דבר ("and bring back a report to us", Deut 1:22, 25; cf. Num 13:26): The phrase indeed stands in the sequence of the Priestly story in Numbers (13:26). However, as we showed earlier, the verse in which it stands is an editorial comment that integrates the two narrative traditions.[28] Whereas the designation of the people as עדה (congregation), the information about מדבר פארן (the wilderness of Paran), and the mention of Aaron alongside Moses, all characterize the Priestly thread of the story (cf. Num 13:3 [cf. 10:12, 12:16], 14:1–2, 5, 10, 26–27, 35–36), the reference to "Kadesh" as the place of embarking on the journey, and the information about the fruit of the land

---

27 See above, 5.1.2.
28 See above, 3.5, footnote 29 (p. 41).

continue the Non-Priestly thread. To these details one can add the expression וישיבו אתם דבר ("they brought back word to them"), which could be part of a full sentence in the Non-Priestly thread.

4. וטפכם אשר אמרתם לבז יהיה ("And as for your little ones, who you thought would become booty", Deut 1:39; cf. Num 14:3, 31): This reference is absent from the Greek translation to Deut 1:39. Cf.:

καὶ πᾶν παιδίον νέον, ὅστις οὐκ οἶδεν σήμερον ἀγαθὸν ἢ κακόν, οὗτοι εἰσελεύσονται ἐκεῖ, καὶ τούτοις δώσω αὐτήν, καὶ αὐτοὶ κληρονομήσουσιν αὐτήν	וטפכם אשר אמרתם לבז יהיה ובניכם אשר לא ידעו היום טוב ורע המה יבאו שמה ולהם אתננה והם יירשוה
LXX: And every young child who this day knows not good or evil, – they shall enter therein, and to them I will give it, and they shall inherit it.	**MT:** And as for your little ones, who you thought would become booty, and your children, who today do not yet know right from wrong, they shall enter there; to them I will give it, and they shall take possession of it.

The Greek might indicate a stage in which the comment about the "little ones" (Deut 1:39) did not yet stand in the Hebrew text. The comment was added to the Hebrew text sometime after the creation of the Greek version, probably due to familiarity with the already merged text in Numbers 13–14.[29] We can imagine a reader annotating the margins of the text with a quotation known from another occurrence of the story. While there was no necessity to add words to the story, the reference scribbled onto the edge of the text was absorbed into the text during the next round of copying the chapter. Thus, of the two consequent notes about the people's children in verse 39, the first one seems to be a gloss, based on the language known from the Priestly account: "*And as for your little ones, who you thought would become booty*, and your children, who today do not yet know right from wrong, they shall enter there; to them I will give it, and they shall take possession of it" (Deut 1:39).

The list above undermines the likelihood that the Deuteronomic account has literary connections with the Priestly version of the spy story or with the combined text of Numbers 13–14. Nevertheless, while a literary affinity with the Non-Priestly version seems more likely, we need to ask about the direction of influence between

---

29 See also Tov 1985, 9. See in contrast Wellhausen's view and McEvenue's that Deut 1:39 influenced Num 14:3, 31 (Wellhausen 1899, 102; McEvenue 1971, 92).

the texts, and thus what was the role of the scene of the threat of destruction in the literary process.

5.2.3 Deuteronomy 1 and the Non-Priestly version: Who took from whom?

Tracing literary similarities in two texts requires a further discussion regarding the direction of influence between the texts. In the case of Numbers 13–14 and Deuteronomy 1, the latter should not be automatically considered secondary solely because it gives a retrospective description of the event. Thus, based on the minor role of the spies in Deuteronomy 1, Frankel argues that the text pre-dated Numbers 13–14, which was a later elaboration and development of the narrative in Deuteronomy.[30] According to Frankel, the initial narrative recounted a refusal of the people to conquer the land out of generalized fear (cf. 1:27), and not because of a report they heard. Indeed, Caleb's exemption in verse 36 is insufficiently connected with the spy operation, and the spy mission is not mentioned in the divine verdict (vv. 34–40), or in the people's remorse (v. 41).[31]

Without the material of the spy incident in Deuteronomy 1, the narrative matches the remark in Deuteronomy 9 about the people's past refusal to "go up and occupy" (v. 23), stated without a connection to a report about the land: "And when the LORD sent you from Kadesh-barnea, saying, 'Go up and occupy (עלו ורשו, cf. 1:21) the land (את הארץ, cf. 1:21) that I have given you', you rebelled against the command of the LORD your God (ותמרו את פי יהוה אלהיכם, cf. 1:26), neither trusting him nor obeying him" (Deut 9:23). But the comparison with Deuteronomy 9 actually indicates the different nature of Deuteronomy 1, which puts both the initial reluctance of the people and the later refusal to conquer the land within the framework of the spy mission (vv. 22, 26–27). While the account indeed highlights the people's responsibility, the report from the land is used as part of the people's attempt to justify their disobedience and to explain their rebellion. As such, the spy element seems integral in the story,[32] though it is used in a way that conveys the people's accountability in the event, stressing their wrong interpretation of the message.

---

30 Frankel 2002, 147–148, 166–167.

31 A similar idea was suggested by Van Seters (1994, 370–378), who claims that the original tradition of the spies did not include Caleb. The latter was added to the story when there was a need to support the legitimacy of the dwelling of the Calebites in Hebron. Note, however, that Deuteronomy 1 does not contain a reference to Hebron (cf. Josh 14:13–15, 15:13).

32 See similar views in: Boorer 1992, 370–389; Nicholson 2002, 138, 153, 175–179; Haran 2004, 197.

This assumption suggests that the Deuteronomic narrative is secondary to and based on the Non-Priestly version of the spy story in Numbers 13–14,[33] while devoting less "story-time" to the role of the spies. As we will see, the difference between the two accounts is due to the Deuteronomic writer's attempt to correct elements that seemed unjustifiable in the context of Numbers 13–14. One of these elements is the scene of God's threat to destroy the people.

5.2.4 The contribution of the Deuteronomic rewriter

The retrospective reference to the spy story in Moses' speech in Deuteronomy 1 relates that the people requested spies be sent to the land and that Moses agreed and carried this out: "The plan seemed good to me, and I selected twelve of you, one from each tribe" (v. 23). The goals of this plan are presented in the terms of the people's request: to know the accessible routes and the cities where the people are heading: "…Let us send men ahead of us to explore the land for us and bring back a report to us regarding the route by which we should go up and the cities we will come to" (v. 22). This outline of the mission's goals is briefer than the one found in the Non-Priestly story, according to which the spies' mission intended to examine both the military and the agricultural aspects of the land:

> 18 (A)nd see what the land is like,
> and whether the people who live in it are strong or weak,
> whether they are few or many,
> 19 and whether the land they live in is good or bad,
> and whether the towns that they live in are unwalled or fortified,
> 20 and whether the land is rich or poor,
> and whether there are trees in it or not.
> Be bold, and bring some of the fruit of the land (Num 13:18–20)

While, these tasks, according to the Non-Priestly narrative in Numbers, are almost entirely fulfilled by the spies (Num 13:18–20, 27–29), they are still followed by God's harsh verdict of a near destruction (14:11–12). As we saw, whether the verdict is a response to the spies' slight deviation according to the story (13:27–29), or to the people's rebellious initiative against the leader (14:4), the determination

---

[33] It should be noted though that this conclusion does not determine the discussion about the place of Deuteronomy 1 within the rest of the book of Deuteronomy. Whether one relates the chapter to a Deuteronomistic editor who produced a prolog about the inheritance of the land (cf. Noth 1981, 15), or one predates the chapter to the stage of Deuteronomic creation (Haran 2004, 196–197), we cannot deny the traces in the text of the Non-Priestly version from Numbers 13–14.

to destroy the people seems unjustifiable in the context.[34] This difficulty disappears in the Deuteronomic version of the story, in which the people themselves initiate sending spies to the land (Deut 1:22). While Moses indeed approves the request (v. 23), he does not set goals for the mission, and thus the results of the initiative seem due only to the people's interpretation of the mission (vv. 27–28). Accordingly, the negative information about the land is known, as we saw, only through the people's complaint, with no affirmation that they actually received a report with this kind of content. In this way, the people's fear turns into a groundless excuse for not conquering the land. At the same time the spies themselves are associated with positive references by presenting the fruit of the land and describing the place as "good" (v. 25). This description detaches the later reaction of the people from any ostensibly "objective" information, and thus highlights their invalid and unjustified objection. In this way a closer connection is made between the supposed sin and the final consequences.

A similar impact arises from the absence in the plot of the scene of God's threat of destruction. In the new Deuteronomic context the risk of destruction relates only to the threat of the Amorites: "...It is because the LORD hates us that he has brought us out of the land of Egypt, to hand us over to the Amorites to destroy us" (v. 27). Beyond that there is no mention of any danger of annihilation from God. Accordingly, there is no hint of Moses' pleading to God in order to prevent annihilation (cf. Num 14:13–19). Instead, we hear Moses' reproach to the people (Deut 1:29–33), which stands in contrast to his silence in the Non-Priestly version in Numbers 13–14.[35]

While the Non-Priestly account does not contain any scene of a reprimand from Moses to the people, numerous details in the reprimand in Deuteronomy 1 repeat details found in the scene of God's threat of destruction and of Moses' attempts to mitigate the verdict. Thus, in both texts the people are accused of lack of trust in God (Num 14:11; Deut 1:32) and God is mentioned as loyal to the people, by "going before them" (לפניכם /לפניהם הולך, Num 14:14; Deut 1:33), in the form of fire by night and cloud by day:

---

34 See above, 3.6.
35 See the supposition that the phrase "to Moses" (למשה) in Numbers 13:30 implies an attempt to quieten the people "for Moses" (ויהס כלב את העם) so that they will listen to his words (Van Seters 1994, 375). This suggestion was raised also by the medieval commentator, Hezekiah ben Manoah (Chizkuni), in his commentary to Num 13:30: "'Caleb silenced the people toward Moses': From this line you can glean what must have been left out here, i.e. that Moses was trying unsuccessfully to interrupt the report of the spies, until Caleb managed to silence them, even if only briefly. Thirty-eight years later in Deuteronomy 1:29 Moses reminds the people that he had tried to give them encouragement to proceed with carrying out God's command to mount an attack against the inhabitants of that land" (Chizkuni to the Torah. Translation from Hebrew: *Sefaria* website).

Numbers 14	Deuteronomy 1
11 And the LORD said to Moses, "How long will this people despise me? And how long will they **refuse to believe in me** (לא יאמינו בי) ...	32 But in spite of this, you have **no trust in the LORD your God** (אינכם מאמינם ביהוה אלהיכם),
13 But Moses said to the LORD ... 14 for you, O LORD, are seen face to face, and **your cloud** stands over them **and you go in front of them** (הלך לפניהם), **in a pillar of cloud by day and in a pillar of fire by night**.	33 who **goes before you** (ההלך לפניכם) on the way to seek out a place for you to camp, in **fire by night**, and **in the cloud by day**, to show you the route you should take.

Similarly, the sequential clause in Moses' speech in Deuteronomy 1, detailing the punishment pronounced on the people, further echoes the scene of the threat of destruction in the Non-Priestly account. Both accounts describe God's oath (Num 14:21; Deut 1:34) that prohibits the people from seeing the land (Num 14:23; Deut 1:35),[36] while referring to a previous oath given to the forefathers concerning the giving of the land (ibid.). Additionally, the two texts mention the promise to Caleb as a reward for his fidelity to God (מלא אחרי יהוה. Num 14:24; Deut 1:36):

Numbers 14	Deuteronomy 1
21 nevertheless – **as I live** ... 23 **shall see the land that I swore to give to their ancestors** (הארץ אשר נשבעתי לאבתם אם יראו את); none of those who despised me shall see it. 24 **But my servant Caleb**, because he has a different spirit **and has followed me wholeheartedly** (וימלא אחרי), I will bring into the land into which he went, **and his descendants shall possess it**.	34 When the LORD heard your words, he was wrathful and **swore**: 35 **"Not one of these** – not one of this evil generation – **shall see** (אם יראה איש באנשים האלה) the good **land that I swore to give to your ancestors** (את הארץ [הטובה] אשר נשבעתי לתת לאבתיכם), 36 except **Caleb son of Jephunneh**. He shall see it, and to him **and to his descendants** I will give the land on which he set foot, **because of his complete fidelity to the LORD** (אשר מלא אחרי יהוה)."

Deuteronomy 1 attests an affinity in terminology and ideas with the scene of the divine threat of annihilation in Num 14:11–25, indicating the possible existence of the latter passage in the hands of the Deuteronomic author.[37] The content of the scene itself is excluded from the rewritten account probably due to the disparity of the idea of destruction from the central theme of Deuteronomy 1. This is expressed

---

36 See the different terminology in the Priestly version, even though referring to an oath: "...'As I live,' says the LORD '...not one of you shall come into the land in which I swore to settle you...'" (Num 14:28–30).
37 See also Keunen 1886, 247; Boorer 1992, 400.

by the prominent use of the verbs ירשׁ (take possession) and נתן (give) (vv. 8, 20, 21, 25, 36, 39), conveying the task of inheriting the land,[38] and specifying its legitimate heirs (vv. 36–39).[39] Within this context there is no place to question whether an inheritance will occur at all or whether the people's existence will continue.

Through this change, the account of Deuteronomy 1 also "improves" the issue of coping with the people's crisis. According to the Non-Priestly version, Caleb alone, with no assistance from the leadership, tries to encourage the people after receiving the report from the spies (Num 13:30). However, Caleb's encouragement refers to the people's capacity to conquer the land without mentioning God's role: "...'Let us go up at once and occupy it, for we are well able to overcome it'" (ibid.).[40] By claiming the people's strength as sufficient, with no mention of God, and with no record of the leadership's response, Caleb's appeal might cause both theological and political inconvenience. Deuteronomy 1 resolves these problems. It removes Caleb's words from the plot and breaks Moses' loud silence. Within this new format, it is not Caleb, the military man, who deals with the rebellion, but Moses, the leader and the messenger of God, who stands up and confronts the people.[41] He clarifies to the people that their achievement is a result of God's will and power, and that as such there is no room to be afraid of the land's physical features: "I said to you, 'Have no dread or fear of them. The LORD your God, who goes before you, is the one who will fight for you, just as he did for you in Egypt before your very eyes, and in the wilderness, where you saw how the LORD your God carried you, just as one carries a child, all the way that you traveled until you reached this place'" (Deut 1:29–31). According to the rewritten work Moses' efforts are not about dealing with God but about teaching and educating the rebellious people.

Nevertheless, as noted, the scene of God's threat of destruction emerges from the scene of Moses' response to the people and from the mention of God's verdict (Deut 1:32–36). This conclusion leads to the assumption that the rewriter worked with a version of the spy story that already included the account of God's threat

---

38 Within this context, however, the reference to the appointment of the people's judges seems secondary. As shown by Loewenstamm (1969, 99–100) the repeat of the expression "at that time" (Deut 1:9, 18), that bracket the section, might indicate a literary expansion.

39 And see the argument above (5.2) about the secondary nature of vv. 37–38.

40 Cf. the significant role given to God in Caleb and Joshua's response in the Priestly version of the story (Num 14:8–9).

41 This assumption disagrees with Noth's suggestion that there is no mention of Caleb's actions in Deuteronomy 1 because his role was familiar to the readers and hence it was sufficient to mention only the right he was granted following the incident (Noth 1981, 29).

of annihilation and Moses' intercession (Num 14:11–25).[42] Thus, together with the amendment of the image of the protagonists, the Deuteronomic rewriter corrects the disturbing discrepancy in the Non-Priestly narrative, namely the disproportion of the divine wish for fatal punishment for the people (Num 14:11–12), despite the efficient conduct of the spies (13:27–29), and the justifiable concern of the people (14:1b, 4).

The deduction that the author of Deuteronomy 1 worked with and revised the scene of the divine threat of destruction known from Numbers 14 leads to an assumption that the scene was interpolated into the Non-Priestly version of the story before the combination with the Priestly version. Indeed, we cannot be sure that the Non-Priestly version preceded the very existence of the Priestly story, as the latter may preserve an alternative, independent tradition,[43] but as shown, the Priestly thread seems to be not known to the Deuteronomic rewriter. With this assumption, the analysis of the account in Deuteronomy 1 contributes to the investigation of the formation of the text found in Numbers 13–14. This will be further elaborated.

5.2.5 Num 13–14 once again: What does Deuteronomy 1 reveal about the compilation of the two rival theological perspectives

Among his other arguments, Frankel reached a conclusion opposite to the one stated above, namely that the unit of the divine threat of destruction in Numbers 14 (vv. 11–25) was attached to the spy story found in Numbers 13–14 in a post-editorial phase, after combining the Priestly and the Non-Priestly versions.[44] Frankel stresses that the proclamation about the actual punishment

---

42 See the discussion above (3.6) regarding the secondary and transplanted nature of the divine verdict in the Non-Priestly account in Numbers 13–14.

43 We should not rule out the possibility that the Priestly narrative already existed when Deuteronomy 1 was created. This can be assumed for example as part of the hypothesis that there was a gap between the time of the composition of the Priestly source, ostensibly in the First Temple period, and the time of its publication, during the period of the return to Zion (Haran 1981, 328–330). According to this hypothesis, until its publication, the Priestly source was kept within a closed circle, that pictured a utopian world without much connection to contemporary social life. The writings became known to the public only during the days of the return to Zion, as reflected in the reading of the Torah in Nehemiah 8–10. This proposal can be found in De Wette's work in the early 19th century, who regarded the Book of Deuteronomy as the last stage in the formation of the Torah, while claiming that the Priestly material was not yet known in the period before the exile (De Wette 1806, 265–266). See the rejection of this theory in Blenkinsopp 1996, 505.

44 Frankel 2002, 160–164. A similar proposal appears briefly in Levine 1993, 376–377.

of the Israelites that they would not see the land (14:22–23) could manifest the divine forgiveness stated in v. 20 only in light of the information about the survival of the offspring, affirmed in the Priestly material (vv. 31–33).[45] Accordingly, the affinity between God's reference to his "glory" in the threat of destruction (הראים את כבדי, Num 14:22), and the mention of God's glory in the Priestly version (כבוד יהוה, Num 14:10), indicates a further literary influence of the Priestly on the unit of destruction.[46] The meaning of this suggestion is that although the story already contained a closure with God's response and the people's punishment (Num 14:26–38), the editor felt a need to intensify the suspense by adding a scene of God determining to destroy the rebellious people. By that he pointed out the shakable nature of the relationship with God and the uncertain existence of the people.

This proposal in itself is not impossible. A case in which a verdict against the people was expanded with details about God's determination to destroy the people was traced in the restoration of the compilation process of the Golden Calf story in Exodus 32.[47] But to assume that the unit of the threat of destruction was later than the combined text of the spy story in Numbers 13–14, one would expect to find a reference to both Caleb and Joshua in the "new" verdict, in accordance with the data in the Priestly account. This, alongside the abovementioned evidence from Deuteronomy 1, indicates that it is more plausible that the scene of the threat of destruction was embedded in the text when it still existed as only one version.

This possibility is reinforced by recognizing what the Priestly account contributes to questions that arise when reading the unit of the divine threat as part

---

45 While, according to Frankel, the proclamation of turning Moses into "a nation greater and mightier than they" (Num 14:12) is a polemic against the account about Moses' death due to the people's sins (Deut 1:37), clarifying that there was no intention to punish Moses even when the whole generation was at risk (Frankel 2002, 193). However, as we suggested above, the Non-Priestly version in Num 13–14 seems to be earlier than the rewriting in Deuteronomy 1, while the remarks about Moses' (and Joshua's) fate in Deut 1:37–38 appear to be even later than the surrounding text, derived from later engagement with the question of Moses' end (cf. Num 20:13; Deut 3:26, 4:21. See Kugler 2018, 195–201).

46 The image of the appearance of God's glory (*kabod*) is indeed significantly prominent in the Priestly literature (Exod 16:10, 29:43, 40:34–35; Lev 9:6, 23; Num 16:19, 17:7 [16:42], 20:6). But whereas these occurrences point to substantial presence, mainly in the tabernacle (cf. Num 14:10), the references in Num 14:21–22 point to the *kabod* that fills the whole earth, as is better known from prophetic and psalmic references: Isa 6:3; Ps 57:6, 12, 72:19 (cf. the appearance of the *kabod* in specific parts of the earth: Isa 35:2, 60:13; Ezek 31:18; Hab 3:3). For more about the notion in the Ancient Near Eastern context see: Weinfeld 1995, 27–31.

47 See above, 2.6.

of the Non-Priestly version. One example is the difficulty in understanding God's forgiveness in Num 14:20 followed by his proclamation that the people will not see the land (vv. 22–23).[48] Thus, the divine verdict and its execution according to the Priestly version (vv. 26–38) present an extensive breakdown of the people's sentence, which leaves no ambiguity in this regard. It points to the spies who defamed the land as the first to be punished (v. 37), and to the people aged twenty and over as condemned to die (vv. 29, 32–35). Accordingly, it stresses that the generation of the offspring is granted survival, alongside Caleb and Joshua (vv. 30–31).[49] This promises a continuity of the nation and survival of the relationship with God, while also refining the political message, namely that the representative not only of Judah (Num 14:24), but also of the future northern kingdom, Ephraim, will have a foothold in the land (vv. 30, 38).

The clarification found in the second divine response (14:26–38) leads some to the assumption that this unit was written in response to the difficulties appearing in the earlier verdict (vv. 11–25). Widmer reads the two verdicts synchronically, in a way that enables, according to his view, an in-depth and multi-dimensional understanding of the story.[50] Thus, while not ruling out completely the historical-literary analysis of Numbers 13–14, Widmer argues that a sequential reading of the two divine responses better exposes the authors' full intentions and reveals the use of the contradictions for rhetorical purposes. With this method he explains mismatched notions in the verdicts as a reflection of elements mentioned earlier in the plot. Thus, the silence about Joshua in the first statement (Num 14:24), as opposed to his mention in God's second response (14:30), match

---

48 This difficulty is resolved in the LXX through the phrase added to Num 14:23 (inspired probably by Deut 1:39) that guarantees an exemption of the offspring of the desert generation: ...ἀλλ' ἢ τὰ τέκνα αὐτῶν, ἅ ἐστιν μετ' ἐμοῦ ὧδε, ὅσοι οὐκ οἴδασιν ἀγαθὸν οὐδὲ κακόν, πᾶς νεώτερος ἄπειρος, τούτοις δώσω τὴν γῆν ("but their children which are with me here, as many as know not good or evil, every inexperienced youth, to them will I give the land"). However, as shown above (3.5), already in its MT version, the verdict in Num 14:22–23 points out that the punishment is applied only to the generation of the adults, namely "... the people who have seen my glory and the signs that I did in Egypt and in the wilderness..." (v. 22).

49 See Sakenfeld (1975, 322), who argues that verses 30–33 in the second divine response in Numbers 14 should be connected to the Non-Priestly version of the story (see also Milgrom 1990, 112). But these verses stand in direct affiliation with the description of the complaint elaborated in the plot of the Priestly thread (Num 14:2–3), while mentioning Joshua alongside Caleb (v. 6). And see the discussion above, 3.3, footnote 8 (p. 34).

50 Widmer 2004, 275–280. See also Wenham's suggestion that the duplications and tension in Numbers 13–14 are a result of the final design of the story (1981, 125–126; 1997, 75–80).

respectively the absence and then the appearance of the protagonist in earlier stages of the narrative (13:30, 14:6).[51]

But such a reading does not sufficiently explain the noticeable contradictions found in the text. While the second divine verdict provides answers for issues that arise in the previous one, it leaves other difficulties that seem less plausible to be raised by an editor who attempts to solve literary problems. These include the mismatch in God's addressees (Moses and Aaron in 14:25 as opposed to Moses alone in v. 11), and the abovementioned contradiction in regard to the rewarded spies (Caleb and Joshua in vv. 30, 38 as opposed to Caleb alone, in v. 24). A synchronic reading of Numbers 13–14 misses the variety of ideas hidden in the minor details.

We can therefore suggest the following assumption: an editor received two separate stories of a similar tradition, containing parallel components and conflicting details. In an attempt to preserve the varied versions of the tradition, the editor combined them, while modifying and reshaping them to create a tenable sequence. Thus, he added emphases in one version based on details found in the other, and amended or omitted details according to the needs of the new sequence.[52] The outcome, however, did not completely avoid some duplications and contradictions.

With this conclusion, we return to the analysis with which we began, of two separate and parallel narrative threads woven into a canonical epic. The two threads preserve different concepts about the relationship of God and the people. The thread considered Priestly seems to reflect a story about a harsh punishment for the people's sinful conduct, without considering the possibility of an end to the people or to the relationship. The tradition found in the Non-Priestly (and Pre-Deuteronomic) thread presents an image of a plausible destruction of

---

51 Widmer ibid., 271–272.

52 The major amendments in the Priestly version led scholars to talk about a Priestly author-editor or an editor from the Priestly school (Gray 1903, 129; Noth 1968, 101–102; McEvenue 1971, 96; Sakenfeld 1975, 328–330; Widmer 2004, 251–253). But since, as shown, both versions seem to have been amended in the course of the literary process, we should define the editor as mainly "neutral". This conclusion corresponds in a way with Frankel's view that the editors were committed to ancient Priestly material contained in the series of stories of complaint in the wilderness. In Frankel's words: "The priestly murmuring narratives reflect a long and complex history of growth and development and consist of a wide variety of forms and traditions, just as do the non-priestly murmuring stories. The priestly stratum preserves not only supplementary material that expands earlier tradition, but also independent narratives that bear the strong stamp of antiquity" (Frankel 2002, 314). Cf. Gray's view of the multiple layers in the Priestly source, which attests to the activity of scribes over hundreds of years (Gray 1903, XXXIII).

the people despite their exclusive ties to God. This tradition included the notion of intercession that granted the ability to awaken the compassion of God and thus assist the nation (and the story) to continue.

The final story found today in Numbers 13–14 reflects the editors' willingness to preserve not only the narratives and the linguistic richness of the two versions, but also alternative models of the nature of the relationship between God and the people. This has been revealed to us through historical-literary analysis of Numbers 13–14 together with an investigation of one of the secondary interpretational rewritings of the story, in Deuteronomy 1.

5.3 Deuteronomy 9: The Calf event as the people's destroyer: Why was Israel not destroyed?

5.3.1 Speech devoted to destruction

Unlike Moses' retrospective report in Deuteronomy 1, the speech in Deuteronomy 9, continuing in 10:1–10, devotes a central role to the notion of divine destruction. It begins with a declaration of God's plan to annihilate the peoples who dwell west of the Jordan valley, stating that their extermination will enable the Israelites to possess the destined land (9:2–3). Nevertheless, while the extinction of the native peoples of the land is considered to be for the benefit of the Israelites, the speech clarifies that this campaign will not occur thanks to the Israelites themselves, as their moral qualities do not entitle them to inherit the land. This idea is stated emphatically as an overview of the people's rebellious behavior in the desert:

> ...do not say to yourself, "It is because of my righteousness that the LORD has brought me in to occupy this land...". It is not because of your righteousness or the uprightness of your heart that you are going in to occupy their land... Know, then, that the LORD your God is not giving you this good land to occupy because of your righteousness... (Deut 9:4–6)

As opposed to other Deuteronomic proclamations which relate the fate of the Israelites to the love and choice of God (Deut 4:37, 7:6–8, 10:15, 14:2, 23:6), the speech in Deuteronomy 9–10 expresses no positive motivation for their fate. The privileged future of the Israelites is rather portrayed as an outcome of the wicked, and therefore vulnerable, nature of the foreign nations, together with God's earlier commitment to the fathers. As stated: "It is not because of your righteousness... but because of the wickedness of these nations the LORD your God is dispossessing them before you, in order to fulfil the promise that the LORD made on oath to your ancestors, to Abraham, to Isaac, and to Jacob" (9:5).[53]

That the Israelites lacked any moral claim to inherit the land is strenuously asserted in the speech by mentioning the threats of destruction uttered against the people on the way to the land. This idea is stated repeatedly in the review, opening with the introduction to the event at Horeb: "Even at Horeb you provoked the LORD to wrath, and the LORD was so angry with you that he was ready to destroy you" (v. 8); continuing by citing God's verdict at the event: "... Let me alone that I may destroy them and blot out their name from under heaven..." (v. 14); proceeding with the explanation of Moses' engagement with a plea to God on behalf of the people: "For I was afraid that the anger that the LORD bore against you was so fierce that he would destroy you..." (v. 19); "...when the LORD intended to destroy you" (v. 25); and ending with Moses' specific words to God: "Lord GOD, do not destroy the people who are your very own possession, whom you redeemed in your greatness, whom you brought out of Egypt with a mighty hand" (v. 26).

Triggered by the Israelites' provocative and rebellious behavior in the desert (v. 7), their risk of near destruction equates the people of Israel with the native peoples of the land. As with these nations, the Israelites are sentenced to total destruction because of their behavior, while no repentance or change in behavior is suggested in their regard (vv. 5, 27). This resemblance then raises a question: what exempts the Israelites from being treated like the inhabitants of the land? What saves the Israelites from destruction and even allows them to win the land, although, as recounted, they were completely undeserving of it?

5.3.2 How did the people of Israel survive?

How and why, then, would the people gain control over the land if their fate was supposed to be like that of their predecessors? If the people demonstrated no change, what then led God to abandon his plan to destroy them? Hayes explains that the distinction between the "wicked" nations and the "unrighteous" Israelites, according to the speech, relies on the virtuous ancestors of the latter (v. 5. Cf. 4:31).[54] But if the commitment to the fathers ensured the people's continuity, the idea of destruction should not have arisen so decisively in

---

53 An allusion to the same idea is found in the account of the covenant with Abraham, clarifying that a dispossession cannot take place yet as "...the iniquity of the Amorites is not yet complete" (Gen 15:16).
54 Hayes 2004, 77.

the first place. Thus, while the commitment to the fathers is indeed an advantage to the Israelites (9:5), it did not necessarily secure protection for them (cf. 6:15–18).

The key explanation for the people' survival should be traced in the declarations about Moses' role in the event, stated at the beginning and the end of the speech: "For I was afraid... that he would destroy you. But the Lord listened to me that time also" (9:19); "And once again the Lord listened to me. The Lord was unwilling to destroy you" (10:10). The statements indicate Moses' active involvement in protecting the people from the fate of potential destruction. Whereas Moses' words on behalf of the people in the event are cited only later in the account, the speech contains a recurring motif of Moses' presence on the mountain for "forty days and forty nights", pointing out the constant interaction with God, and thus Moses' effective engagement with the threat of destruction:

> When I went up the mountain to receive the stone tablets, the tablets of the covenant that the LORD made with you, I remained on the mountain **forty days and forty nights**; I neither ate bread nor drank water (Deut 9:9)
>
> At the end of **forty days and forty nights** the LORD gave me the two stone tablets, the tablets of the covenant (9:11)
>
> Then I lay prostrate before the LORD as before, **forty days and forty nights**; I neither ate bread nor drank water, because of all the sin you had committed, provoking the LORD by doing what was evil in his sight (9:18)
>
> Throughout the **forty days and forty nights** that I lay prostrate before the LORD when the LORD intended to destroy you (9:25)
>
> I stayed on the mountain **forty days and forty nights**, as I had done the first time. And once again the LORD listened to me. The LORD was unwilling to destroy you (10:10)

As Lohfink claims, these recurrences of the "forty days and nights" phrase do not mean to point to the number of times Moses actually ascended the mountain and contacted God. They rather draw attention to the central theme in the speech, that is the continuity of the covenant.[55] Thus, the phrase is mentioned in regard to the tablets received, in regard to their shattering, in the context of the atonement over the violation of the covenant, and in regard to the covenant's restoration. Moreover, one should notice that the "forty days and nights" motif in the account, rather than pointing to the stability of the covenant, signals the increasing engagement of Moses with God at the time, and highlights Moses' distinct role in preventing the threatened disaster of the people.

Whereas the first occurrence of the motif is mentioned when Moses obtains the two tablets on behalf of the people (9:9–10), the second occurrence intro-

---

55 Lohfink 1963, 214–216.

duces God's message to Moses about both the plan to destroy the people and the intention to make Moses the beginning of a new nation (vv. 11–14). The third occurrence already prefaces Moses' active role in intervening on behalf of the people and Aaron (vv. 18–20), while not yet citing the intercession itself but rather detailing Moses' action at the foot of the mountain (vv. 17, 21). Only the fourth recurrence of the phrase introduces Moses' prayer (v. 25), followed by the specific words (vv. 26–29). This forms the climax of the event, namely Moses' use of his (physical) closeness to God to act as advocate for the people.

The prayer terminates in verse 29, but the following section, in chapter 10, presents its outcomes, and thus completes the story: God instructs Moses to "Carve out two tablets of stone like the former ones" and to bring them to him "on the mountain" (10:1), in order to write on them "the same words as before, the ten commandments that the LORD had spoken..." (v. 4). This indicates the success of Moses' prayer in preventing the threat: Moses pleads that God will allow the people to continue (9:26–29), and God indeed renews the tablets, and thus continues the covenant with the people (10:4). In this context the repeated motif occurs for the last time (10:10) follows the description of the successful outcome of the prayer, i.e. the obtaining of the second tablets (10:1–5).[56] As opposed to the previous occurrences of the refrain, the "forty days and nights" in 10:10 is mentioned with a reference to another supposed occurrence in which a similar effective prayer of Moses had occurred. Moses mentions the "earlier days" (כ]ימים הראשנים]),[57] in which God listened to him "once again" (גַם בַּפַעם הַהִוא). Does this imply an additional intercession in the past aimed at preventing destruction?

---

56 The motif in chapter 10 comes after a deviation about Aaron's death and the Levites' role (vv. 6–9). While this segment strays from the main theme of the account it juxtaposes elements in it. The reference to Aaron's death during the journey (vv. 6–7) resonates with the earlier reference about his sentence of death (9:20), stressing that he eventually died a natural death after Moses' successful pleading on his behalf. The reference about the Levites' special role in carrying the ark (10:8–9) relates to the introduction of the ark in 10:1–5 as a preface to the later account of the Levites' duty (Deut 31:9, 26). Thus, while 10:1–5 accords with the account in Exodus 34 about the making of the second set of stone tablets (Exod 34:1–3), the pericope in Deuteronomy 10 adds information about the ark, stressing that its function was defined only then, as a storage place for the tablets rather than as a sacred artifact of God's presence (cf. Exod 25:10–22; Num 10:35–36; 1Sam 5:11; Ps 132:7–8). On the Deuteronomist's tendency to demythologize, see Nelson 2002, 127.

57 The NRSV translates the phase as "as I had done the first time", pointing to Moses' action as the repetitive element. The Hebrew text though does not specify it. Cf. KJV "according to the first time".

The beginning of the speech points to Horeb as the place where God wished to destroy the people of Israel (9:8). More specifically it refers to "the mountain" (vv. 9, 10, 15, 21; continuing in 10:1, 3–5, 10), and points to a transgression in the making of an image (מסכה, 9:12. Cf. Exod 34:17; Lev 19:4; Num 33:52; Deut 27:15), a calf (עגל, Deut 9:21. Cf. Exod 32:19–20, 24, 35), or an image of a calf (עגל מסכה, Deut 9:16. Cf. Exod 32:4, 8). Thus, the speech relates God's determination to destroy the people and Moses' intercession on behalf of the people to an occasion known from the story told by the omniscient narrator in Exodus 32. Is it possible that by referring to Moses' successful appeal to God in the past (Deut 10:10) the speech alludes to an additional incident in which Moses prevented an annihilation of the people?

5.3.3 Instances of the threat of destruction: Why the Golden Calf and not the spy incident?

Horeb is not the only place mentioned in the speech. The scene of Moses' intercession to God on behalf of Israel follows a list of other places in the wilderness where the people provoked God's wrath and rebelled against his commandants, as stated:

> 22 at Taberah also, and at Massah, and at Kibroth-hattaavah, you provoked the LORD to wrath. 23 And when the LORD sent you from Kadesh-barnea, saying, "Go up and occupy the land that I have given you," you rebelled against the command of the LORD your God, neither trusting him nor obeying him. 24 You have been rebellious against the LORD as long as he has known you (Deut 9:22–24)

Can the references to Taberah, Massah, Kibroth-hattaavah and Kadesh-barnea allude to other occasions when God initiated the people's extermination? Preceded by the reminder of the threat of destruction (vv. 19–20), and followed by Moses' plea not to destroy the people (v. 25), and his specific words to God (vv. 26–29), the reference to the other occurrences in the desert supposedly point to further events of God's destructive initiative against the people. Particularly, the occasion that took place at Kadesh-barnea (v. 23) could seemingly allude to the scene of the threat of destruction recounted in Numbers 13–14 (14:11–12), which is implicitly connected with Kadesh (13:26). But when comparing the reference in Deuteronomy 9 with the text of Numbers 13–14, the literary relationship is limited. Instead, the reference in Deuteronomy 9 resonates with the account of the spy story recounted in Deuteronomy 1, which does not mention a potential risk of destruction:

Deuteronomy 9:23	Deuteronomy 1
And when the LORD sent you from **Kadesh-barnea**, saying, "**Go up and occupy** (עלו ורשו) **the land** that **I have given you**,"	19 ...we set out from Horeb and... until we reached **Kadesh-barnea.** 21 See, **the LORD your God has given the land to you; go up, take possession** (עלה רש)...
you rebelled against the command of the LORD your God,	26 But you were unwilling to go up. **You rebelled against the command of the LORD your God.**
neither trusting him nor obeying him (ולא שמעתם בקלו)	32 But in spite of this, **you have no trust in the LORD your God.** 43 Although I told you, **you would not listen** (ולא שמעתם). **You rebelled against the command of the LORD...**

Both Deuteronomy 1 and 9 refer to "Kadesh-barnea" (קדש ברנע, 1:19, 9:23) as the place where the Israelites were instructed to "go up and inherit the land" (עלה רש, Deut 1:21; עלו ורשו, 9:23). This differs from the mention of "Kadesh" in the combined text in Numbers 13–14 (13:26),[58] referring to the place to which the spies returned, while the context relates instructions directed to them alone, requiring them to "tour" and "see" the land (ראה, תור, Num 13:2, 17–20). Further like the reference in Deuteronomy 9, the account in Deuteronomy 1 portrays the people's behavior as demonstrating distrust in God and disobedience to him (Deut 1:26, 32, 43. Cf. 9:23),[59] rather than allegations such as despising, testing and complaining against God, as mentioned in the accounts in Numbers 13–14 (נאץ, 14:11, 23; נסה, v. 22; לון, v. 27).

The supposition of a literary affinity between Deut 9:23 and Deuteronomy 1 rather than Numbers 13–14 requires further effort to determine the direction of influence between the texts. Frankel, as we saw, argues that the concise reference in Deuteronomy 9, which mentions neither the spies nor the journey's outcomes, was the literary inspiration for the "spy stories" in Numbers 13–14 and Deuteronomy 1.[60] But it is hard to find justification for a process in which a sweeping rejection of the people (Deut 9:23) would be reduced to a transgression by individuals, while still asserting a collective punishment that stemmed from it, as recorded in Numbers 13–14. It is also difficult to accept Frankel's suggestion

---

58 As shown above, the verse in Num 13:26 seems to be a result of editorial work that combined the information of the Priestly account about the spies' departure from the wilderness of Paran (Num 13:3, 17), with a possible narrative about departing from Kadesh-barnea, as preserved in Deuteronomy 1. See above, 3.5 and 5.2.2.

59 According to Deuteronomy 1 the people initially violate God's instruction by refusing to go up to the land (v. 26), and later by insisting on doing so despite God's prohibition (v. 43).

60 Frankel 2002, 147–148, 166–167. And see above, 5.2.3.

in regard to the account of Deuteronomy 1, where the information about the spies seems integral to the plot.[61]

The brief reference to Kadesh-barnea in Deuteronomy 9 seems to summarize a wider account, with a function similar to that of the other events mentioned in the toponym list – Taberah, Massah, and Kibroth-hattaavah, which seem to point to narratives known in a more detailed form.[62] In fact, when compared with these three events, the reference to Kadesh-barnea is quite elaborate. While the first three references share the information that the people "provoked the LORD to wrath" (מקצפים הייתם את יהוה, v. 22), the reference to Kadesh-barnea mentions both God's instruction to the people, and the people's rebellious response in the event (v. 23). As such, the incident at Kadesh-barnea is the climax of an implied "three and four" list, following references to three events with equal value.[63] The information about Kadesh-barnea therefore points to a decisive moment in the wilderness, when an opportunity to enter the land was lost. This opportunity, as stated, is described in detail in Deuteronomy 1, and only repeated briefly here, in Deut 9:23.

The possible literary influence of the narrative in Deuteronomy 1 on Deut 9:23 rules out the option that the latter alludes to the idea of threat of destruction. The rest of Deuteronomy 9, in contrast, indeed refers to the notion of the potential destruction of the people, but with a focus on the event at Horeb. This is indicated by the use of definite articles in verse 25 that points back to the event at Horeb mentioned in verse 18, with no mention of the other events that occurred in the desert (vv. 22–24):

9:25	9:18
Throughout **the forty days and the forty nights** (את ארבעים היום ואת ארבעים הלילה) **that** (אשר) I lay prostrate before the LORD when the LORD intended to destroy you.	Then I lay prostrate before the LORD as before, **forty days and forty nights**; I neither ate bread nor drank water, because of all the sin you had committed, provoking the LORD by doing what was evil in his sight.

The reference to verse 18 connects the prayer detailed in the next section (vv. 26–29) with the incident at Horeb. The other events from the days in the wilderness (vv. 22–24), in contrast, interrupt the sequence of Moses' actions after

---

61 See the discussion above, 5.2.4, about the rewritten principles of Deuteronomy 1, which involve an attempt to reinforce the people's guilt.
62 Cf. Taberah: Num 11:1–3; Massah: Exodus 17:1–7, Deut 6:16; Kibroth-hattaavah: Num 11:4–34.
63 On implied as opposed to explicit models of the "three and four" lists see Zakovitch 1978, 2–3, 24.

discovering the people's transgression at Horeb: breaking the tablets (v. 17); lying prostrate before God on behalf of the people (vv. 18), and on behalf of Aaron (v. 20); burning the calf and grinding it and casting its dust into the stream (v. 21); and uttering a prayer to God (vv. 25–29). Without the list of events in vv. 22–23, and the conclusion in verse 24, the text deals first and foremost with the threat of annihilation that was heard at Horeb, as proclaimed in verse 8: "Even at Horeb you provoked the LORD to wrath, and the LORD was so angry with you that he was ready to destroy you".

Verses 22–24, in contrast, point to the people's other sins and rebellions, as does the statement regarding the general behavior of the people in verse 7: "Remember and do not forget how you provoked the LORD your God to wrath in the wilderness; you have been rebellious against the LORD from the day you came out of the land of Egypt until you came to this place". The repetition of the verbs "provoke" (קצף) and "rebel" (מרי) in verses 7 and 22–24 creates a framework that manifests the people's general sinful and rebellious behavior in the desert:

9:7	9:22–24
Remember and do not forget how you **provoked the LORD your God to wrath** in the wilderness; you have been **rebellious against the LORD** from the day you came out of the land of Egypt until you came to this place.	At Taberah also, and at Massah, and at Kibroth-hattaavah, you **provoked the LORD to wrath.** And when the LORD sent you from Kadesh-barne a, saying, "Go up and occupy the land that I have given you," you **rebelled against the command of the LORD** your God, neither trusting him nor obeying him. You have been **rebellious against the LORD** as long as he has known you.

This framework may have been created by a later Deuteronomist author who wished to place the incident at Horeb in the broader context of the rebellious nature of the people in the wilderness.[64] But it is also plausible that these events were written by the author of the other parts of the chapter, one who introduced the past event with a general warning to the people: "Remember and do not forget how you provoked the LORD your God to wrath in the wilderness..." (v. 7). The author then moved to illustrate it with one concrete event, using the same term, "provoke" (הקצפתם את יהוה, v. 8). In this way he placed a long and detailed story of one specific occasion, alongside a brief review of other events (vv. 22–24), that allegedly required no elaboration.

---

64 As argued by Bertholet 1899, 32; Von Rad 1966(a), 78; Mayes 1981, 196–198, 201–202; Weinfeld 1991, 407, 414.

Whether the verses in Deut 9:7, 22–24 were secondary to the story about Horeb or were written together with the account in the first place, the interruption of the main narrative conveys the idea that the Horeb incident was only one in a sequence of rebellious and provocative actions by the people. As such, the reference to the other events intensifies the criticism against the people, but also strengthens the potential contribution of Moses' intercessory prayer, since it may concern to further mutinies that exhausted God's patience.

The allusion to the other events in verses 22–24, however, does not frame the events as part of the context of the threat of annihilation. None of the events is mentioned as a further motive for the severe threat, not even the one at Kadesh-barnea. Instead, they serve as a footnote for the proclamation about the people's rebellious behavior. Contrary to the story of the spies in Deuteronomy 1, which avoids reporting about the threat of destruction associated with the incident,[65] the absence of the threat of destruction in regard to the other events in Deuteronomy 9 seems to derive from the literary sources used by the author. Thus, the reference to Kadesh-barnea was based on a version that did not contain the information regarding the risk of extermination, like the one in Deuteronomy 1.[66]

The incident at Horeb, thus, is the only event, according to the speech, in which God wanted to terminate the people's existence, as stated: "Even [better: "And"] at Horeb you provoked the LORD to wrath, and the LORD was so angry with you that he was ready to destroy you" (v. 8). The near destruction is mentioned with the verb שמד (Deut 9:8, 14, 19–20, 25), which is common to the Deuteronomic terminology: in regard to both Israel's potential destruction (Deut 1:27, 4:26, 6:15, 7:4, 28:20, 24, 45, 48, 51, 61, 63), and the determined extermination of the other nations (2:12, 21–23, 4:3, 7:23–24, 9:3, 12:30, 31:3–4, 33:27). This replaces the root כלה that is used in the Calf episode in Exodus 32 (ואכלם, "and I may consume them", Exod 32:10). This root in the meaning of destruction appears only once in the book of Deuteronomy, in the context of the annihilation of the nations: כלתם (Deut 7:22). However, a related root, אכל, indicating potential destruction of the

---

65 See my arguments above, 5.2.4.

66 The discussion about the direction of influence between Deuteronomy 1 and Deuteronomy 9 also concerns the broader debate about the extent of Deuteronomic and Deuteronomistic material in the chapters. While one cannot resolve the uncertainty about it by engaging with only one episode, it can still be deduced that if the comment in Deut 9:23 belongs to the chapter's author rather than to the editor, it is less plausible that Deuteronomy 1 (together with chapters 2–3) was a later historiographical framework based on other Deuteronomic materials (as argued by Noth 1981, 15). See Haran's argument about the existence of Deuteronomic material in Deuteronomy 1–3 (Haran 2004, 196–197).

Israelites, appears in chapter 4 in the context of warning the people against committing idolatry: יהוה אלהיך אש אכלה ("the LORD your God is a devouring fire", 4:24. Cf. v. 23).

Indeed, the portrayal of the event at Horeb as the ultimate cause of destruction, according to Deuteronomy 9, corresponds with the Deuteronomic prohibition against making "an idol in the form of anything" (Deut 4:23), as mentioned in the background of the reference to the people's gathering at Horeb.[67] The law warns that in a case of acting corruptly by "making an idol in the form of anything..." (v. 25), and thus representing the essence of evil "...in the sight of the LORD your God, and provoking him to anger" (ibid.), the people "...will soon utterly perish... will not live long on it, but will be utterly destroyed" (v. 26). This emphasis emerges after the description of the theophany at Horeb in the previous verses, which clarifies that during the stay at the foot of the mountain, the people heard only "the sound of words", and encountered no visual manifestation of God: "Then the LORD spoke to you out of the fire. You heard the sound of words but saw no form; there was only a voice" (Deut 4:12. Cf. v. 15). As such, any attempt to envisage a physical manifestation of God, even without an intention to deviate from the engagement with God, is wrong, and will lead to an abolition of the covenant in the most serious way.

While there are no allusions in the speech in chapter 9 to other occurrences when destruction was threatened, it nevertheless implies that Moses' prayer in the incident was not his first appeal to God. The phrase כראשנה ("as before") in 9:18 alludes to an appeal that occurred in the past, and the proclamation ההוא וישמע יהוה אלי גם בפעם ("But the LORD listened to me that time also") in verse 19, states that the past appeal received God's approval. Without a threat of destruction in the background, the references to the past can allude to traditions of further prayers of Moses during the time in the wilderness. Driver points to the prayers recorded in Exod 15:25, 17:4–5 and Num 11:2, 12:13–14, 14:13–20, 21:7–9.[68]

---

67 See Johnstone's claim (2014, 22) that the ritual customs of the northern kingdom were, according to the Deuteronomistic school, the ultimate explanation for the exile (2Kgs 17:16–23). Johnstone equates it with the role of the Golden Calf in explaining Israel's destiny. However, he relates the Golden Calf sin to the forty-years wandering as the punishment, based on the references in Deut 1:35, 2:14, while in fact, the literary context of these references is the event at Kadesh-barnea.

68 Driver 1901, 115. And see also the medieval commentator Ibn Ezra on Deut 9:19: "For he had previously prayed for Israel when they were at the Sea. *Wherefore criest thou unto me* (Exod 14:15) is proof of the latter. Furthermore, Scripture states, *and he cried unto the Lord; and the Lord showed him a tree* (Exod 15:25)" (Strickman and Silver 2001, 63). It is less plausible though that the chapter refers to the prayer known from the incident of the spies (Num 14:13–20). While there

In a similar way to the abovementioned suggestion, the reference in 10:10 that associates Moses' action with an occurrence from "the earlier days" (כ[י]מים הראשנים) seems to be a reminder of past interactions between Moses and God rather than a reference to a prayer at Horeb.[69] And indeed, the comment כימים הראשנים is missing from the Septuagint to 10:10, which can indicate a perception of the phrase as redundant in the context. The other statement in 10:10 about God's previous listening to Moses וישמע יהוה אלי גם בפעם ההוא ("and once again the Lord listened to me"), repeats word by word the statement in 9:19, but with the addition of the result, that "...The LORD was unwilling to destroy you" (לא אבה יהוה השחיתך, 10:10), thus stressing Moses' specific prayer on the mountain.

The account in Deuteronomy 9 (and 10:1–10) depicts the event at Horeb as the ultimate setting for the threat of destruction of the people, while emphasizing the dramatic role of Moses in sustaining the people. To retell the story with these emphases, the Deuteronomic author modifies elements in the known story. In some cases, as we will see, this helped to amend problematic issues in the narrative.

5.3.4 The imprint of the Deuteronomic rewriter

The retrospective account in Deuteronomy 9–10 recounts God's past intention to destroy the people of Israel in response to the idolatry at Horeb. Like the account in Exodus 32, Deuteronomy 9 mentions the instruction given to Moses to descend from the mountain, followed by a proclamation of a threat of destruction: "Get up, go down quickly from here... Let me alone that I may destroy them..." (Deut 9:12–14; cf. Exod 32:7–10). But in contrast to the narrative in Exodus 32, that relates Moses' approach to God as a response to the threat (Exod 32:11–13), the account in Deuteronomy recounts that Moses descended immediately from the mountain, carrying down the tables of the covenant: "So I turned and went down from the mountain, while the mountain was ablaze; the two tablets of the covenant were in my two hands" (Deut 9:15).

---

is an allusion to the spy story in Deut 9:24, it seems to represent, as we saw, a version of the story without Moses' intercession.

69 Rashi and Nachmanides in contrast relate the reference in Deut 10:10 to Moses' further prayer when he received the second set of tablets. As Rashi states: "'And I remained on the mount' [Deut 10:10] – to receive the last (second) tablets" (Rosenbaum and Silbermann 1965, 55). And Nachmanides (to Deut 10:10): "'And the Eternal hearkened unto me that third time also [as] when the Eternal passed by before him, and proclaimed: The Eternal, the Eternal, God, merciful, etc [Exod 34:6–7]" (Chavel 1976, 125).

According to the review in Moses' own words in Deuteronomy 9, Moses' approach to God occurred only later in the sequence (vv. 26–29), after his return to the people and dealing with the idolatry himself (vv. 16–21). The narrative in Deuteronomy 9–10 reports only one prayer of Moses to God, uttered after the occurrence at the foot of the mountain. This differs from the narrative of the omniscient narrator in Exodus 32 that reports two prayers that took place on the mountain, before Moses' descent from the mountain (Exod 32:11–13) and after his conduct on the ground and re-ascent of the mountain (vv. 30–32).[70]

What is the reason for the different information about Moses' prayers in the two accounts of the story? Was the Deuteronomic writer not familiar with the specific account in Exodus 32? Otherwise, was one of the intercessions intentionally omitted from the narrative? The medieval Jewish commentator, Nachmanides, argues that the account in Deuteronomy 9–10 alludes to the two separate prayers of Moses known from Exodus 32 (vv. 11–12, 31–32):

> …In the Book of Deuteronomy Moses narrated the account in another order, stating that God had told him, *Let Me alone, that I may destroy them* (9:14), he said, *So I turned and came down* (v. 15). The reason [for this change in the narrative] is that Moses was listing to them there [in Deuteronomy 9] all their transgression, and the pains he took for them… he went back to the matter of his prayers which he had mentioned, and set down in order the two prayers, saying, *So I fell down before the Eternal the forty days and forty nights that I fell down; because the Eternal had said He would destroy you* (v. 25) – until I prayed, *destroy not Thy people* (v. 26). It was not necessary for him to mention the second prayer because he had already said there that he prayed for them forty days, and even here it does not mention [all the prayers he recited], for who can write down the many supplications and entreaties that he prayed for them during the forty days (Nachmanides on Exod 32:11)[71]

Though the author of Deuteronomy 9–10 might be conscious of more than one prayer, nevertheless, the account does not cite it. The prayer that is cited (Deut 9:26–29) corresponds in content and wording with the first prayer in the sequence in Exodus 32, taking place prior to the descent from the mountain (Exod 32:11–13). Thus, like the first prayer in Exodus 32, the prayer in Deut 9:26–29 mentions Moses addressing God's intention to destroy the people and his success in dissuading

---

70 In the broader context of Exodus 32 further entreaties to God are recorded in 33:12–16 and 34:9.
71 Chavel 1973, 560–561. And see above, 2.5.

God from carrying out the plan (Deut 9:26; Exod 32:12).[72] In addition, as with Exod 32:11–13, the prayer mentions God's deliverance of the people from Egypt and his promise of the land to the patriarchs (Deut 9:26–27; Exod 32:11, 13).

The literary connection of the prayer in Deuteronomy 9 with the first prayer in Exodus 32, together with the mismatch between the number of prayers in the two chapters, led scholars to argue that the wording in Exod 32:11–13 was added to the context of Exodus 32 on the basis of the prayer in Deuteronomy 9.[73] This suggestion is supported by the presence of the Deuteronomistic term זכר in Exod 32:13 (cf. Deut 7:18, 8:18, 9:7, 27), as well as the several Deuteronomistic elements found in the verses surrounding the prayer in Exodus 32: סרו ("turned aside", Exod 32:8; Deut 9:12, 16, 11:28, 31:29; Judg 2:17), מהר ("hurry", Exod 32:8; Deut 4:26, 7:4, 9:3, 12, 16, 28:20; Josh 2:5; Judg 2:17, 23), and אשר ציויתם ("that I commanded them", Exod 32:8; Deut 9:12, 17:3, 18:20, 31:5, 29).

But a further linguistic comparison of the prayer segments (Exod 32:11–13; Deut 9:26–29) reveals more Deuteronomistic phrases in the prayer in Deuteronomy 9 than in the one in Exodus 32:11–13. Such phrases include: עמך ונחלתך ("your very own possession", Deut 9:26, 29; cf. 4:20; 1Kgs 8:51), פדית ("redeemed", Deut 9:26; cf. 7:8, 13:6, 15:15, 21:8, 24:18; 2Sam 7:23), חטאתו ("their sin", Deut 9:27; cf. 1Kgs 12:28–30, 13:34, 14:15–16, 15:3, 26, 30, 34; 2Kgs 17:16–22), שנאתו ("his hatred", Deut 9:28; cf. 1:27), and בכחך הגדל ובזרעך הנטויה ("by your great power and by your outstretched arm", Deut 9:29; cf. 2Kgs 17:36; Jer 27:5, 32:17).

The Deuteronomistic language featuring in the prayer in Deuteronomy 9 is thus likely to be a development of the text in Exod 32:11–13 and not vice-versa.[74] In addition, the different placement of the prayer in the structure seems aimed to resolve the dissonance found in Exodus 32, caused by a second request for

---

72 In contrast to the terminology of the second prayer in the sequence of Exodus 32, requesting the forgiveness of God without mentioning the risk of destruction (Exod 32:31–32).

73 See: Coats 1968, 184–191; Hyatt 1971, 301–303; Noth 1972, 268–271; Childs 1974, 559; Aurelius 1988, 41–44. Others suffice with identifying the Deuteronomistic nature of the prayer in Exodus 32. Lewy (1959, 321), for example, ascribes the pericope in Exodus 32 to a Deuteronomistic editor from "the men of Hezekiah" (cf. Prov 25:1), who added it as part of the promotion of the reform in the cult and the denunciation of the worship practised in the northern kingdom. For further proposals regarding the Deuteronomistic intervention in Exodus 32 see: Holzinger 1900, 108; Balentine 1989, 609; Blum 1990, 73, 185–187; Boorer 1992, 209–210; Propp 2006, 148–149. Van Seters, in contrast, discerns a post-Deuteronomistic intervention in the text: Van Seters 1994, 302–303, 308–318.

74 For the argument that the prayer in Exod 32:7–14 is a pre-Deuteronomistic text and earlier than Deut 9:25–29 see: Beyerlin 1965, 21, 126, 133; Greenberg 1978, 21–35; Moberly 1983, 182–185; Weinfeld 1991, 414, 426–428; Hayes 2004, 72–93; Baden 2009, 162, 166.

God's mercy (Exod 32:31–32) after the threat had already been removed (v. 14).[75] The prayer from Exodus 32:11–13 is adopted by the Deuteronomic author, but placed more suitably in the structure, after a scene conveying Moses' own reaction to the people's transgression (Deut 9:16–21).[76] Thus, after presenting the earthly sentence to the people, the leader can approach God with a request for compassion (vv. 18, 25–29).

One could suggest that the author of Deuteronomy 9–10 was not familiar with the other prayers mentioned in the story in Exodus (32:31–32, 33:12–16, 34:9). But the description of Moses' interaction with God – in this he moves from the mountain (Deut 9:9–14), to the base of the mountain (vv. 15–21); and again up to the mountain (vv. 25–29), down to the plain (10:1–3), up (v. 4), down (v. 5), and up again (v. 10) – alludes to the variety of locations for Moses' prayers, as known from Exodus 32–34. The writer might be familiar with the concept of more than one prayer in the account, as he hints at the various stages in Moses' efforts. Nevertheless, he mentions only the content of the prayer that succeeded in saving the people from destruction.

While the retelling of the story in Deuteronomy 9–10 leaves only one prayer and transfers it to a later stage in the narrative, it adds a preceding reference to the prayer, in 9:18–19, which ahead of time reveals its successful result. This "spoiler" is located in the middle of the report, and appears as another occurrence of the "forty days and forty nights" motif that stresses the crucial role of Moses in protecting the people from the fate of the other nations – annihilation. Thus, even though the text focuses on one appeal to God, Moses' crucial role is highlighted by building up the *mise en scène* until its final climax, that is Moses' engagement with God on behalf of the people.

The change in the sequence of events also allows the removal of a problem of possible disobedience by Moses implied in the narrative. Exodus 32 recounts that

---

75 See the discussion above (2.5) about the mismatch between the two intercessions in Exodus 32. Cf. Ibn Ezra's commentary to Exod 32:11 (above, p. 22) that supposes that the Golden Calf incident contained only one prayer, after the descent from the mount: "... this prayer should have been recorded following Moses's return to the mountain (Exod 32:31). Therefore the Lord repented of the evil (v. 14) after Moses prayed and fell upon his face for forty days (Deut 10:10). If God repented first, what reason was there for Moses to say, *peradventure I shall make atonement for your sin* (Exod 32:30)? The sequence of events was as follows: Moses descended, burned the calf, and killed its worshippers. He then returned to pray to God on behalf of Israel and on behalf of Aaron... Actually, this chapter (Exod 32:11–14) should have been written after *And Moses returned unto the Lord* (v. 31). However, there is no chronological order in the Torah."

76 Cf. Hayes, who argues that the omission of Moses' first intercession in Deuteronomy 9 underscores Moses' later argument in the appeal to God: "... for that argument to work the people must believe at this point in the retelling that their lives hung by a thread" (Hayes 2004, 75).

instead of immediate obedience by Moses, descending from the mountain as God ordered ("Go down at once!", Exod 32:7), Moses approaches God with a request (v. 11). The author of Deuteronomy 9 prevents this discrepancy by describing Moses as immediately fulfilling the instruction to go down from the mountain: "Then the Lord said to me, 'Get up, go down quickly from here...'. So I turned and went down from the mountain..." (Deut 9:12, 15). Only after obeying God by descending from the mountain, and then observing the situation and reacting to it himself (vv. 16–21), could Moses intercede with God in order to save the people from a deadly destiny (vv. 25–29).[77]

The work of the Deuteronomic rewriter is thus evident from both the wording of the prayer (Deut 9:26–29) and its placement in the structure (cf. vv. 12–15). Another contribution of the rewriter appears in the scene when Moses burns the calf (Deut 9:21), which equates to the description in the Exodus 32 version, except at the last stage:

Exod 32:20	Deut 9:21
He **took** the calf that they had made,	Then I **took** the sinful thing you had made, the calf,
burned it with fire,	and **burned it with fire** and crushed it,
ground it to powder (עד וטחן	**grinding it thoroughly**,
(אשר דק,	**until it was reduced to dust** (טחון היטב עד אשר דק לעפר);
scattered it on the water,	**and I threw the dust of it into the stream** that
and made the Israelites drink it.	runs down the mountain.

The Deuteronomic report ends with a description of scattering the dust of the Calf into the stream (v. 21), though nowhere earlier do we hear about any nearby stream. Further, nothing is said about making the Israelites drink the mixture of dust and water, as recounted in Exodus 32. This variant seems to result from the author's avoidance of the association with a familiar cultic action of drinking the water, even though this was not necessarily the intention of the narrative of Exodus 32.[78] Alongside the removal of the potentially cultic connotation of the action, the amendment of this scene makes Moses' actions resonate with the purification reform to be conducted by King Josiah in the far future (2Kgs 23:12. Cf. v. 6). This assumption suggests dating the account in Deuteronomy 9 to the period after condemnation of the northern kingdom had developed (cf. Hos 8:5–6, 13:2),[79] but not before the seventh century reform of Josiah.

---

77 As we saw, Moses' "disobedience" in Exodus 32 results from the textual intervention in the chapter, namely, the addition of the dialogue in verses 9–14. See above, 2.6.
78 See: Weinfeld 1972, 233–234, 1991, 411–413; Begg 1985, 208–210, 247–248.
79 See above, 2.3.

The text of Deuteronomy 9–10:10, thus, seems to have worked with the story or with a version of what is known today from Exodus 32, which already included the scene of God's threat of annihilation and Moses' intercession on behalf of the people.[80] However, the work of the Deuteronomic author was more than a direct copy. He adopted key points of the story by the omniscient narrator and amended others, while stressing his central concern – the fundamental role of Moses in ensuring the continued existence of the people.

5.4 Joshua 14: Instead of annihilation: Tradition of settlement and apologetics

5.4.1 Caleb's right over Hebron: An exclusive promise from the past

The account in Joshua 14 retells the episode of the spies with no reference to the threat of destruction. In this way, the account is similar to the recounting of the spy event in the other retrospective reports: Numbers 32, Deuteronomy 1 and Deuteronomy 9. As opposed to these accounts, however, Joshua 14 narrates the spy event not in Moses' own words, but as a testimony of Caleb, another participant in the affair.

Caleb's recounting of the spy event in Joshua 14 follows an introduction by the narrator about the division of the land by lottery amongst the tribes of Israel (vv. 1–5), and a reference to the members of the Judean tribe that approach Joshua "at Gilgal" (v. 6aα). This reference continues only in the next chapter in a detailed report about Judah's inheritance (15:1–12, 20–63), a report which seems to derive from a Priestly workshop.[81] This sequence is interrupted by the account of Caleb's speech in chapter 14 (vv. 6aβ–15), shifting the setting from "the Gilgal" in the scene with the Judeans (v. 6aα) to "the mountain" in Caleb's monologue (v. 12), and from dealing with the mission of parcelling the land that is ostensibly already

---

80 Which was added to the narrative in one of the latest stages of its compilation. See above, 2.6 and 2.7.

81 The Priestly characterization of Josh 14:1–5 is attested from the mention of Joshua and the priest Eleazar, standing together alongside "the heads of the families of the tribes" (Josh 14:1), as mentioned elsewhere in writings from the Priestly school (cf. Num 27:18–21, 31:26, 32:28, 34:17, 36:1; Josh 17:4, 19:51, 21:1). Correspondingly, the boundaries of Judah as portrayed in Joshua 15 contain names of places found mainly in Priestly texts (Num 20:1, 27:14, 33:36, 34:3–5; Deut 32:51; Ezek 47:19). For more Priestly characterization of the texts see: Holzinger 1901, 55; Cooke 1918, 131–132, Woudstra 1981, 225; Nelson 1997, 176–177, 185–191.

in the people's possession (vv. 2, 5), to a discussion over territory that had yet to be conquered (v. 11–12).

The interruption in the account of the Judeans' territory reveals the secondary nature of the story recounted by Caleb in the text.[82] The story was attached to a document about the Judean territory (14:1–5, 6aα, 15:1–12, 20–63. Cf. 15:13–19) probably thanks to the content of Caleb's request, i.e., to obtain Hebron – a portion in the territory of Judah (cf. Josh 20:7, 21:11). Additionally, the supplement might be due to the known tradition about Caleb's connections to Judah (cf. Num 13:6, 34:19; Josh 15:13; 1Sam 30:14; 2Sam 3:8).

According to Joshua 14, the spy story is recounted by Caleb as part of his endeavor to receive a territory that was promised to him in the past. To this end Caleb repeatedly mentions the divine origin of the promise: "You know what the Lord said…" (14:6); "as you see, the Lord has kept me alive, as he said…" (v. 10); "…give me this Mountain of which the Lord spoke on that day… It may be that the Lord will be with me… as the Lord said" (v. 12). Additionally, he mentions the assurance he received from Moses in this regard: "And Moses swore on that day, saying: surely the land on which your foot has trodden shall be an inheritance for you and your children forever, because you have wholeheartedly followed the LORD my God" (v. 9). Moses' endorsement of the promise verifies Caleb's rights to the land. Moreover, it points to Joshua as the official responsible for bestowing the privilege, as with other decrees he carries out by virtue of his role as Moses' successor (cf. Josh 1:13, 4:12, 8:35, 9:24, 11:15, 17:4, 20:2, 21:2, 8). In addition, the validity of the promise is also asserted in Caleb's speech by presenting it as being familiar to Joshua from his own personal experience, since he himself was given a divine promise at the same time as Caleb: "You know what the LORD said to Moses the man of God in Kadesh-barnea concerning you and me" (14:6b).[83]

A promise, addressed to both Caleb and Joshua, is indeed known from the Priestly version of the spy story in Numbers 13–14, which presents the two protagonists as spies delivering a positive report about the land. The narrative recounts the two protagonists' embarking, together with others, on a tour of the land (Num 13:6, 8); it recounts their effort to address the people's fear (14:6–9), opposing the negative report brought by the other spies (13:32–33); and it narrates the congregation's violent reaction to the two figures for presenting a different view (14:10). Due to this conduct, according to the Priestly narrative, the two

---

82 See Herrington (1976, 108) for more arguments about the secondary nature of Josh 14:6aβ–15.
83 In contrast, the story as told by the omniscient narrator in Numbers 13–14 does not disclose if and how Caleb or Joshua were informed about the consequences of the event for their future (Num 14:24, 30. Cf. Num 32:12, Deut 1:36).

protagonists are entitled to an exemption from the spies' punishment, and a promise of a future in the land (vv. 30, 38; cf. 32:12).[84]

In Caleb's report in Joshua 14, however, the reference to Joshua (v. 6) does not point to the latter's part in the event. Joshua is not mentioned alongside Caleb in the departure of the mission ("...Moses the servant of the LORD sent me [Caleb] from Kadesh-barnea to spy out the land...", Josh 14:7a), nor is he mentioned in regard to the delivery of the "honest report" about the land (v. 7b). The honest report is credited to Caleb alone, who "...wholeheartedly followed the LORD" (v. 8b), while his companions "...made the heart of the [rest of the] people melt..." (v. 8a). Hence, apparently, the divine decision was directed to him alone, as stated by Caleb in the name of Moses: "...'Surely the land on which your foot has trodden shall be an inheritance for you and your children forever, because you have wholeheartedly followed the LORD my God'" (v. 9).

An attempt to explain the story told by Caleb in Joshua 14 in accordance with the Priestly narrative that attributes a central role equally to Joshua (cf. Num 13:16, 14:6, 30, 38. Cf. 26:65, 32:12) suggests that Caleb deliberately ignores the past partnership with Joshua, to highlight the consequences related to him, Caleb.[85] But the narrative in Joshua 14 does not seem to be concerned about an alteration of the past legacy, or about a possibility that the esteem for the leader is downgraded by one of his subjects. On the contrary, Caleb's request in the context wins a favorable reply from Joshua (Josh 14:13).

Another explanation for Joshua's peculiar role in Caleb's account is that the reference to the shared promise to Joshua and Caleb ("concerning you [Joshua] and me [Caleb]", Josh 14:6) was added to the narrative at a secondary stage, in order to associate it with the narrative in Numbers 13–14.[86] But this supposed addition in Josh 14:6 did not manage, and seems not to have attempted, to solve the broader mismatch with the narrative of Caleb as the sole loyalist. An alternative solution to this inquiry might be found in the account in Deuteronomy 1, which mentions a divine promise to Joshua alongside a specific promise made to Caleb for his participation in the spy mission.

---

84 Cf. the Non-Priestly version in Numbers 13–14 in which Joshua is not mentioned at all. Caleb alone opposes the people's resistance (13:30) and receives an exemption from the punishment of his generation (14:24). For the differences between the Priestly and the Non-Priestly versions see above, 3.2.

85 See Woudstra 1981, 228–229. See also Malbim's commentary (19th century) to Josh 14:6: "...he meant that he [Joshua] would bring him to the land where he had come, that is Hebron, and that his descendants would inherit Hebron, and therefore he mentioned what the Lord had said 'concerning' Caleb and Joshua [v. 6], that this would prove what he spoke earlier in regard to Caleb [Num 14:24], to give him Hebron" (my translation).

86 Dillmann 1886, 517; Cooke 1918, 132–133.

Below we will trace the literary sources of Joshua 14:6b–15, one of which seems to be Deuteronomy 1. We will examine the formation of the account in Joshua 14, which will shed light on the use and meaning of the spy story in this context, as well as on the broader theme of our investigation – the threat of annihilation, and specifically here, its absence from the passage.

5.4.2 Literary sources and the absence of punishment and destruction

A tradition of Caleb's privileged claim on the land is known from the story of the spy mission as told in several places: Numbers 13–14, Numbers 32 (cf. Num 26:65) and Deuteronomy 1. Among these texts, Deuteronomy 1 seems to have the closest affinity to Joshua 14. In the terminological aspect, Deuteronomy 1 describes Caleb's visit to the land with the verb דרך ("set foot", Deut 1:36), like the account in Joshua 14 (Josh 14:9). This differs from the use of the verb בוא in Numbers 14 ("the land into which he went", v. 24), and from the absence of any term in Numbers 32. Additionally, like Joshua 14, Deuteronomy 1 uses the verb רגל to describe the spy mission ("to spy out", Deut 1:24; Josh 14:7), unlike the verbs used in Numbers: תור ("to scout", Num 13:2, 16, 17, 21), עלה ("go up" 13:17, 21, 22, 32:9) and ראה ("see" 13:18, 32:9). Moreover, terms that describe the impact of the spies on the people, as mentioned in the people's words in Deuteronomy 1: אחינו המסו את לבבנו ("our brothers made our heart fail", Deut 1:28), resonate with the description in Joshua 14 of the influence of the spies on the people's spirit: המסיו את לב העם ("made the heart of the people fail", Josh 14:8). Both texts also share the word בנים (children), in mentioning Caleb's descendants (Deut 1:36; Josh 14:9), while Num 14:24 uses the word זרע ("seed"),[87] and Numbers 32 makes no reference to the offspring of the participants in the event. In terms of content, Joshua 14 and Deuteronomy 1 differ from the other versions of the story in their portrayal of the role of Joshua in the event. Both texts indicate Joshua obtained a divine promise at Kadesh-barnea,

---

87 The reference to Caleb's descendants (זרעו , "seed") in Num 14:24 could be understood as conveying that Caleb's sons alone will possess the land, due to the standard meaning of the verb in use, ירש, in *hiphil*, "to destroy" (e.g., Num 21:32; Josh 13:12; Judg 1:19). (see Rashi's commentary to the verse). If this was the case, though, the phrase in Num 14:24 would preserve a tradition that has not survived elsewhere, granting Caleb the privilege of entering the land, but allowing only his descendants to occupy it. Nevertheless, the verb ירש in *hiphil* also has a rare use to mean the transfer of an inheritance, i.e., giving possession to the next generation (Judg 11:24). This meaning is used in the occurrence in Num 14:24 by the Samaritan Pentateuch, which modifies the verb to q*al*: וזרעו יירשנה. The same meaning is understood by the Deuteronomic writer, recounting that Caleb will receive the land together with his descendants: "to him (Caleb son of Jephunneh) and to his descendants I will give the land on which he set foot" (Deut 1:36).

alongside Caleb (Deut 1:36–38; Josh 14:6). But whereas Caleb is seen as meriting an award in the wake of his visit to the land (Deut 1:36; Josh 14:7), Joshua's promise is not related to his role in that event (Deut 1:38; Josh 14:6–7).

With these deductions about the close affinity between Joshua 14 and Deuteronomy 1,[88] the latter can be considered the literary source of the former. Deuteronomy 1 points out the consequences of the event for the entire people (vv. 35, 39), while elaborating who was to perish and who was to stay alive to participate in the next stage of history. Caleb is mentioned as one in a list of the people who will enter the land. Joshua 14, in contrast, focuses upon the consequences for the one protagonist, Caleb, without elaborating the outcome for the rest of the people, even though acknowledging their existence (Josh 14:8. Cf. Num 14:23, 29, 32, 35, 32:11; Deut 1:35). The narrative about the collective public (Deuteronomy 1) is thus reduced to an allusion to the individual (Joshua 14). In the latter, the mention of the other individual, Joshua (Josh 14:6), matches the list of survivors found in Deuteronomy 1, which records a promise to Joshua as Moses' successor rather than as a faithful spy.[89]

The use of Deuteronomy 1 in creating Joshua 14 may also explain the laconic description of Caleb in the report in Joshua 14. The report defines Caleb's performance as in accord with his heart (ואשב אתו דבר כאשר עם לבבי, "and I brought him an honest report", Josh 14:7), since he "wholeheartedly followed the LORD my God" (ואנכי מלאתי אחרי יהוה אלהי, v. 8), while it omits the details provided in the narrative in Numbers 13–14, about Caleb's courageous opposition to the other spies (Num 13:30), and his definition as a servant of God with a "different spirit" (Num 14:24). The lack of these elements seems to be a result of creating the text in Joshua on the basis of Deuteronomy 1, which, as we saw, has deliberately reduced the information about Caleb, to enhance the impression of Moses' conduct in the crisis (Deut 1:29–33).[90]

The assumed direction of literary influence from Deuteronomy 1 to Joshua 14 may also explain the mismatch regarding the area of land that was promised to Caleb in the terms of his speech. Thus, whereas at first Caleb points to God's detail about "the land on which you set foot" as indicating his potential inheritance

---

88 See also: De Vaux 1970, 110; Herrington 1976, 117. See in contrast Schart's conclusion that "Josh 14 knew the J-layer of Num 13–14", missing some of the aforementioned arguments about Deuteronomy 1 (Schart 2013, 189).

89 Cf. the narrative provided in the Priestly thread, according to which Joshua survived the generation's death thanks to his faithful conduct in the spy mission alongside Caleb. As some scholars suggest, the Priestly thread itself might have absorbed this idea only in a secondary stage (Loewenstamm 1992[a], 138; Kislev 2017, 54–55).

90 See above, 5.2.4.

(הארץ אשר דרכה רגלך בה, Josh 14:9), he later defines "this mountain" (ההר הזה) as the territory "of which the Lord spoke on that day" (v. 12). Nelson, and then Butler, argue that the different expressions were put in Caleb's mouth with an attempt to point out and criticize his excessive request.[91] But the conclusion about the use of Deuteronomy 1 provides a better explanation. The reference to the broader land in Caleb's words (Josh 14:9) echoes the general information about Caleb's visit to the land, as mentioned in Deut 1:36. Caleb's reference to the mountain (Josh 14:12) then, links back to the specific place explored by the spies in the journey, as mentioned in Deut 1:24.[92]

Finally, the deduction about the Deuteronomic source of Joshua 14 seems to explain the silence regarding the threat of annihilation in the context. Similar to the allusion to the spy mission in Deuteronomy 9 (verse 23), the reference to the event in Joshua 14 was taken from a text which did not include a divine threat of destruction (in contrast to Num 14:11–12).[93] It should be noted, however, that as opposed to the allusion to the incident in Deuteronomy 9, in the case of Joshua 14 there is no expectation of a statement about the issue of the people's destruction. This notion is recounted in the Non-Priestly version of the spy story as a matter that was discussed privately between Moses and God (Num 14:11–25), and therefore was not necessarily known or revealed to the others. As opposed to the case of Deut 9:23, which is supposedly spoken by a protagonist who is familiar with the events, Joshua 14 would have no reason to note the risk of annihilation from Caleb's perspective.

The narrative in Joshua 14, however, lacks not only the divine threat of destruction, but also any mention of the death sentence passed on Caleb's fellow spies, or information about the lengthy stay in the desert as their punishment. The latter indeed appears in the version of Deuteronomy 1 (v. 35) and thus could be known to the author of Joshua 14, who alludes to the collective misconduct in the event (Josh 14:8. Cf. Deut 1:28). Nevertheless, the narrator of Joshua 14 focuses on the deeds of and the consequences for the one protagonist, Caleb.[94] In this way it provides further support for the protagonist's virtue, as part of a general apologetic about his right over the land. For more on the apologetic nature of the account of Caleb in Joshua 14, see the appendix below.

---

91 Nelson 1997, 179; Butler 2014, 88.

92 The two geographic areas are implied in the Non-Priestly story (Num 13:22, 14:24), which, as we saw, seems to be the literary source of the account in Deuteronomy 1. See above, 5.2.2.

93 See 5.3.3 above on the literary sources of the reference to the spy account in Deuteronomy 9.

94 This stands in contrast to Numbers 32, which alludes to the wrongdoing of the spies as part of a criticism against the Transjordanian tribes, and to Deuteronomy 9, which alludes to the transgression of the entire nation.

5.4.3 Appendix: The purposes of the spy narrative in Caleb's account in Joshua 14

Three noticeable elements in Joshua 14 are not found in the text's literary source in Deuteronomy 1. These are the number of years since the incident at Kadesh (Josh 14:10. Cf. Num 14:33–34, 32:13); the reference to Hebron (Josh 14:13–14; Num 13:22); and the mention of Caleb's "Kenizzite" origin (Josh 14:6, 14. Cf. Num 32:12). An examination of these elements in the story of Caleb, and an analysis of their literary sources, indicate the apologetic nature of the account in Joshua 14, and thus might reveal more regarding the rewriter's goals and intentions.[95]

Forty-five years after the event: Acknowledging Caleb's courage
The information in Joshua 14 about the forty-five years that passed since the promise to Caleb (Josh 14:10) is not mentioned in the main source of the account, Deuteronomy 1. While similar data are indeed found in the Priestly version of the story in Numbers 13–14 (14:33–34), and in the retrospective account in Moses' speech to the tribes in Numbers 32 (v. 13), the author of Joshua 14 does not necessarily use these texts as his sources. The tradition of the time in the wilderness could reach the author from other sources, such as those known from Deuteronomy with no connection to the spy episode (Deut 2:7, 8:3–4 and 29:4). Moreover, the fact that the length of the period mentioned – forty-five years until the entrance into the land – deviates from the typological number forty, indicates the author's lack of commitment to the known tradition. Instead, it is possible that he worked with or assumed another counting tradition, such as the one reflected in Deuteronomy 2:14.[96] Why then was the precise number "forty-five years" stressed in the narrative?

The information about the forty-five years stands in Caleb's account alongside other numerical data, which together seem overly detailed. Apart from the forty-five years since the promise (Josh 14:10), Caleb mentions his current age, eighty-five (v. 10), after already stating that he was forty years old in the time of the mission (v. 7). The carefully detailed equation highlights Caleb's extreme determination to receive the promise made to him. He proclaims that despite his mature age and the many years of expectation, he is "...still as strong today as I

---

95 For further discussion on the apologetic nature of Joshua 14 see my article, Kugler 2017, 570–580.
96 See the sages' assertion in the Bavli, Zevahim 118b, based on the reference in Deut 2:14, that the wandering in the desert continued for thirty-eight years, and was then followed by seven years of conquest of and settlement in the land.

was on the day that Moses sent me; my strength now is as my strength was then, for war, and for going and coming" (v. 11).[97]

Caleb's declaration that he is still strong enough to "go and come" (לצאת 14:11 ולבוא) conveys his willingness to obtain his inheritance by virtue of his own effort and not as an outcome of passive means, such as the lottery for the tribes (cf. Josh 15:1, 16:1, 17:1 etc.). His readiness to fight for his piece of land stands in sharp contrast to the attitude of the Josephite tribe, whom the book of Joshua describes as fearful and reluctant to embark on a battle with the Canaanites in order to increase their territory (17:16b), despite the Josephites' great number and might (vv. 14, 17). Caleb, on the contrary, approaches Joshua with an offer to deal with the inhabitants of the land himself (14:11–12).[98] Moreover, while the Josephites complain about the size of the portion they obtain (17:14, 16a), Caleb is ready to fight only for Hebron, even though he initially requested "this hill", with the "great fortified cities" (14:12), pointing ostensibly to the broader land on which he "set foot" (v. 9. Cf. Deut 1:36).

Thus, without describing the battle itself,[99] the text stresses its results, confirming the protagonist's possession of the territory up "to this day" (Josh 14:14), and proclaiming that with the end of the battle "...the land had rest from war" (14:15b). Together with the recollection of the promise of God, and with Moses' and Joshua's confirmation, Caleb's military motivation and capability despite his advanced age further approve his claim on the land. This reflects the endeavor to defend and justify his right to the land. At the same time, this move attests that Caleb alone, and no one else, fought and defeated the inhabitants of the place. This suggestion is elaborated in the following discussion.

---

97 This message resonates with the description in Joshua 13 of Joshua's old age and his resultant incapacity to complete the occupation. As the text might derive from a relatively late stage in the creation of the book (see below, footnote 102), it might be written after the narrative in Joshua 14 and perhaps with some relation to it. The statement about Caleb's ability resonates also with Moses' statement about his lack of capacity (or of God's approval) "to go and come" (לצאת ולבוא) at the age of a hundred and twenty (Deut 31:2). For the military aspect of the phrase "to go out and to come in" see: 1Sam 8:20, 18:13, 16. See also Van der Lingen 1992, 62.

98 It should be noted that Caleb's claim here regarding his power and abilities is accompanied by a declaration of trust in God: "... it may be that the LORD will be with me, and I shall drive them out, as the LORD said" (Josh 14:12). This differs from the missing reference to God in the statement attributed to Caleb in Numbers 13: "...Let us go up at once and occupy it, for we are well able to overcome it" (v. 30).

99 The text might rely on another reference to Caleb's war such as the one in Josh 15:14. See below "Caleb's Kenizzite roots", p. 121.

The conquest of Hebron – Caleb and not Joshua

The second element which does not appear in Deuteronomy 1, the main literary source of Joshua 14, is the mention of Hebron.

The legitimacy of Caleb's claim on Hebron, stated in Josh 14:13, is proved, according to the book of Joshua, in Caleb's military performance, described in a short and fragmentary account in 15:13–17.[100] This account demonstrates Caleb's military skills (15:14), thereby justifying his acceptance as the forefather of the Calebites (v. 17). In the final form of the book of Joshua, this account of the actual conquest of Hebron follows the official approval for Caleb to conquer the territory, based on a divine promise and the leadership's support (14:6b–15). As such, the two sequential narratives in Joshua 14 and 15 point to the period of the settling in the land as the time of conquering Hebron, and to Caleb as the approved military executor of the possession. This background stands in marked contrast to the information given elsewhere in the book of Joshua about the conquest of Hebron.

The first part of the book of Joshua, chapters 1–12, portrays the conquest of Canaan as an extensive campaign conducted by Joshua. In the campaign, Joshua captures the northern and southern areas of the land (11:16–17, 23), destroys the surrounding towns (v. 21), and kills the entire population (v. 20), including the giant inhabitants of Hebron ("the Anakim", Josh 11:21. Cf. 10:36–37, 12:7, 10). At the end of the campaign, apparently, "the land had rest from war" (11:23), as there was no further need to deal with local inhabitants. According to this narrative, only after the completion of the conquest campaign could the next stage begin: the division of the land among the tribes of Israel.

In contrast to this description, the second part of the Book of Joshua (chapters 13–21) presents the process of settling in the land concurrently with the (unfinished) mission of the occupation. This was the case especially in regard to the two and a half central tribes, Judah, Ephraim, and the western half of the tribe of Manasseh,[101] which gain a portion by lot while still being required to determine the tribal boundaries by local military maneuvers. This is learned from the stories about Caleb's initiatives at Hebron (14:6–15, 15:13–15); from the action of Othniel and Achsah (15:18–19); from the demand of the daughters of Zelophehad (17:3–6); and from the aspiration of the tribe of Joseph to expand their inheritance (17:14–18). All these references reflect the view that the process of settlement was interwoven with the incomplete endeavors of the occupation.[102] This

---

100 See Wright 2014, 186, 201.

101 For the definition "two and a half central tribes" in regard to the tribes of Judah and Joseph see: Wazana 2011, 492.

102 The incompleteness of the occupation is explicitly acknowledged by the sweeping claim in Josh 13:1–6, that Joshua never completed the task of the conquest: "Now Joshua was old

is further indicated by the mentions of the residents remaining in the territories (15:63, 16:10, 17:11–12, 16), in contrast to the many references in the first part of the book that claim a total destruction of the residents of the land, with almost no remnants (6:21, 8:2, 22–26, 10:20, 28, 32, 35, 37, 39, 40, 11:11, 14, 19–20).[103]

Following Martin Noth, scholars have defined the account of the pan-Israelite conquest of Canaan in the first part of the book of Joshua as the work of a later Deuteronomistic editor who collected earlier "local" sources, and put them in a so-called general "national" framework.[104] This hypothesis suggests that the local traditions were amended to establish Joshua as the primary hero of the conquest of the land, so that after his campaign it was possible to proclaim that "the land had rest from war" (Josh 11:23b).

According to this suggestion, the reference to Hebron in 11:21 (cf. 10:36–37) took into consideration earlier traditions about local battles that took place in Hebron.[105] But this suggestion is difficult to accept with regard to the account in Joshua 14. First, as we saw, the account of Caleb in Joshua 14 is itself a later supplement in the broader context of the second part of the book of Joshua.[106] Moreover, the account of Caleb in chapter 14 seems to be familiar with the story about Joshua's campaign in chapter 11, by concluding with the same distinctive phrase: "and the land had rest from war" (והארץ שקטה ממלחמה, 11:23b, 14:15b).[107]

and advanced in years; and the LORD said to him, 'You are old and advanced in years, and very much of the land still remains to be possessed. This is the land that still remains…'" (Josh 13:1–2). It should be noted that the comment does not refer to the "nations that remain" as mentioned elsewhere in the second part of the book (Josh 15:14, 17:12–13, 16, 23:4, 7, 12. Cf. Judg 2:21, 23, 3:1), but rather to the "land that still remains" (Josh 13:2), that is, the geographical area that was intended for the people. The verses therefore present the potential, or ideal, territory of the land, whose possession is to be realized at an unknown time in the future. This can be regarded as a certified promise, designed to create a utopian picture of the country. As such, Wazana dates the text to the post-exile era, when there was a need to encourage the returnees that the territory of the country would expand by virtue of a divine promise (Wazana 2011, 494, 2013, 231–239).

103 This marked contradiction emerges, for example, from a comparison of the list of dead kings in 12:9–24 and the list of undefeated cities in 16:10 and 17:11–18.

104 Noth 1953, 57, 1981, 38–39; Herrington 1976, 110; Boling 1982, 317; Weinfeld 1992, 70; Aḥituv 1995, 176; Na'aman 2005, 326.

105 Including the tradition that links the conquest of Hebron with the Judeans (Judg 1:10, 20). See also: Moore 1895, 23; Cooke 1918, 134; Boling 1982, 355, 360.

106 See above, 5.4.1.

107 The phrase echoes the expression "and the land had rest (ותשקט הארץ) X years", in Judges (Judg 3:11, 30, 5:31, 8:28), but has its own specific and unique wording in Joshua 11 and 14: והארץ שקטה ממלחמה (11:23b, 14:15b).

The phrase "and the land had rest from war" fits the story of the mighty Joshua, who conquers the whole land and eliminates its entire population (11:21–23). The phrase stresses that the campaign is over, and the land is peaceful since no more local people remain. This phrase, in contrast, has little credibility in the case of Caleb, whose battle had, presumably, less impact on the state of the whole land.

Boling suggests that the phrase "and the land had rest from war" in Josh 14:15b is an appendix to the narrative.[108] But the phrase seems relevant to the view implied in the account, that Joshua is not the ultimate executor of the possession of the land, that is of the specifically named area of Hebron. The text alludes to a continuity from Caleb's unique behavior in the past to his brave conduct in the later situation: just as he had acted without partners in the past, he would overpower the Anakim of Hebron by himself, even without Joshua's assistance. Thus, the place name, which is absent in the literary source in Deuteronomy 1, is explicitly emphasized in this context.[109] Conveying such a message, the text can be termed "a hidden polemic",[110] that challenges the accepted image of Joshua as the primary conqueror of the land.[111]

Why and when would an author attribute the possession of Hebron to Caleb, thus enhancing his image and justifying his achievement? This will be examined through the third and last new element in the text – Caleb's Kenizzite roots.

Caleb's Kenizzite roots

The third and last element in Joshua 14 that is not known from its Deuteronomic source is the naming of Caleb as "the Kennizite" in verses 6, 14.[112] The existence of this element in the account may be of further help in tracing the text's aims and messages, while revealing the text's setting and the circumstances of its composition.

In the fragmentary text about Caleb's military performance at Hebron in Joshua 15, Caleb's connection to the Kennizite is implied by a reference to Caleb's

---

108 Boling 1982, 358.

109 The existence of multiple, sometimes contradictory references to the conquest of Hebron (Josh 10:23, 36, 39, 11:21, 12:10, 14:13–15, 15:13; Judg 1:10, 20) indicates the significance of the place in the ethos of the people, and thus the question of who can claim past engagement with it. See Butler 1989, 170, and more extensively: Wright 2014, 209–213.

110 For the term "hidden polemic" see: Amit 2000, 93.

111 Moreover, as a settler who receives his portion by a divine verdict, Caleb is implicitly equated with Joshua, the only other person to obtain his own land through a specific decision by God (Josh 19:50).

112 Cf. Deut 1:36.

brother, Othniel, the son of Kenaz (Josh 15:17. Cf. Judg 1:13, 3:9). While this reference does not directly connect Caleb to Kenaz, it leaves ambiguous information
about Caleb's paternity with two potential fathers, Jephunneh (Josh 15:13) and
Kenaz (v. 17). The account in Joshua 14, in contrast, points to only one father,
Jephunneh, and uses the name Kenaz as the basis of Caleb's title, "the Kennizite",
thus pointing to his broader ethnic origins.

As a more constructed and elaborate text, the narrative in Joshua 14 seems to
be a later expansion of the fragmentary account about Caleb in Joshua 15, which
preserves a local, "secular" tradition about Caleb's military success at Hebron.[113]
As such, the text in chapter 14 not only resolves the supposed problem about the
identity of the father,[114] but also changes the focus of the narrative from the family
to the nation.[115] Butler interprets the ethnic use of "Kenaz" in Joshua 14 as a reflection of the attempt of various groups, like the Benjaminites, to gain control over
Hebron by using the Calebites to that end.[116] But the information about Caleb's
ethnic roots in Joshua 14 seems first and foremost to promote the right of the
Calebites themselves.

The text emphasizes Caleb's foreign origins: while it could refer to Caleb as
only "the son of Jephunneh" (Josh 14:13),[117] it adds his ethnic background in both
the introduction to and the epilogue of the account (14:6, 14). The motivation to
add the ethnic title to Caleb in Joshua 14 can be deduced from the use of the
phrase "to this day" in the account (14:14). By stating that Caleb owned Hebron
until the "present" time, the dwelling of "Calebite" descendants in Hebron may
be an indication of the time of telling the story or even of writing the text. When
could this occur?

Archaeological discoveries show that at the end of the First Temple period
the southern territory of Judah, which included Hebron, had been settled by
Edomites alongside Judeans. Evidence for this includes finds of Edomite ostraca

---

113 The two traditions, though, may be integrated in the introductory statement in 15:13.
See Cooke 1918, 141; Butler 1983, 185–186. In contrast, Wright suggests that the narrative in
Joshua 14 presupposes the narrative in Joshua 15, including the "gloss" in verse 13 (Wright
2014, 185, 201).
114 Cf. the sages' resolution by pointing to Kenaz as Caleb's step father (Bavli, Sotah 11:2).
115 Elsewhere Caleb is mentioned with his patronym ("son of Jephunneh", Num 13:6, 14:6, 30,
38, 26:65, 34:19; Deut 1:36; I Chr 4:15), and at times with an affiliation to Judah (Num 13:6, 34:19).
These occurrences led Wright and others to argue that Caleb was considered a Judahite aristocrat
detached from the Kennizites. See: Wright 2014, 168–173. See also: Galil 1983,194–200; Weinfeld
1992, 63.
116 Butler 1989, 171.
117 Some LXX manuscripts contain the name "Kenizzite" alongside "the son of Jephunneh" in
Josh 14:13, in line with the occurrences in verses 6, 14.

and inscriptions among the many Hebrew ostraca in the area, along with numerous examples of Edomite pottery located with Israelite material.[118] An additional indication is the reference found in the Hebrew "Arad 24" ostracon about the Edomites' infiltration into the southern region.[119] Indeed, according to traditions implied in genealogical lists in Genesis and Chronicles, Kenaz was considered to belong to a leading Edomite family, descendants from Esau's elder son, Eliphaz (Gen 36:11, 15, 42; 1Chr 1:36, 53).[120]

The account in Joshua 14 indicates familiarity with the existence of Edomite families in the Hebron area, and even association with them as fellow citizens. As opposed to the prominently acerbic antagonism towards Edom and Edomites,[121] the apologetic message of Joshua 14 indicates acceptance of the Edomites within the Judean population, attributing to them a share in the tribal ethos. The information about Caleb's ethnic origin stands alongside a message about the validity of his possession of the land, being an implementation of a divine plan through human efforts and skills.[122]

This pro-Edomite approach adheres to the Deuteronomic view about legitimate coexistence with the Edomites, as mentioned in Deut 2:1–8 and 23:8–9.[123] In addition, it reflects an understanding of the need to protect foreign residents who live among the more privileged majority.

---

118 See: Beit-Arieh and Cresson 1985, 96–101; Beit Arieh 2003, 70.

119 See: Alt 1925, 108; Noth 1963, 256; Ferris 1992, 107–108; Lemaire 2006, 418; Aḥituv 2012, 88, 124–125.

120 Alongside these references the Bible preserves evidence of a complete integration of the Kenizzites into Judah, as might have happened to other groups of inhabitants who dwelled in the south of the country (see Galil 1983, 194, 196–200; Weinfeld 1992, 63; Jeremias 2017, 152). This is illustrated by the genealogical list in 1 Chronicles 4 that includes the sons of Kenaz (1Chr 4:13, 15), and in the more general reference to the Canaanites in the story of Judah's marriage with the daughter of Shua the Canaanite (Gen 35:2). The fact that in other places Caleb is mentioned only as the "son of Jephunneh" (Num 26:65, Deut 1:36 and supposedly also Josh 15:13), or as a Judean hero with no allusion to "Kenaz" (Num 13:6, 34:19), might indicate a stage of assimilation with no residue of any foreign origin.

121 As strongly represented in prophetic texts: Isa 63:1–6; Jer 49:7–22; Ezek 25:12–14, 35:1–6; Joel 4:19; Amos 1:11–12; Obad 1:1–21; Mal 1:2–5 (cf. Ps 137:7).

122 See above, 5.4.1 and 5.4.3 ("Forty-five years after the event: Acknowledging Caleb's courage").

123 When not used in the limited family sense, the term אח ("brother") in Deuteronomy mainly refers to an Israelite as opposed to an alien (Deut 1:16, 15:2–3, 7, 9, 11, 12, 17:15, 23:19–20). The term אחיך ("your brother") in Deut 23:8 (v. 7 in some editions) thus conveys that Edomites should be treated almost as fellow Israelites (see: Barlett 1989, 92). This view corresponds with the Deuteronomic version of the traveling of the Israelites in the boundaries of the land of Edom in Deut 2:1–8 (as opposed to Num 20:14–21), describing the Edomites as "...your kindred (אחיכם), the descendants of Esau, who live in Seir...".

The retelling of the incident about the spies in the words of Caleb in Joshua 14 justifies the existence of foreign settlers within a Judean majority. Derived from a story about a national incident in the desert (Deuteronomy 1), the focus changes to a justification of inter-tribal relationships, while undermining another ethos about the well-known and undisputed military leader. With relatively minor variations, the story in front of us is one of the interesting incarnations of a tradition that elsewhere ends with the near destruction of the whole nation.

6 Reviewing the past in light of the present plight: Nehemiah 9

In chapter 4 we dealt with the retrospective review in Psalm 78 of the time in the wilderness. While the notion of near destruction is implied in the account, the narratives of the Calf and the spies are absent and seem not to be known to the psalmist.[1] In this chapter and the two that follow we will examine three texts in the Hebrew Bible that mention the two events from the desert or the consequences of the threat of destruction as part of pointing to landmarks from the people's biography. We will analyze the image of the past preserved by the historiographers, we will trace the literary material with which they worked, and we will assess the contributions of the authors to the myths of the past as a reflection of their own interests and concerns.

The reviews will be presented here according to my presumed dating of their composition, beginning with Nehemiah 9, dated, as will be argued, to the First Temple period.

6.1 The Calf and spy episodes with no threat of destruction

Nehemiah 9 reports an event involving a collective confessional prayer uttered by Jeshua, Bani, Kadmiel, Shebaniah, Bunni, Sherebiah, Bani, and Chenani the Levites, who "...cried out with a loud voice to the LORD their God..." (9:4). This event occurs in Jerusalem on the "twenty-fourth day of this month" (v. 1), that is, the seventh month (8:2, 14), while the Israelites, assembling "...with fasting and in sackcloth, and with earth on their heads... separated themselves from all foreigners, and stood and confessed their sins and the iniquities of their ancestors" (9:1–2).

Recorded within the abovementioned framework, the prayer is ascribed to the days following Ezra and Nehemiah's return from Persia, some ninety years after Cyrus' edict of restoration. Thus, after reading from the Torah (8:1–3, 7–8, 13), followed by the celebration of the festival of Succot (vv. 16–18), the returnees confess "...their sins and the iniquities of their ancestors" (9:2), and cry out "... with a loud voice to the Lord their God" (v. 4). Their prayer itself opens with a lengthy historical review, from the creation (v. 6), to the covenant with Abraham (vv. 7–8), and moves on to the distress in Egypt and the crossing of the sea (vv. 9–11), and the wandering in the wilderness (vv. 12–23), concluding with the

---

1 See 4.3.

https://doi.org/10.1515/9783110609905-006

conquest and possession of the land (vv. 24–31).[2] In this way, while focusing on God's devotion to the Israelites, the prayer marginalizes the people's part, assigning to it a mere three verses (vv. 16–18).[3] Nevertheless, within this limited statement, the review in the prayer mentions the two incidents from the days in the desert, the Calf and the spies, though in the opposite order to their appearance in the Pentateuch (Exodus 32; Numbers 13–14).[4]

The first reference is to the mention of the people's determination "to return to their slavery in Egypt" (Neh 9:17). This resonates with the account of the spies as it appears in Numbers 14:[5]

Nehemiah 9:17

| ...They appointed (נתן) a leader (ראש) | ויתנו ראש |
| to return (שוב) to their slavery in their rebellion | לשוב לעבדתם במרים |

Numbers 14:4

| ...Let as appoint (נתן) a leader (ראש) | נתנה ראש |
| and [we will] return (שוב) to Egypt | ונשובה מצרימה |

Like the account in Numbers 14, the review in Nehemiah 9 uses the phrase "give [one as a] head" in the meaning of appointing a leader,[6] together with the use of שוב in regard to the people setting off back to Egypt. In addition, במרים ("in their rebellion") in the Nehemiah phrase echoes the word מצרימה ("to Egypt") in Numbers 14, as the former could stand for the word במצרים ("in Egypt"), which would contain only one additional letter (במרים – במצרים), and thus could also point to Egypt. This possibility is evident in the Greek translation of the verse of Nehemiah: καὶ ἔδωκαν

---

2 Verses 22–23 should be attributed to the segment of the wandering in the desert as they mention the kings of the area (v. 22) and the plan of bringing the people to the land (v. 23). The next segment moves directly to the fulfillment of the promise of inheritance: "So the descendants went in and possessed the land..." (v. 24).

3 In contrast, for example, to the extensive engagement with the people's wrongdoing in the desert in the retrospective review of Psalm 78, which repeatedly describes actions of rebellion, lack of faith and testing God: Ps 78:17–20, 22, 32, 36–37, 40–43.

4 This order also reverses the order of the other text that recalls the events together, Psalms 106 (vv. 19–27). In contrast, the prior position of the spy story in the sequence corresponds with the order of the stories in the reviews within Moses' speeches in the final form of Deuteronomy (chapters 1 and 9).

5 The verses here are presented with my translation. The NRSV does not sufficiently convey the similarity of the two phrases (ויתנו ראש – נתנה ראש).

6 As opposed to the appointment of "head" by God: "The LORD will make you the head, and not the tail..." (Deut 28:13). Cf.: "... the LORD your God will set you high above all the nations of the earth" (28:1); "I will make him the firstborn, the highest of the kings of the earth" (Ps 89:28).

ἀρχὴν ἐπιστρέψαι εἰς δουλείαν αὐτῶν ἐν Αἰγύπτῳ (in Egypt) (LXX to Neh 9:17). But the variant במרים in Nehemiah 9 could also be a deliberate amendment of the word במצרים, to stress the nature of the people's behavior in the event, i.e., "in their rebellion" (במרים). This works well with the other variant in the verse, the reference "to their slavery" (לעבדתם), which points to and mocks the actual meaning of the people's aspiration. The critical tone of Nehemiah 9 is further manifested with the reference to the wish in the desert as a *fait accompli*: "They appointed a leader", as opposed to the neutral less defined format in Num 14:4, that refers to the people's plan to return as a wish only: "let us appoint a leader".

Further in Nehemiah 9, an allusion to the incident of the Calf resonates with the account in Exodus 32:

Nehemiah 9:18

Even when they had cast an image of a calf for themselves and said, 'This is your God who brought you up out of Egypt'...	עשו להם עגל מסכה ויאמרו זה אלהיך אשר העלך ממצרים

Exodus 32:4

[He] ... formed it in a mold, and cast an image of a calf; and they said, 'These are your gods, O Israel, who brought you up out of the land of Egypt!'	ויעשהו עגל מסכה ויאמרו אלה אלהיך ישראל אשר העלוך מארץ מצרים

Similar to the story in Exodus 32, the reference in Nehemiah 9 mentions the statue as "an image of a calf" (עגל מסכה) and points to its construction with the root עשה (v. 18). Additionally, the Nehemiah reference recounts the people's proclamation about the calf with almost the same wording as in the story in the Pentateuch, differing only in the demonstrative pronoun and the form of the verb. This differentiation is in fact a correction of the grammatical mismatch in Exod 32:4 that uses a plural form when pointing to only one statue.[7] While Exodus 32 equates the calf with the notion of gods, by using plural with "god" (אלה אלהיך... העלוך, Exod 32:4. Cf. 1Kgs 12:28), Nehemiah 9 describes the calf as the people's representation of the one God (זה אלהיך... העלך, v. 18).

Alongside the abovementioned similarities, Nehemiah 9 contains two expressions known from the two stories in the Pentateuch, though using them in the opposite order to their appearance in the stories. The review in Nehemiah 9 refers to the people as having stiffened their necks when expressing the wish to return to Egypt: ויקשו את ערפם ויתנו ראש לשוב לעבדתם במרים ("...but they stiffened their necks and determined to return to their slavery in Egypt...", 9:17). This differs from the use

---

7 This in itself results from the attempt in Exodus 32 to vilify the worship of the northern kingdom by embedding the words of the future king, Jeroboam, in the context of the people's sin from the past. For this likely editorial process occurring in Exodus 32 see above, 2.2 and 2.3.

of "stiffened neck" in the Pentateuch in regard to the incident of the Golden Calf (Exod 32:9).[8] Likewise, the phrase "great blasphemies" in Nehemiah 9 (נאצות גדלות, Neh 9:18) is used in regard to the erection of the Calf (ibid.), while in the Pentateuch it is known from the story of the spies (Num 14:11, 23). These cross references connect the events from the wilderness, implying their close ties to each other.[9]

The link between the two past events is further manifest in the prayer by the proclamation that in both cases God has not forsaken the people: "...and you did not forsake them" (Neh 9:17) "You... did not forsake them in the wilderness..." (v. 19). Notably, the reference to this divine determination not to forsake the people is not associated with the narrative of the people's near destruction, extensively recounted in the Pentateuchal stories (Exod 32:10–13; Num 14:12–19. Cf. Deut 9:8–29). Thus, as the risk of extermination does not play a role, no allusion is made to Moses as the people's advocate who eased God's verdict (cf. Exod 32:11–13; Num 14:13–19; Deut 9:18, 20, 25–29; Ps 106:23). Instead, the willingness of God not to forsake the people, according to the review, resulted from the divine attributes of grace, mercy and steadfastness, as stated: "...But you are a God ready to forgive, gracious and merciful, slow to anger and abounding in steadfast love, and you did not forsake them" (Neh 9:17); "you in your great mercies did not forsake them..." (v. 19).[10] Together with this, the review does not mention the threats of punishment made to the people in the events. The fate of the forty-year wandering is mentioned not as a realization of the penalty uttered against the generation in the desert (cf. Num 14:32–34), but as God's opportunity to demonstrate his favor for the people: "Forty years you sustained them in the wilderness so that they lacked nothing; their clothes did not wear out and their feet did not swell" (Neh 9:21).[11]

---

8 Most occurrences of the expression, especially in the Deuteronomic and Deuteronomistic literature, are used to demonstrate the people's sinful nature: Deut 9:6, 10:16, 31:27; 2Kgs 17:14; Jer 7:26, 17:23.

9 The two expressions, "stiffened their neck" and "great blasphemies", appear again in the context of the people's wrongdoing during the time in the land (vv. 26, 29), a further indication of the people's sinful nature in contrast to God's restrained responses.

10 God's merciful image is further emphasized by the absence of features of rebuke and revenge such as נקה לא ינקה ("yet by no means clearing the guilty", Exod 34:7; Num 14:18) or פקד עון על אבת ("visiting the iniquity of the parents upon the children", ibid.; ibid.). In this matter it is difficult to accept Beyerlin's assertion (1965, 137–138) that the absence of these attributes is a result of the reforms to the concept of retribution according to Jeremiah's and Ezekiel's call (see also: Sakenfeld 1985, 147–152; Boda 1999, 151). As indicated in the closing verses (and see further below, 6.3), the prayer ascribes the present suffering (Neh 9:32) to deeds committed by past leaders and earlier generations (v. 34), thus expressing acceptance of the assumption that the nation's fate depends on actions of those both within and between the generations.

11 This notion is known from the description of God's care of the people in the wilderness in Deut 8:4, and might even rely on it (see Batten 1980, 368; Williamson 1985[a], 314). However, the

The review therefore notes the sinful events from the days of the desert without the punishments that accompanied them. In the case of Psalm 78 we related the silence regarding the calf and the spy incidents to a lack of familiarity with the stories.[12] This explanation cannot be applied to the absence of the idea of near destruction in Nehemiah 9. The very association between the Calf and the spy events in the prayer indicates the author's familiarity with the one common motif of the stories – the tradition of the threat of annihilation, even if it is not stated explicitly.

Like the numerous traditions from various Pentateuchal sources with which the text shows familiarity,[13] the prayer alludes to the broader contexts of the calf and the spy narratives. This assumption leads to the almost inevitable conclusion that the presentation of the stories in the prayer is both consciously and unconsciously affected by the author's position. To understand why the Calf and the spy stories were mentioned without an explicit reference to the risk of annihilation, we need to trace the time and place of the text composition, specifically the circumstances that might have affected decisions about the literary design.[14]

6.2 Date of composition

6.2.1 The prayer's unity

The circumstances of the prayer in Nehemiah 9 can be learned from the final verses of the chapter,[15] which move the focus from past events to the current situation, by approaching God with a plea for this moment: "Now therefore, our God..."

---

information regarding the forty years wandering in Nehemiah 9 does not present the divine plan as pedagogic in purpose (cf. Deut 8:16; also 29:4–5), but rather as God's opportunity to demonstrate his mercy towards the people (cf. Deut 2:7; Jer 2:2, 31:1–2).

12 See above, 4.3.

13 The textual and linguistic affinities with Pentateuchal passages suggest that the author was acquainted with Priestly, Non-Priestly, and Deuteronomic material. Thus, **vv. 7–8** resonate with Gen 15:7, 18–21, 17:2, 5, 7–10; **v. 9** – Exod 3:7, 4:31; **v. 10** – Deut 4:34, 7:19, etc.; **v. 11** – Exod 14:21, 15:5; **v. 12** – Exod 13:21; Num 14:14; **v. 13** – Exod 19:11, 20; **v. 15** – Exod 6:8, 16:4; Num 14:30; Deut 11:31; **v. 21** – Deut 2:7, 8:4, 29:4; **v. 22** – Num 32:33; Deut 2:3; **v. 23** – Gen 22:17, 26:4; Exod 32:13; Deut 1:10, 10:11, 22; **v. 24** – Deut 4:1, 7:24, 8:1, 9:3, 10:11, 11:8; **v. 25** – Deut 3:4–6, 6:10–11, 8:7–8, 9:1. See more on the connection of the prayer with the Pentateuchal literature: Myers 1965, 167–170; Rendtorff 1997, 115; Boda 1999, 89–185.

14 This research task is clarified by Rendtorff: "...The more interesting question is what kind of theological consequences he [the author] himself drew from these traditions for his own situation and that of his people" (Rendtorff 1997, 111).

15 The conclusions of this section and some of the historical-literary arguments about the chapter are summarized in my article: Kugler 2013, 616–626.

(v. 32). Pointing first to the community's leaders and the former generations (vv. 32–35), the speakers mention the sins and distresses that accompanied the nation, and then focus on their own suffering, of being slaves in their land: "Here we are, slaves to this day – slaves in the land that you gave to our ancestors to enjoy its fruit and its good gifts. Its rich yield goes to the kings whom you have set over us because of our sins; they have power also over our bodies and over our livestock at their pleasure, and we are in great distress" (vv. 36–37).

Moving from past events to the current ordeal, the discourse changes to a first-person address (vv. 32–37) that replaces the third-person employed in the retrospective review (vv. 6–31). Despite this diversity, the two units are inseparable in the prayer, as indicated by the similar themes and terminology they share. Thus, the reference to God as צדיק ("just", v. 33) in the speakers' plea goes back to the call to God as צדיק in the historical review (v. 8), conveying the idea that God can be trusted to fulfill his promises. Similarly, the root עוד in *hiphil*, in the meaning of God's warnings and commandments used in the speaker's assertion (v. 34), resonates with the triple use of the root throughout the earlier review (vv. 26, 29, 30). This is also true of the triple reference to the patriarchs in the closing verses (vv. 32, 34, 36): they go back to the threefold mentions of the fathers in the retrospective review (vv. 9, 16, 23). The reference to the speakers' "great distress", צרה גדלה (v. 37), also echoes the afflictions the people had suffered in the past, namely the צרות (sufferings) and the צרים (enemies) that share the same Hebrew root (v. 27). The wordplay on the root צרה further connects the two literary units.

The final verses also connect to the previous review by shedding an ironic perspective on the image of the past. While the past is characterized by possession of "...a rich land..." full of "hewn cisterns, vineyards, olive orchards, and fruit trees in abundance..." (v. 25), the present circumstances, according to the speakers' appeal, know this prosperity mostly through its use as tribute for foreign kings: "...slaves in the land that you gave to our ancestors to enjoy its fruit and its good gifts. Its rich yield goes to the kings whom you have set over us... and we are in great distress" (vv. 36–37). Nevertheless, as the prayer emphasizes, in both periods the varied scenarios of prosperity and slavery were planned by God: while in the past the people had "...delighted themselves" in God's great goodness (v. 25. Cf. v. 8), in the present the rich yield of the land goes to the kings whom God set over the people (v. 37).

6.2.2 The speakers' current distress

The crisis which the speakers report as occurring in their own day fails to match the prayer's framework presented in the beginning of the chapter, relating the prayer to the days of the return to Zion (Neh 9:1–5). A document from the period of the return to Zion would be expected to deal with the issues of a returning community and the challenges of reestablishing life on the land.[16] But the speakers' appeal in Nehemiah 9 emphasizes the servitude and oppression of the community, indicating a period when independence is being lost as a result of the presence of foreign powers in the land, as stated: "Here we are, slaves to this day – slaves in the land that you gave to our ancestors to enjoy its fruit and its good gifts. Its rich yield goes to the kings whom you have set over us because of our sins; they have power also over our bodies and over our livestock at their pleasure, and we are in great distress" (vv. 36–37).

The subjugation and oppression by the kings mentioned in the appeal cannot be identified as imposed by the rulers of the empire at the time of the return to Zion. Nowhere in the writings of the return to Zion (Ezra-Nehemiah or second Isaiah) do we find a hint of the desire to be freed from the burden of the Persian Empire and its foreign kings.[17] On the contrary, the common message of the writings of the period is that the sovereignty in the land at the return to Zion was achieved thanks to the mercy of the Persian kings, who redeemed the people from "...the kings of the lands" to whom the people were handed over (Ezra 9:7). Thus, the kings of Persia were the tool of God to realize the nation's redemption, as stated in Ezra's prayer: "For we are slaves; yet our God has not forsaken us in our slavery, but has extended to us his steadfast love before the kings of Persia, to give us new life to set up the house of our God, to repair its ruins, and to give us a wall in Judea and Jerusalem" (Ezra 9:9. As well as: Isa 44:28, 45:1–3; Ezra 1:1–4, 6:14, 7:11–26; Neh 2:1–8; 2Chr 36:23). This portrayal does not concur with the view in the last verses of Nehemiah 9 of the harsh conditions under the government of foreign kings.[18]

---

16 E.g., building the temple and the wall (cf. Neh 2:17), dealing with intermarriage (cf. 13:23–28), or hoping for the renewal of the kingdom of David (Hag 2:23; Zech 12:10).

17 Contra McConville (1986, 216–217), who argues that Ezra's supplication in Ezra 9 ("For we are slaves", 9:9), indicates the people's subjugation to the Persian kings. Likewise, the account of the political upheavals in Haggai – "and to overthrow the throne of kingdoms; I am about to destroy the strength of the kingdoms of the nations..." (Hag 2:22) – outlines a general and universal wish rather than an urge to rebel against the empire. Historical evidence indeed indicates that while other provinces in the Persian Empire rebelled during Darius' reign, Judah remained loyal to the Empire (see Tadmor 1999, 407).

18 In this matter I disagree with Duggan (2001, 229, 231), who suggests that the presentation of the foreign kings in Nehemiah 9 has evolved over time, from esteem and admiration (Ezra 9:9; Neh 1:11) to this hostile image offered by Nehemiah 9 (vv. 32, 37). As mentioned, outside the prayer of Nehemiah 9 there is no evidence for such a supposed development in the people's perception of the Persian kings.

While the writings on the return to Zion indeed mention taxes that were collected for the Persian Empire (אפתם מלכים, "royal revenue", Ezra 4:13), nowhere is it suggested that the taxes were gathered in a way that caused injury or enslavement. On the contrary, elsewhere it is pointed out that specific sectors in the society were tax exempt according to the empire's legislation (Ezra 7:24). In fact, the burdensome taxes of the period were often initiated by the people's local governors, namely the Judean officers, as stated by Nehemiah, who identifies his role as similar to theirs, but differentiates himself by practice: "The former governors who were before me laid heavy burdens on the people, and took food and wine from them, besides forty shekels of silver. Even their servants lorded it over the people. But I did not do so, because of the fear of God" (Neh 5:15). As the demands of these local governors add to the burden the creditors imposed on the people (vv. 1–5), Nehemiah indeed urges the latter to cancel the debts of the poor as a solution to an economic recovery of the society (vv. 7–13).[19] His engagement therefore, is not with conditions of servitude to foreign governors of an intimidating empire. Such an engagement is only found in Nehemiah 9.

6.2.3 Optional datings

The surprisingly negative image of the foreign kings mentioned in the speaker's appeal in Nehemiah 9 should be regarded alongside the fact that the prayer as a whole makes no reference to the period in which the appeal supposedly occurs. This absence is striking in comparison to Ezra's prayer in Ezra 9, which, together with the positive description of the kings of Persia, refers to the construction of the temple and the wall in Jerusalem: "... but [God] has extended to us his steadfast love before the kings of Persia, to give us new life to set up the house of our God, to repair its ruins, and to give us a wall in Judea and Jerusalem" (Ezra 9:9). The absence of references to the time's characteristics in Nehemiah 9 indicates the incongruity of the prayer with the literary context that surrounds it, and leads to the assumption that the prayer does not belong to the circumstances stated in the chapter, namely to the period of the people's return to Zion.

---

19 Nehemiah stresses that as a governor he acted differently from his predecessors ("...neither I nor my brothers ate the food allowance of the governor", Neh 5:14), implying that the matter was at the discretion of these local rulers. This indicates that the tax, at least in part, was intended for the local government and not for the empire. On Nehemiah's alternative leadership style see Bedford 2002, 156–157.

The disparity between the prayer in Nehemiah 9 and its literary context was recognized by Torrey in the late 19th century, as part of an investigation of the scope of the secondary text in the book of Nehemiah (chapters 8–9, 9–10, 8–10 or only 9), and of any relation to "Ezra's memories".[20] In the wake of Torrey's work, scholars have suggested that the prayer should be dated to a period earlier than Nehemiah. Welch, for example, ascribes the text to the days of the northern kingdom's exile in the eighth century BCE, pointing to the reference to the Assyrian kings in v. 32 as an indication of the author's personal experience of the Assyrian oppression and the northern exile.[21] This proposal, though, does not emerge from the prayer's literary context. While the Assyrian monarchs are related to the last stage of the historical review (vv. 32–37), they appear in a "...עד ...מ" formula ("**since** the time of the kings of Assyria **until** today", v. 32), that points to two separate moments in that stage of the people's life: "the time of the kings of Assyria" and "today". With this reading, an overlap between the time of the Assyrian kings and the days of the speakers is impossible.[22] The reference to the Assyrian monarchs, however, helps to indicate the *terminus a quo* of the text composition, after the exile of the northern kingdom and even after the days of Sennacherib's campaign in Judah (2Kings 18–19). In contrast to the *terminus a quo*, less obvious is the *terminus ad quem* of the text, i.e., the latest date at which the text could be written.

Boda points to the elements shared between Nehemiah 9 and the aspirations of Haggai and Zechariah (Hag 2:20–23; Zech 1:7–17), and thus dates the prayer of Nehemiah 9 to the beginning of the Persian period, during the reign of Darius I, namely around fifty years earlier than the days of Nehemiah.[23] But the prophecies in Haggai and Zechariah express hope for a wide-ranging religious and national restoration, a hope that does not appear to be the background of the speakers' cry in Nehemiah 9. It is also difficult to accept the argument that the economic pressure reflected in Nehemiah 9 (vv. 36–37) echoes the difficulties mentioned

---

20 Torrey 1896, 31–34. For further discussion on the secondary nature of chapters in Nehemiah see: Rudolph 1949, 154, 181; Myers 1965, 165, 186; Batten 1980, 352–353; Talmon 1987, 358; Japhet 1994, 120; Williamson 2004, 282.
21 See Welch 1929, 130–137. Together with the allusion to the Assyrian kings at the end of the prayer (v. 32), Welch points to the comment about the prostration of the host of heaven (v. 6), which he regards as a polemic against specific contemporary Assyrian religious tenets. This argument is well refuted by Boda (1999, 12–14), claiming that beliefs related to the heavenly army were also prevalent in other periods and among other nations.
22 Welch's proposal meets another difficulty in light of the literary evidence in the review that attests familiarity with varied sources of the Pentateuch (see above, footnote 13), including Deuteronomic literature, most of which is later than the eighth century BCE.
23 Boda 1999, 189–194, 197.

by Haggai and Zechariah (Hag 1:5–6; Zech 8:9–13),[24] as the latter deal with lack of resources due to natural and divine causes (cf. Hag 1:10–11), and not with oppression by foreign kings.[25]

Continuing the pursuit of the circumstances of the composition of the prayer in Nehemiah 9, the final verses of the chapter should be further considered. These verses, as mentioned, refer to the presence of foreign kings that enslave the people (v. 37), alongside the mention of the nation's own rulers: מלכינו ("our kings", vv. 32, 34). This information, together with the reference to the people being handed over "...to the peoples of the lands" in the previous section (v. 30), led Werline to locate the text in the time of the Babylonian exile, when the Judean monarchy came to an end.[26] Similarly, Williamson ascribes the prayer to survivors of the 586 BCE exile that remained in the land and sought to defend their claim to be the legitimate heirs of Abraham (vv. 7–8. Cf. Ezek 33:24).[27] But the reference to the local kings alongside the other institutions of the nation (Neh 9:32, 34) indicates that the text does not consider the kings as suppressed or dethroned. Neither the final verses nor the retrospective review mentions the downfall of the local monarchy, even though it could demonstrate the people's loss of independence (vv. 36–37. Cf. v. 30). In addition, at no point in the review do the speakers mention a destruction or a population transfer into exile.[28]

---

24 Ibid., 180–185, 196–197.

25 It is also less plausible that the mention of prophets and priests side by side in Nehemiah 9 reflects the approach found in Haggai (1:14) that attributes prophetic qualities to Joshua son of Jehozadak, the high priest (see Boda 1999, 191). As we will see below (6.3), unlike Haggai, the references in Nehemiah 9 distinguish the prophets from the priests and the rest of the leadership (vv. 32, 34), and do not associate the two institutions. Similarly, it is impossible to connect the Israelites' ad hoc fast, mentioned in the prayer's framework in Nehemiah 9, with the official fasts mentioned in Zechariah (8:19), as Boda suggests (ibid. 192–193).

26 Werline 1998, 57.

27 Williamson 1985(a), 309, 1985(b) 129–131, 2004, 282–283, 2007, 167–168, and see Frankel's similar conclusion: 2011, 13–14. Attributing the text to the survivors who stayed in the land sheds an ironic light on history, as in the period of the return to Zion the descendants of these supposed speakers will be insulted with the derogatory name "the people of the land" (Ezek 4:4) and considered unfit to build the Temple.

28 Cf. Ezra's reference to the past, when stating the magnitude of the salvation in his day: "... and for our iniquities we, our kings, and our priests have been handed over to the kings of the lands..." (Ezra 9:7. Cf. Neh 1:8–10). See Duggan's suggestion (2001, 229, 232) that the absence of a reference to the exile is an outcome of the relative remoteness of the prayer in Nehemiah 9 from the exile, compared to the prayers in Ezra 9 and Nehemiah 1. For an opposite view about the precedence of the prayer in Nehemiah 9 to the other prayers, see below 6.3, 6.4.

6.2.4 My suggestion

By referring to foreign conquerors who imposed tribute on the people in their land (v. 37), the prayer should be considered not only as prior to the return from exile but also earlier than the departure itself. Such were the times of the kings Jehoiakim and Zedekiah. In Jehoiakim's days the Judean monarchy was subordinate to Egypt (2Kgs 23:34), and thus obliged to pay them tribute (v. 35). When supremacy in the international arena moved to Babylon (24:1), the economic and political burden of subjection to Babylon was felt in the days of Zedekiah. These circumstances might also be reflected in the historiographical choices of the retrospective review in the prayer, with the focus on periods when the people, while in their own land, were dominated by foreign rulers (Neh 9:27–30). This political setting is emphasized at the expense of other periods of national independence, governed by the monarchy and the temple, so the review matches the conditions and concerns contemporary with the speakers' time.

6.2.5 Linguistic support

The plausibility of the claim that the prayer was composed just before the Babylonian exile is further supported by grammatical and lexical features in the text that share elements with Ezekiel's prophecies, most of which reflect the period before the final days of Judah:[29]

1. The expression in Nehemiah 9 אשר יעשה אדם וחיה בהם ("by the observance of which a person shall live", Neh 9:29) is almost identical to a saying repeated three times in Ezekiel 20: אשר יעשה אותם האדם וחי בהם ("by whose observance everyone shall live", Ezek 20:11, 13, 21). The shorter verb וָחַי in Ezekiel 20 is considered a variant of earlier Hebrew,[30] but elsewhere in Ezekiel the longer form of the verb is in use (Ezek 18:23, 33:11),[31] just as it is in Nehemiah 9.[32]

---

29 On the close correspondence between the content of Ezekiel's prophecies and the dates mentioned in the title of each, see Greenberg, who dates the writing to 593–585 BCE (Greenberg 1983, 3–17), unlike Zimmerli who dates some of the prophecies as late as 571 BCE, i.e. to the period after the destruction (Zimmerli 1979, 9–16).

30 See occurrences in texts considered pre-exilic: Exod 33:20; Lev 25:35–36; Num 21:8–9; Deut 4:42, 5:24, 19:4–5, as opposed to the use of וחיה in late biblical Hebrew: Ecc 6:6; Esth 4:11; Damascus Document 3:15–16. See Hurvitz 1982, 46–47; Rooker 1990, 82.

31 The short form וָחַי in Ezekiel 20 may be due to the use of the citation from Lev 18:5 (אשר יעשה אתם האדם וחי בהם), or, as Hurvitz claims, a result of Ezekiel's place in an intermediate stage between early and later biblical Hebrew (Hurvitz 1982, 48).

32 I thus disagree with Rendsburg's argument (1991, 362) that the incidence of וחיה in Nehemiah 9 is an indication of the restoration period.

2. Nehemiah 9 employs an unusual usage of the direct object marker את before subjects: אל ימעט לפניך את כל התלאה אשר מצאתנו (v. 19); את עמוד הענן לא סר מעליהם (v. 32); ואת מלכינו שרינו כהנינו ואבתינו לא עשו תורתך (v. 34). While this phenomenon exists in later biblical Hebrew (cf. Hag 2:17; Zech 7:7; 2Chr 31:17), it is particularly common in Ezekiel's prophecies: e.g.: ואת כל מברחיו ... יפלו (Ezek 17:21. And see: 10:22, 29:4, 35:10, 44:3).

3. Nehemiah 9 contains the interchanged roots צעק (v. 27) and זעק (vv. 4, 9, 28) to express the people's crying out to God. Surveys of the roots elsewhere in the Bible distinguish the former (צעק) as earlier in usage, and the latter (זעק) as a characteristic of later biblical Hebrew.[33] While Ezekiel makes use of only the so-called later root זעק (Ezek 9:8, 11:13, 21:17, 27:28, 30), the prayer in Nehemiah 9 contains both roots (זעק, vv. 4, 9, 28; צעק, v. 27), thereby indicating a transition stage of the language.

4. The plural construct עמי הארצת ("the peoples of the lands") in Nehemiah 9 (v. 30) is found elsewhere only in the restoration-period literature (Ezra 3:3, 9:1, 2, 11; 2Chr 13:9, 32:13).[34] But in the context of Nehemiah 9 the sense of the phrase does not match the meaning intended in this literature, namely as referring to the population that remained in the land after the exile. Instead, in Nehemiah 9 it points to the enemies that threatened peace in the land (vv. 27–28). This resonates with the expression עמי הארץ ["the peoples of the earth"] in the Deuteronomistic literature (Deut 28:10; Josh 4:24; 1Kgs 8:43, 53, 60), and more significantly with the use in Ezekiel in regard to the relations between Egypt and the peoples of the region (Ezek 31:12).

The close affinity of the prayer in Nehemiah 9 with linguistic characteristics of the Ezekiel literature supports the claim that the prayer should be dated to the days before the Judean exile.[35] Despite that, as we will see further, the prayer

---

33 Compare, for example, Esau's "exceedingly great and bitter cry": ויצעק צעקה גדולה ומרה (Gen 27:34) with Mordecai's "wailing with a loud and bitter cry": ויזעק זעקה גדולה ומרה (Esth 4:1). Similarly, the phrase ויצעקו בני ישראל ("the Israelites cried out to the LORD", Exod 14:10) with *Targum Onkelos* (Aramaic translation) to the verse: ויזעקו בני ישראל; and Isaiah's statement אף יצעק אליו ולא יענה ("If one cries out to it, it does not answer", Isa 46:7) with the reading in the Isaiah Scroll: אף יזעק עליו ולוא יענה (4QIsaa). See Rooker 1990, 134–138.

34 The peculiar form of plural construct is commonly considered a mark of later biblical Hebrew (e.g., גבורי חילים, 1Chr 7:5, 7). Nevertheless, it is also found in earlier Hebrew: שרי החילים (1Kgs 15:20; vs. שרי החיל, 2Sam 24:4); אנשי מדות (Num 13:32; vs. אנשי מדה, Isa 45:14); לוחת האבנים (Deut 9:9; vs. לחת האבן, Exod 24:12).

35 This conclusion opposes Rendsburg's contention that the prayer reflects Second Temple Hebrew (1991, 362–363), based on the order of the attributes of God in the prayer, חנון ורחום (Neh 9:17), which like occurrences in several psalms (Ps 111:4, 112:54, 145:8), stand in reverse

of Nehemiah does not necessarily derive from the same literary and ideological circle as Ezekiel's.[36]

6.3 Negligible self-criticism and a minor request

The prayer in Nehemiah 9 is customarily associated with the three confessional prayers recorded in the Second Temple period writings: Dan 9:5–19; Ezra 9:6–15, Neh 1:5–11.[37] These prayers appear in a narrative context in which they are ascribed to people who take an action, specified by the root ידה in *hithpael*: Dan 9:4, 20; Ezra 10:1; Neh 1:6, 9:2–3.

The verbal form ידה (התודה) appears prominently in the Priestly literature in conjunction with references to ritual acts.[38] The abovementioned prayers, in contrast, refer to the notion of confession (ידה) with no association with a ritual, ceremonial or sacrificial offering, indicating the evolution of the concept from focus on a ritual act to a mode of invocation. Thus, the narrative contexts of the prayers point to the participants' words: "I prayed to the LORD my God and made confession, saying..." (Dan 9:4); "While Ezra prayed and made confession, weeping and throwing himself down before the house of God..." (Ezra 10:1); "...the prayer of your servant that I now pray... confessing the sins of the people of Israel..." (Neh 1:6); "...read from

---

order to the "original" expression in Exod 34:6, רחום וחנן. But the evidence from the psalms is insufficient support, as the variants there derive from literary and structural considerations such as creating an alphabetic acrostic, and thus do not testify to a fixed use of the phrase (cf. other psalms that contain the so-called "early" form of the expression: Ps 86:15, 103:8). Likewise, it is difficult to accept Rendsburg's argument that the ending ות for nouns in Nehemiah 9 (עבדות, v. 17 and מלכות, v. 35) reflects Second Temple Hebrew, as this ending also occurs in texts composed prior to the restoration: כסות (Gen 20:16); גאות (Isa 9:17); דמות (Isa 13:4); מלכות (Jer 49:34); זנות (Hos 4:11). Joosten's argument (2006, 143, 2012, 398), that the peculiar form *weyiqtol* in vv. 27–28 in the prayer (ותציל ם, ויושיעום) reflects late biblical Hebrew, must, however, take into consideration the rarity of this form (Ecc 8:10; Neh 3:14; 2Chr 24:11) and the possible existence of the form in earlier Hebrew as preserved in the *qri* [reading] tradition to Josh 19:29.

36 In contrast to Chrosotowski's suggestion (1990, 259–261) that the prayer was written within circles associated with Ezekiel. See below 7.6.

37 See Duggan 2001, 228–229; Rom-Shiloni 2006, 51; Schuller 2007, 3. Cf. Weinfeld 2004, 126.

38 E.g. Lev 5:5–6: "When you [Heb. he] realize your [his] guilt in any of these, you [he] shall confess והתודה the sin... And you [he] shall bring to the LORD... a female from the flock, a sheep or a goat, as a sin offering...". Cf. Lev 16:21; Num 5:7. An exception is the statement in Lev 26:40 "But if they confess their iniquity and the iniquity of their ancestors..." (והתודו את עונם ואת עון אבתם), as it lacks an allusion to ritual action, apparently due to the principle that sacrifices are not to be offered in exile (see Milgrom 1991, 301). For the affinity between the confessional ritual in the Priestly literature and Second Temple period prayers see Hogewood 2006, 71, 82.

the book of the law of the LORD their God for a fourth part of the day, and for another fourth they made confession and worshiped the LORD their God" (Neh 9:3).

The four prayers noted above also share several elements of phraseology: an affirmation of God's righteousness and his just judgment (Dan 9:14; Ezra 9:15; Neh 9:8, 33), a description of God as "great and awesome" (Dan 9:4; Neh 1:5, 9:32), references to the people's leadership (kings, priests) and ancestors (Dan 9:6; Ezra 9:7; Neh 9:32, 34), a recognition of the prophet's commissioning (Dan 9:6, 11; Ezra 9:11; Neh 9:30), and employment of the term ועתה "and now" in the actual appeal to God (Dan 9:15, 17; Ezra 9:8, 10, 12; Neh 9:32). Alongside these linguistic characteristics, the prayers contain two substantive components that characterize the texts as confessional documents: the speakers' recognition of their sinful behavior (Dan 9:5–6, 8–11, 15; Ezra 9:6–7, 10, 13, 15; Neh 1:6–7), and a request for divine deliverance and redemption (Dan 9:17–19; Ezra 9:8; Neh 1:8–11).[39] These two components are almost non-existent in our text, the Levites' prayer in Nehemiah 9.

6.3.1 A limited acknowledgement of sin

While the phrases "we have acted wickedly" (Neh 9:33) and "our sins" (v. 37) reflect a measure of self-condemnation, they do not represent the general tone of the prayer, which mainly ascribes responsibility to people other than the speakers, who thus absolve themselves of blame. The prayer frequently accuses the speakers' former generations from the time in the desert and during the dwelling in the land (vv. 16–18, 26, 28–29). Similarly, it ascribes responsibility to the people's leaders, who "...have not kept your law or heeded the commandments and the warnings that you gave them" (v. 34).

This tendency to blame others is noteworthy in the distinction made in the prayer between the sufferers and the sinners, whether in the past or in contemporary times (vv. 32–34). In v. 32 the "sufferers" are listed as "our kings, our officials, our priests, our prophets, our ancestors, and all your people"; however, in v. 34 the sinners are apparently only "our kings, our officials, our priests, and our ancestors", while "our prophets" and "all your people" are mentioned as subordinates of the sinner groups, indicated by the use of the possessive marker (מלכינו שרינו כהנינו ואבתינו).

---

[39] For the centrality of these two elements in confessional prayers see: Quanbeck 1962, 667; Jacobs 1989, 759; Schuller 1996, 129. See also Hiller 1936, 561–562, on Azariah's prayer in the LXX additional section to Daniel, which likewise contains both components.

As the speakers themselves, thus, have not committed actual sins but were only subjected to sinful leaders, their confessional statements – "we have acted wickedly" (v. 33), "our sins" (v. 37) – seem no more than lip service to their utterances about the Lord: "You have been just...[and in contrast] we have acted wickedly" (ואתה צדיק...ואנחנו הרשענו, v. 33). This supposed confession indeed stands with no details of sins, contrary to the information regarding the accused leadership groups who "...have not kept your law or heeded the commandments and the warnings that you gave them... they did not serve you and did not turn from their wicked works" (vv. 34–35).

The limited self-criticism in the prayer stands in contrast to the centrality of the motif in the three other Second Temple period prayers. While focusing on past and present sins and transgressions (Dan 9:5–6, 8–11, 15; Ezra 9:6–7, 10, 13, 15; Neh 1:6–7), the three prayers point out the speakers' essential role in the collective misconduct: "...because of our sins and the iniquities of our ancestors" (Dan 9:16); "From the days of our ancestors to this day we have been deep in guilt, and for our iniquities..." (Ezra 9:7); "...confessing the sins of the people of Israel, which we have sinned against you. Both I and my family have sinned" (Neh 1:6). This acknowledgment from the speakers relates to the sins of the present day ("because of our sins", "our iniquities", "we have sinned") in association with sins that have accumulated since the days of the forefathers. Contrary to this approach, the prayer in Nehemiah 9 employs third-person rather than first-person discourse, accusing the leadership and the ancestors for "not keeping (the laws)" (לא עשו), "not heeding" (לא הקשיבו), "not serving" (לא עבדוך), and "not turning (from their wicked works)" (לא שבו) (Neh 9:34–35). Such assertions dissolve the already minimal level of accountability taken by the speakers.

6.3.2 A small request

Equally negligible and inconsequential is the appeal to God in the prayer in Nehemiah 9. The speakers make a minor request at the beginning of their appeal: "Now therefore, our God... do not treat lightly all the hardship that has come upon us..." (v. 32). Unlike the pleas for national salvation in Daniel (9:16–17) and Ezra (9:8–9), and the request for personal success in the confessional prayer in Nehemiah 1 (v. 11), the request in Nehemiah 9 does not yearn for any fundamental change in the speakers' conditions. Their request is only that their hardships not be treated lightly (see אל ימעט לפניך, v. 32), so that they may achieve recognition for the tribulations that occurred to the people. Instead of words of supplication, the main content of the prayer in Nehemiah 9 is a review of the past (vv. 6–31), focusing on God's deeds for the people. As such, while mentioning troubles that have visited the people in the past and the present, the prayer makes no specific request for change in the *status quo*.

The request for an acknowledgment of the people's suffering reflects the hope that God will regard the tribulations that have occurred so far as sufficient. Such an attitude is appropriate in a record made during difficulties that threaten to deteriorate. This is less likely to characterize the period defined in the chapter's opening verses, namely the period of the restoration, and may be better suited to circumstances when the speakers struggled to maintain independence and resilience while still in their land. This possibility ties in with our view about the dating of the prayer, based on the historiographical information it contains and its linguistic characteristics.

6.4 The past in the service of the present: Silencing the tradition of near destruction

This prayer, possibly from the First Temple period, survived and reached the communities of the Second Temple period due to its liturgical function in the years following the exile.[40] Its dissemination prior to writing might have been the basis for the creation of other manifestations of this unique genre, containing similar features, such as appear in Daniel 9, Ezra 9, and Nehemiah 1.[41] The "old" prayer was eventually inserted into "Nehemiah's memoirs" about the time of the return to Zion due to the need to demonstrate the returnees' familiarity with events mentioned in the Torah that was supposedly distributed on those days (Nehemiah 8), as well as the need to point out the returnees' connection with the national ancestry (cf. Neh 9:7). The prayer was attached to the current context by the opening verses that defined the prayer as a confession of the Levites (vv. 1–5), even though the prayer in its original incarnation had another purpose – to assure immunity from further troubles. This original purpose of the prayer may explain the way the Golden Calf event and the spy episode were used and presented in the prayer. This will be our concern in the final stage of the analysis of Nehemiah 9.

The speakers' limited hope to avoid further troubles can be understood, as said, in light of the possibility that the text was composed in a period of political

---

40 The possibility that the text has been used in liturgical contexts may be indicated by the presence of its wording in later fixed prayers, such as *Pesuqei Dezimra* (cf. Neh 9:5a–11), *Seder Taḥanun* (cf. Neh 9:33), and the *Day of Atonement prayer* (cf. Neh 9:17).

41 This conclusion differs from Duggan's proposal, which identifies the prayer in Nehemiah 9 as secondary to the prayer in Ezra, based on the repeated mention of the groups of the leaders and the patriarchs in the two texts (Neh 9:32, 34; Ezra 9:7) (Duggan 2006, 176, 179).

instability and threat to the people's life, that is on the eve of the destruction of the Judean kingdom. The threats from Babylon, and perhaps the incursions of 597 BCE, caused distress and anxiety among the inhabitants of the land and gave rise to fears of worse scenarios. Within this literary and historical context, the references to the Calf and the spy traditions play an important role in the review of the past.

The phenomenon of reviewing the past as part of an appeal to God is not common in the Hebrew Bible. Other historical reviews, such as those in Ezekiel 20, and in Psalms 78, 105 and 106, are used as a reproach to or consolation for the audience. The review in Nehemiah 9, in contrast, addresses God and expresses longing for his attention (and for this reason has been employed as a confessional prayer). Within this framework, God's merciful behavior in the past is seen as a possible precedent for the current time.

Highlighted in the review are two periods when God acted mercifully towards the people: the days of the wandering in the desert and the days in the land. During the time in the desert, as soon as God "...performed signs and wonders..." in Egypt (v. 10) and saved the ancestors (v. 9) from their "pursuers" (v. 11), he guided the people by a pillar of cloud and a pillar of fire in the desert (v. 12), he gave them ordinances and laws (v. 13), he fed them with bread from heaven and watered them with water from the rock, and he renewed the promise of the inheritance of the land (vv. 12–15). The people themselves, however, "...acted presumptuously and stiffened their necks..." (v. 16), as they expressed their will "...to return to their slavery in Egypt..." (v. 17), and committed great blasphemies (נאצות גדלות) by casting an image of a calf and pointing to it as "God who brought you up out of Egypt" (v. 18).

The people' sins are presented in these verses as recurrent and intersecting, indicating the repeated display of their contemptuous attitude:

> Neh 9:16: ... **stiffened their necks** (ויקשו את ערפם)
> and **did not obey** (ולא שמעו) your commandments;
> v. 17: **they refused to obey** (וימאנו לשמוע)
> ...but they **stiffened their necks** (ויקשו את ערפם)...

In addition, the term הזידו ("acted presumptuously") in verse 16 resonates ironically with the description of the attitude of the Egyptians towards the Israelites in Egypt: הזידו עליהם (v. 10). The people's despising of God (v. 16) was expressed by the wish to return to Egypt (v. 17), the homeland of the people by whom the Israelites themselves had been despised (v. 10).

The review stresses, though, that despite the people's sinful behavior God maintained his favorable attitude towards the people. He continued to guide them in the desert with a pillar of cloud and a pillar of fire (v. 19); he gave them his good spirit "to instruct them" (להשכילם, v. 20); [42] he persisted in providing supplies that enabled them to cross the desert (vv. 20–21), and finally, he guided the people to the inheritance of the promised land (v. 23). The structure of these details in the review creates a schema that symbolizes the gap between God's consistent conduct and the people's ingratitude:

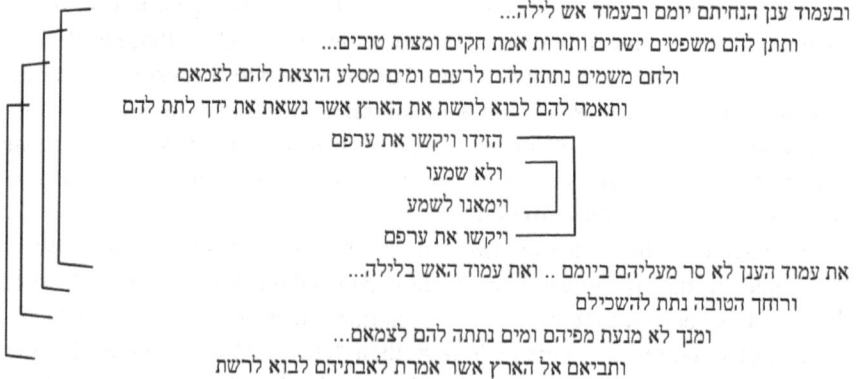

ובעמוד ענן הנחיתם יומם ובעמוד אש לילה...

ותתן להם משפטים ישרים ותורות אמת חקים ומצות טובים...

ולחם משמים נתתה להם לרעבם ומים מסלע הוצאת להם לצמאם

ותאמר להם לבוא לרשת את הארץ אשר נשאת את ידך לתת להם

הזידו ויקשו את ערפם

ולא שמעו

וימאנו לשמע

ויקשו את ערפם

את עמוד הענן לא סר מעליהם ביומם .. ואת עמוד האש בלילה...

ורוחך הטובה נתת להשכילם

ומנך לא מנעת מפיהם ומים נתתה להם לצמאם...

ותביאם אל הארץ אשר אמרת לאבתיהם לבוא לרשת

God's compassion to the people is further stressed in the review of the time of the people's settlement in the land (vv. 24–30), even though it does not indicate concrete events as in the former section. This is manifested by converting two sequential cycles in history to a repeated pattern, reminiscent of the historiographical framework of the Book of Judges.[43] Thus, both cycles relate the people's sins (vv. 26, 28), God's punishments, the people's appeals to God, and God's attention to and rescue of the people (vv. 27, 28). This description indicates, apparently, that the entrance to the land begins a new era of normalization, in which divine compassion was not granted automatically as in the days of the wanderings. Rather it was given only after a stage of retribution.[44] During the time of the settlement, then, the people began

---

42 See the use of this verb in the context of God's commandments: Deut 29:8; Josh 1:7–8; 1Kgs 2:3. The reference to God's "good" spirit in the prayer (Neh 9:20) resonates with the mention of the "good" commandments given to the people prior to their sins: "…right ordinances and true laws, good statutes and commandments" (Neh 9:13).

43 See the definition of the pattern in the introductory part of the book: Judg 2:11–21, as well as in specific references to periods in the people's life: 3:7–11, 12–15, 4:1–3, 6:1–6, 10:6–10.

44 The idea that the entry into the land ended the time of people's immunity from punishment echoes the description in Jeremiah about the change in the relationship between God and the people. After walking through the desert under the auspices and protection of God (Jer 2:6) the people entered the land and defiled it, provoking God to accuse the people: "I brought you into

suffering the consequences of their behavior: their sovereignty was undermined by abandonment (ותתנם, ותעזבם, vv. 27, 28) into the hands of their enemies. Within this new weakened situation, pleas and cries to God played a larger role, as they invoked God to save the people from the punishment imposed on them: "...Then in the time of their suffering they cried out to you and you heard them from heaven, and according to your great mercies you gave them saviors who saved them..." (v. 27); "...yet when they turned and cried to you, you heard from heaven, and many times you rescued them according to your mercies" (v. 28).[45]

The two abovementioned cycles, describing the dynamic of the people's relationship with God at the time of the settlement, are followed in the review by a third cycle of this dynamic. However, while, like its predecessors, it addresses the people's sin (vv. 29–30a) and the punishment by God (v. 30b), the third cycle omits any reference to supplications that preceded the divine redemption: "... Therefore you handed them over to the peoples of the lands. Nevertheless, in your great mercies you did not make an end of them or forsake them, for you are a gracious and merciful God" (v. 30b–31).

This tendency resonates with the events from the time in the wilderness, when God exercised his attribute of compassion and, without receiving a plea from them, refrained from forsaking the people (vv. 17, 19). These references – the "third cycle" and the two allusions from the past – share similar terminology:

> *On the land* (Neh 9:31) Nevertheless, in your **great mercies** (ברחמיך הרבים) you did not make an end of them or **forsake them** (ולא עזבתם), for you are a gracious and **merciful** (רחום) God.

In the Spies segment (v. 17): ...But you are a God ready to forgive, gracious and **merciful** (רחום), slow to anger and abounding in steadfast love, and **you did not forsake them** (ולא עזבתם)	*In the Calf segment* (v. 19): you in your great **mercies** (ברחמיך הרבים) **did not forsake them** (לא עזבתם)...

---

a plentiful land to eat its fruits and its good things. But when you entered you defiled my land, and made my heritage an abomination... Therefore, once more I accuse you, says the LORD, and I accuse your children's children" (Jer 2:7–9).

45 These descriptions differ from the ancestors' "cry" mentioned in the previous section of the review (Neh 9:9), which does not refer to an appeal to God, but rather the people's sensate response to hardship, equivalent to the use of עֳנִי (distress) in the verse.

The allusion to the narratives from the days of the desert – the Calf and spies – provides a sense of comfort by guaranteeing that at the very least there is no intention to annihilate the people. Unlike the proactive responses in the previous cycles – sending saviors (v. 27) and rescuing the people from the enemies (v. 28) – the third cycle consists only in non-action by God (v. 31): הלב סתישע אל (you did not make an end of them), סתבזע אלו (you did not forsake them). Evidently the continuity of the very existence of the people, namely, their escape from annihilation, does not require supplication or petition, either from the people themselves, or on their behalf.[46]

The precedents from the wilderness indicate a pledge of non-eradication (vv. 17, 19) performed in times of "acting presumptuously" and "stiffening their necks" (הזידו... ויקשו את ערפם, v. 16). This pledge was also applied in later times when the people were already in their land (v. 30) and were judged guilty of the same transgressions (הזידו... וערפם הקשו, v. 29). Thus, the "third cycle" of the time in the land mentions no cry to God since the basic existence of the people is not dependent upon their supplication. Nevertheless, as Williamson noted, the notion of the people's pleading later in time appears in the final verses of the prayer, through the people's reference to their present predicament: "Here we are... slaves in the land... and we are in great distress" (vv. 36–37).[47] With this plea the speakers turn from historiographers to petitioners concerned about their present plight. Their cry nevertheless counts on the guarantee that God will not allow them to be destroyed in their present crisis. With such assurance, the speakers find a modicum of consolation in days of great distress during the Babylonian threat within their land.

---

46 See in contrast the preoccupation with the danger of annihilation in the period of the return to Zion (Ezra 9:14–15), when the phenomenon of exile is known, and the relatively recent wellbeing is perceived as fragile and conditional.
47 Williamson 1985(b), 125, 2007, 168.

7 The past in the service of God's name: Ezekiel 20

7.1 Threats of destruction recurring throughout Israel's history

God's speech as recorded by Ezekiel in Ezekiel 20 includes a retrospective review of the story of Israel from their dwelling in Egypt (vv. 5–10) until the days in their land (vv. 28–29). It continues with a reproach against the current "House of Israel" (בית ישראל, v. 30) situated in exile (v. 34), and ends with references to a future return to the land of Israel (vv. 35–38, 41–42).

The review recounts that when the people of Israel lived in Egypt God chose them to be his own nation, then swore an oath and revealed himself to them, appointing himself to be their owner (v. 5). These decisions soon led to a demand for exclusivity, that manifested God's unique self-image (v. 7) and his reputation in the sight of the nations (v. 9). This was also the basis for God's decision to take the people out of Egypt into a land that he had searched out for them (v. 6), regardless of their idolatrous culture (v. 7) and their disobedience to the divine requests (vv. 8–10). However, as the people's disobedience did not change after the departure from Egypt (v. 13a), God menaced them with annihilation (v. 13b), and eventually replaced the threat with an embargo on entering the land (v. 15). Parts of this narrative correspond to our two stories about the days of the desert, the Golden Calf and the spies.

The threat of destruction introduced by God according to the Ezekiel review is described with the root כלה: ואמר לשפך חמתי עליהם במדבר לכלותם) ("...Then I thought I would pour out my wrath upon them in the wilderness, to make an end of them", v. 13b). This resonates with the words of God in the context of the Golden Calf in Exodus 32: ויחר אפי בהם ואכלם) ("...so that my wrath may burn hot against them and I may consume them", Exod 32:10. Cf. v. 12).[1] At the same time, the Ezekiel review resonates with the story of the spies in Numbers 13–14 through the idea that the destruction was replaced by a prohibition against entering the land, as stated: "...I swore to them in the wilderness that I would not bring them into the land that I had given them, a land flowing with milk and honey, the most glorious of all lands" (Ezek 20:15); "...none of the people... shall see the land that I swore to give to their ancestors..." (Num 14:22–23).[2]

---

1 This differs from the reference to the potential destruction in the context of the spy story, mentioned with the word דֶּבֶר (pestilence): אכנו בדֶּבֶר ואורשנו ("I will strike them with pestilence and disinherit them...", Num 14:12).

2 Cf. the suggestion of the medieval Jewish commentator RaDaK (Rabbi David Kimhi), who interprets the verse in Ezekiel 20, "Moreover I swore to them in the wilderness" (v. 15), in regard to God's oath in

https://doi.org/10.1515/9783110609905-007

Apart from the shared terminology for the notion of destruction and the account of the modification of the punishment into the rebuff of their entry into the land, a further element in Ezekiel 20 resonates with the two stories from the Pentateuch: the concern about a possible profanation of God's name in the sight of the nations. We hear in the review: "But I acted for the sake of my name, so that it should not be profaned in the sight of the nations, in whose sight I had brought them out" (Ezek 20:14. Cf. vv. 9, 22). Similarly, in the stories in the Pentateuch Moses' argument against the destruction expresses concern about the image of God as perceived by the nations: "Why should the Egyptians say..." (Exod 32:12. Cf. Deut 9:28); "...then the nations who have heard about you will say..." (Num 14:15–16).

The similarities between the retrospective review in Ezekiel 20 and the two Pentateuchal stories, however, draw attention to major differences between the texts. We will mention three issues that are significant for our investigation.

7.1.1 No references to the Calf and the spy events

The review in Ezekiel 20 does not explicitly mention the incidents of the Golden Calf and the spies. Instead, it links the danger of annihilation in the desert to the people's general violation of God's laws at that time (Ezek 20:13). At the center of the laws stands the commandment of the Sabbath (vv. 12–13), the violation of which arouses God's determination to destroy the people (v. 13, cf. vv. 16, 21, 24). Alongside the Sabbath, another demonstration of the people's law violation is their practice of idolatry (גלולים, v. 16. Cf. 8, 24). While the latter might supposedly allude to a story like the Calf incident,[3] no direct reference is made to the spy event.

7.1.2 Extending the threat of extermination to other periods

The review recounts that the people who were taken out of Egypt were threatened with destruction in the wilderness (v. 13). But it also relates an implicit threat of destruction on two other occasions in the people's life: when they were still in

---

the story of the spies: "[God swore to them] regarding spies when he said: 'nevertheless – as I live...' (Num 14:21)" (my translation).

3 However, as argued above (2.2), the occurrence in Exodus 32 was not a story of law violation in the first place. Only at an advanced stage in the process of the narrative composition was the incident portrayed as negative and possibly acted as an influence on the formulation of the final text of the Ten Commandments.

Egypt (v. 8), and in the period of their descendants in the desert (v. 21). In the context of these occurrences, the verb כלה is mentioned, pointing to a fatal punishment that was supposed to be visited on the people in order to give full rein to God's anger: ואמר לשפך חמתי עליהם לכלות אפי בהם ("…I would pour out my wrath upon them and spend my anger against them…", vv. 8, 21, cf. v. 13).

The idea of God's assuaging his anger by causing harm to his people is known from other references in Ezekiel's prophecies (5:13, 16:42, 21:22, 24:13). Specifically, the combination found in our text, כלה and אף ("cease" and "anger"), occurs elsewhere in Ezekiel, pointing out that God's fury is to be "consumed" or allayed only after striking all the people, applying various methods of destruction: pestilence, famine, sword and exile.[4] Thus, the prophecy to Jerusalem proclaims that its annihilation would be caused by pestilence and famine on one third of the city, death by sword on the second third, and scattering "…to every wind and… unsheathing the sword after them" on the last third. This will enable God to "spend" his anger and to "satisfy" himself (5:12–13. Cf. 6:11–12, 7:15).[5]

With the retrospective review in Ezekiel 20, the two references to God's deadly fury – in the time in Egypt and during the second stage in the wilderness, indeed resonate with the Golden Calf story from the Pentateuch, through the phrase לכלות אפי בהם. Cf. :

Ezek 20:8 (cf. v. 21): ...ואמר לשפך חמתי עליהם **לְכַלּוֹת אַפִּי בָּהֶם** בתוך ארץ מצרים

Exod 32:10 (cf. vv. 11, 12): ...ועתה הניחה לי ויחר־**אַפִּי בָהֶם וַאֲכַלֵּם**

The extension of the notion of near-destruction is also evident from the fact that during the two other periods, in the time in Egypt and in the days of the second generation, God refrained from executing his fury for the sake of his name in the sight of the nations. This same motive restrained him from ultimately executing the destruction in the desert: "…I acted for the sake of my name, that it should not be profaned in the sight of the nations…" (Ezek 20:9. Cf. vv. 14, 22).[6]

---

4 Cf. the description of complete destruction by using pestilence, famine, sword and exile in Jer 21:6–7 (cf. 15:2; Lev 26:25–26).

5 Cf. Psalm 78:38, which by way of negation conveys the idea that destruction is an outcome of a full expression of God's fury. Thus, God's ability to "restrain his anger" and "not stir up all his wrath" (הרבה להשיב אפו ולא יעיר כל חמתו, Ps 78:38) prevents a complete destruction: "… and did not destroy them" (ולא ישחית, ibid.).

6 As Osborne states: "[T]he message was clear – the exodus took place in spite of Israel's sin and because of her election and Yahweh's desire for his glory…" (Osborne 2011, 9).

7.1.3 Moses' absence

According to the accounts of the near destruction in the Pentateuch it was Moses who convinced God to lay aside his deadly determination regarding the nation (Exod 32:11–14; Num 14:13–24). The review in Ezekiel 20 does not mention Moses, or his role at the moments when the people faced the danger of destruction. Rather than Moses' confrontation with God on behalf of the people, the review mentions God's own willingness to keep the people alive. The silence regarding Moses' intervention in these events is especially notable in light of the account in Ezekiel 22 concerning God's search for anyone who would "...repair the wall and stand in the breach before me [God] on behalf of the land, so that I would not destroy it..." (22:30. Cf. 13:5; Jer 15:1). While the prophecy describes the futility of the search for a person that could stand "in the breach" in the current time, it does not mention, even for the sake of comparison, the ultimate archetype of this action, Moses, as he is indeed portrayed elsewhere: "...Moses, his chosen one, stood in the breach before him, to turn away his wrath from destroying them" (Ps 106:23).

What can be learned from the discrepancies between the review in Ezekiel 20 and the traditions known from the Pentateuch? Does the description of the threats of extermination in the past, with no mention of the Calf or the spy events or of Moses' role, indicate the limited literary knowledge of the prophet-writer?[7] Such a possibility was suggested, for example, in the case of the review in Psalm 78 that alludes to a risk of destruction in the past without mentioning the relevant events from the Pentateuch.[8] A similar suggestion could ostensibly be made regarding Ezekiel, based, *inter alia*, on the assumption that his prophecies mainly link with the Priestly literature and the Holiness Code,[9] which do not include our

---

7 The question of the identification of the author of the book of Ezekiel is a subject of ongoing discussion among scholars (see Kasher's detailed summary of the matter in 2004, 20–28). From the range of existing proposals, we should note Zimmerli on the one hand, who speaks of an "Ezekiel school" that was involved in various stages of the composition (Zimmerli 1979, 71–74), and Greenberg on the other hand, who attributes most of the writing to Ezekiel, a historical figure, with minor interventions from later editors (Greenberg 1986, 133–135). In light of the correspondence between the principles in Ezekiel 20 and the world-view expressed elsewhere in Ezekiel, we will not distinguish between the author and the prophet Ezekiel.

8 See above, 4.3.

9 The hypothesis about the connection of Ezekiel to the "Holiness Code" in Leviticus 17–26 first appeared in Graf's work (1866, 81) and has since been relatively dominant in scholarship (e.g., Patton 1996, 73–76; Kasher 2004, 56–62). Zimmerli suggests that the direction of influence was actually from Ezekiel to the Holiness Code (Zimmerli 1979, 48–52). I tend to agree with his argument especially concerning the final verses of Leviticus 26 (Kugler 2006, 96–99).

two stories. Indeed, the review in Ezekiel 20 resonates with the Priestly version of the spy story in the Pentateuch because of the reference to the land that "flows with milk and honey" in conjunction with the root תור (Num 14:7–8; Ezek 20:6).[10] But can we conclude from this that the writer did not know the addition to or the "complete" version of the story of the spies? Does the lack of references to specific events from the past prove that the prophet/author adopted the notion of extermination from other narrative contexts?

We will approach these questions gradually, through an examination of the retrospective review in light of the presumed circumstances of the prophecy, with an attempt to understand the author's views and intentions. By these means, we will trace the extent of the Prophet's connection with the national collective memory and the notion of extermination.

7.2 Explaining the exile

The reference in Ezekiel 20:34 to the people scattered among the nations indicates a time of exile as the setting of the prophecy, as is also implied in the chapter's title: "In the seventh year, in the fifth month, on the tenth day of the month..." (20:1). This date might refer to the capture of Jehoiachin and his entourage by the king of Babylon, in 597 BCE (2Kgs 24:8–16).[11]

Spoken to the exiles, the prophecy in Ezekiel 20 responds to inquiries regarding the current situation, presented in the scene of the elders coming to consult the Lord (לדרש את יהוה, v. 1). The inquirers might wish to understand the justification for the exile, as it challenges premises about God's relationship with the people and his fidelity to them. Ezekiel addresses these inquiries by explaining that the situation of the exile is a consequence of the "abominations of their ancestors" (v. 4), demonstrating it with a detailed review of past sins (vv. 5–29). The exile, according to Ezekiel on behalf of God, was a specific response to the ancestors' past crimes in the desert: "... I swore to them in the wilderness that I

---

10 Further traces of the Priestly version of the spy story can be found in other prophecies of Ezekiel. Thus, the instruction to bear the people's sin for forty days as analogous to forty years – "...and bear the punishment of the house of Judah; forty days I assign you, one day for each year" (Ezek 4:6) – resonates with the words of God to Moses and Aaron in the Priestly version of the spy story: "...forty days, for every day a year, you shall bear your iniquity..." (Num 14:34). Another link occurs between the metaphoric assertion in Ezekiel 36: "...You devour people, and you bereave your nation of children" (Ezek 36:13), and the image in the spies' report in Num 13:32 of the land that "devours its inhabitants".

11 This dating is generally acceptable to scholars. See: Eichrodt 1970, 262; Zimmerli 1979, 15, 406; Greenberg 1983, 363; Rom-Shiloni 2005, 8–9; Brettler 2005, 188, 192.

would scatter them among the nations and disperse them through the countries" (v. 23). Its aim in fact was to replace a much harsher sentence for the people (v. 21), portraying the exile as a relatively tolerable compromise compared to the potential destruction in earlier days.

There is no record in the Pentateuch of the idea of early verdict that determined the future exile.[12] Nor should we presume that this concept was common among the prophet's audience.[13] Instead, it seems to be an ad hoc explanation to deal with religious doubts arising among the believers, from their assertion that "The way of the Lord is not just" (Ezek 33:17, 20. Cf. 18:29). The review in chapter 20 gives a theodicial explanation for a current situation, relating it to past sins, while presenting it as a diminished and belated realization of a much harsher punishment – an irreversible destruction. As stated:

> 21 But the children rebelled against me; they did not follow my statutes, and were not careful to observe my ordinances...Then I thought I would pour out my wrath upon them and spend my anger against them in the wilderness. 22 But I withheld my hand, and acted for the sake of my name, so that it should not be profaned in the sight of the nations, in whose sight I had brought them out. 23 Moreover I swore to them in the wilderness that I would scatter them among the nations and disperse them through the countries (Ezek 20:21–23)

While this explanation links the current situation to the deeds of previous generations, it seems to conflict with a prominent view, expressed elsewhere in Ezekiel, that God grants rewards according to one's deeds. The prophecy in Ezekiel 18 teaches that a person is judged not by the deeds of their predecessors (vv. 5–20), but by their personal actions (vv. 21–32). The paradigm that God postpones the rewards to later generations ("vertical retribution") or bestows them on the collective congregation ("horizontal retribution"),[14] is regarded by Ezekiel as

---

12 As RaDaK states in his commentary to Ezekiel: "This we did not find explained in the Torah" (Radak, to Ezekiel 20:23. My translation). Nachmanides' uncertainty regarding the Midrash that associates the people's cry in Num 14:1 with the later destruction of the Temple: "'They [the people] wept for no good reason [in Num 14:1]; therefore I will establish that day as one for weeping throughout their generations' (Bavli, Taanith 29a) – But I do not know from what allusion in this section [of the Torah] the Rabbis deduced this interpretation" (Nachmanides to Num 14:1. Chavel 1975, 133).

13 The other occurrence of this idea in Psalm 106:26–27 was probably derived from Ezekiel's chapter. See below 8.2, and Kugler 2014, 548–549.

14 See Rom-Shiloni's definitions of "diachronic" and "synchronic" sets of retribution that distinguish between the postponement of retribution to the next generation ("vertical") as opposed to bestowing a direct and immediate reward, and the expansion of the reward to the collective generation ("horizontal") as opposed to allocation to the individual (Rom-Shiloni 2009[a], 286, 289–290).

a misconception (cf. 18:2–3). Instead, according to the prophet, God has always rewarded his subjects according to their own actions (cf. 3:17–21, 14:12–23, 18:2–24, 33:7–20).[15]

This view of the divine retribution as direct and individual, decisively promoted by Ezekiel, seems to be undermined by portraying the exile as a predetermined punishment (Ezek 20:23). The idea that the exile is a postponed punishment from God clashes also with elements in the immediate context in the review, such as the description of God's judgment of the people during the redemption process "face to face" (20:35), applying direct and personal measures against the sinners (vv. 35–38).[16] These measures would determine the fate of the individuals – whether they enter the land or not: "... and I will bring you into the wilderness of the peoples, and there I will enter into judgment with you face to face... I will purge out the rebels among you, and those who transgress against me..." (vv. 35–38).[17] We need to ask then, how this theological view could exist with the idea of the exile as a predetermined punishment. An engagement with

---

15 A rejection of the vertical pattern is also promoted by the prophet Jeremiah, who prophesied around the same period as Ezekiel at the end of the Judean kingdom. However, while this view is common to both prophets, their starting point is different. Jeremiah speaks of an innovation, a new system that will occur in the time of the nation's reconstruction (Jer 31:27–30). This implies, according to Jeremiah, that in the meantime God tends to postpone his reactions to the sinners' descendants.

16 For the essential connection of verses 32–44 with the historical review in the previous section (vv. 4–31) see: Greenberg 1964, 434–434, 1983, 377–381; Hoffman 1975, 481–482; Block 1997, 612–613; Kasher 2004, 385–386; Krüger 2010, 167. The primary consideration is the similarly harsh attitude towards the prophet's addressees in both sections. This reading challenges the view of scholars who separate the two sections with an argument that the supposed incentive of the prophecy – the elders' inquiry (לדרש את יהוה, v. 1) – has been answered and completed at the end of the first section (ואני אדרש לכם אם אדני יהוה נאם אני חי ישראל בית לכם אדרש ואני, v. 31). Moreover they claim that the latter section contains words of hope for redemption, which could only be composed after a severe destruction like the one in 586 BCE (see: Eichrodt 1970, 276–284; Zimmerli 1979, 412–414. Rom-Shiloni [2005, 24, 2009(a), 342] argues for the secondary status of verses 39–44, as well as vv. 27–29). But the supposed restoration predicted in the chapter is not like one in a post-exilic text that contains comfort and consolation. Rather it applies the same harshly critical reproach against the people (vv. 34–38, 39), even in the context of restoration, and further elaborates the idea that God acts in the world for his own sake (vv. 42–44).

17 The idea of measuring the individuals is better reflected in the LXX version of the chapter, which in verse 37 contains the words ἐν ἀριθμῷ, "by number", instead of the MT "within the bond of the covenant" (הברית במסרת). This expresses the idea that the returnees will not enter the land automatically, but according to an assessment and as part of a quota. The phrase in the MT verse (הברית במסרת, v. 37) seems to be a distortion of במספר ("by number") due to a dittography influenced by the word וברותי in the following verse: וברותי ...הברית במסרת instead of ובמספר... וברותי. See: Wevers 1969, 159; Zimmerli 1979, 403; Joyce 2006, 120–121.

this tension in the text will help us to further expose the prophet's views and his approach towards the narratives of the past.

7.3 Maintaining sinfulness

The "abominations of their ancestors" mentioned in the review (v. 4) are not considered as a specific act of one generation, but rather as repeated behavior that led, gradually, to the current crisis. This is illustrated by a refrain that describes the people's rebellious pattern in the desert, followed by God's repeated response to them:

Ezek 20:13	Ezek 20:21
But the house of Israel rebelled against me in the wilderness; they did not observe my statutes but rejected my ordinances, by whose observance everyone shall live; and my sabbaths they greatly profaned. Then I thought I would pour out my wrath upon them in the wilderness, to make an end of them.	But the children rebelled against me; they did not follow my statutes, and were not careful to observe my ordinances, by whose observance everyone shall live; they profaned my sabbaths. Then I thought I would pour out my wrath upon them in the wilderness, to make an end of them.
וימרו בי בית ישראל במדבר בחקותי לא הלכו ואת משפטי מאסו אשר יעשה אתם האדם וחי בהם ואת שבתתי חללו מאד ואמר לשפך חמתי עליהם במדבר לכלותם	וימרו בי הבנים בחקותי לא הלכו ואת משפטי לא שמרו לעשות אותם אשר יעשה אתם האדם וחי בהם ואת שבתתי חללו ואמר לשפך חמתי עליהם לכלות אפי בם במדבר

These references follow information about the transgressions of the people while still in Egypt, pointing out that the people disobeyed God in the first moments of their life as a nation. While they did not violate any given law (which would be given only later in time, vv. 11–12, cf. vv. 13, 16, 21, 24), they ignored various instructions given by God: "But they rebelled against me and would not listen to me; not one of them cast away the... things their eyes feasted on, nor did they forsake the idols of Egypt..." (v. 8a). This put the people at risk of being destroyed by God (rather than by Pharaoh): "...Then I thought I would pour out my wrath upon them and spend my anger against them in the midst of the land of Egypt" (v. 8b), similar to the risk that would recur later in the people's life (vv. 13, 21).[18]

---

18 See the suggestion above (7.1.2) that the description of God's intention to "spend his anger" (v. 8; cf. v. 21) conveys the same intention of utterly destroying the people (cf. v. 13).

The review thus recounts that a threat of destruction has accompanied the people throughout history. Paradoxically, however, this constant threat followed numerous opportunities given to the generations to be measured by the quality of their own deeds, in accord with the principle of direct and individual retribution. While provocation of God could lead to a severe reaction (v. 13), avoidance of such behavior could save the people from punishment (vv. 18–20), as stated to the second generation in the wilderness: "...Do not follow the statutes of your parents, nor observe their ordinances, nor defile yourselves with their idols. I the LORD am your God; follow my statutes, and be careful to observe my ordinances" (vv. 18–19).

Nevertheless, in practice, the escape from extermination did not come from the people's repentance. Rather it derived from the provision of alternative punishments specified by God. This had already occurred in Egypt: the danger of extermination was replaced by expulsion from Egypt directly into the desert (v. 10).[19] While this partial penalty allowed the people to stay alive, more importantly it helped God to protect his name (v. 9). From then on, a series of punishments arose to replace the verdict of extermination: prohibition against entering the land (v. 15), an oath to ensure a future exile (v. 23), and legislation of "statutes that were not good and ordinances by which they could not live" (חקים לא טובים ומשפטים לא יחיו בהם, v. 25). The promulgation of the "not good" statutes and deadly ordinances are linked in Ezekiel's review to the punishment of future exile. Like the punishment of the exile, a penalty of "not good" statutes is not known from the Pentateuchal wilderness narrative. Among the various attempts to explain the meaning of the verdict,[20] the literary context of the verse in Ezekiel 20 is most helpful. It conveys an idiosyncratic idea: that God intentionally provides offensive laws,[21] laws aiming to harm the people by causing them to sin more frequently, thus enabling God to execute the consequent punishment – the exile.

According to the review, the "not good laws" were given to the people after they had forsaken God's first laws, that is, the laws that provide life (vv. 11, 13, 21). The nature of the wrong and dangerous new laws seems to contradict the quality

---

19 The punishment is a detour through the desert (v. 10) instead of directly to the "...land that I had searched out for them, a land flowing with milk and honey, the most glorious of all lands" (v. 6). This move is also linked to the enforced departure from Babylon as depicted later in the review (v. 34).

20 For a review of ancient Jewish and Christian engagements with the verse see Van der Horst 1994, 126–145. For tendencies in modern scholarly work see Kugler 2017, 47–49.

21 Surprise at the theology reflected in this verse is expressed even by modern Biblical scholars. See Bewer's statement (1953, 159) that it is hard to believe that God would function "so entirely contrary to his nature", and Heider's words: "these statutes and ordinances... how can they be 'not good' if they are of God?" (Heider 1988, 721).

of the first revivifying ones. Specified in the next verse, an exemplar of the "not good laws" is the requirement to sacrifice the firstborn to God: "I defiled them through their very gifts, in their offering up all their firstborn..." (v. 26a).[22] This law had in itself the potential for harm, causing deadly consequences, as explained in the law's rationale: "... in order that I might horrify them..." (לְמַעַן אֲשִׁמֵּם, v. 26b: שמם, hiphil: "cause to be deserted/desolated"). The idea of child sacrifice appears in Exod 22:28 without a clarifying exemption.[23] The prophet seems familiar with such an idea, but it is difficult to tell whether he regards it as a divine demand,[24] or as a controversial notion that can be used to achieve rhetorical power.

The idea of "not good laws" given by God reflects a concept appearing elsewhere in Ezekiel, that God tends to accelerate consequences once sins are committed. Such is the case of the righteous person who transgresses and fails further because of God's intervention which results in death: "Again, if the righteous turn from their righteousness and commit iniquity, and I lay a stumbling block before them, they shall die..." (3:20). This stands as clearly similar to the "deceived" prophet, who is being further seduced by God, in order to "...stretch out my hand against him, and... destroy him from the midst of my people Israel" (14:9).[25] This was the fate of the second generation in the desert who chose to abandon the revivifying laws (20:21). As the punishment of future exile (v. 23) could not harm them directly, the "statutes that were not good and ordinances by which they could not live" (v. 25) formed their punishment. Moreover, the wrong customs and behavior kept the people in a sinful state that enabled the execution of the other punishment, the exile, in the future. Thus, it ensured the exile in the future was deserved by the next generations as much as their parents deserved it.

This peculiar way of explaining the roots of the current agony is an extreme expression of the notion that God is powerfully dominant in the world. Not only does history reflect God's response to his subjects' actions, but God also directs the choices of his people in a way that allows him to carry out his plans for them. To achieve this God may mislead the people and cause them to fail. The review draws a straight line between the exile in the prophet's day and the past wrongdoing of the ancestors, while somewhat awkwardly still applying the concept of direct and individual retribution.

---

22 On the connection between the two statements (vv. 25–26) see also: Greenberg 1964, 436, 1983, 369; Heider 1988, 721–724; Davis 1989, 114; Block 1997, 640.

23 In contrast to the demand elsewhere to redeem the firstborn of human beings: Exod 13:13, 15, 34:20; Num 18:15–18.

24 As suggested by Fishbane (1985, 185).

25 Cf. elsewhere in the Hebrew Bible, e.g., the references to the "hardening" of Pharaoh's heart (Exod 7:3–5, 9:16, 10:1–2, 14:4, 18), and the misleading of sinful Israel (Isa 6:10, 63:17).

7.4 Generic rather than specific sins

Now we can turn back to our question about the absence of the two Pentateuchal narratives, the Golden Calf and the spies, from Ezekiel's retrospective review. Unlike the review in Psalm 78, to the structure and message of which the two narratives were suited,[26] the agenda of Ezekiel 20 would gain little from these two narratives of the events in the desert. The review in Ezekiel 20 points to the people's habitual tendency of law violation. This had occurred from the days of the patriarchs (Ezek 20:4) until the current time (v. 30). Thus, rather than pointing to concrete, single events, the sinful behavior is better demonstrated by pointing to generic principles and constant violations: performing idolatry (גלולים) and profaning the Sabbath.

The גלולים in the review (vv. 7–8, 16, 18, 24, 31, 39) are a manifestation of the "abominations of their ancestors" (v. 4) and match the central place of the notion of גלולים throughout Ezekiel's prophecies.[27] The cult of the גלולים is called by Ezekiel תועבה ("abomination", Ezek 8:9–10, 18:12, 22:1–4) and טמאה ("uncleanness", Ezek 22:3–4, 36:18, 37:23), and is considered a stumbling block in relations with God (14:3–5). In his vision of the future, Ezekiel predicts that Israel will not look up to the גלולים anymore (6:6; cf. 18:6, 15, 37:21), but rather will be slain in front of them (6:4–5), and the idols themselves will be destroyed as a proof of their transience (v. 6). The review in chapter 20 stresses the continuity of the sin. Instead of mentioning a single event of a ritual deviation from the past, such as the Golden Calf, it describes an ongoing custom continued into the current period (20:31, 39), deriving from the days in the desert (vv. 16, 18, 24, 31), and even from the time in Egypt: איש שקוצי עיניו השליכו ובגלולי מצרים אל תטמאו... את שקוצי עיניהם לא (השליכו ואת גלולי מצרים לא עזבו) ("...Cast away the detestable things your eyes feast on, every one of you, and do not defile yourselves with the idols of Egypt...not one of them cast away the detestable things their eyes feasted on, nor did they forsake the idols of Egypt", vv. 7–8).

In the Pentateuch, indeed, there is no evidence of the idea of idolatry committed in Egypt. Elsewhere in the Hebrew Bible there appears only the single accusation in Joshua 24 about "...the gods that your ancestors served beyond the

---

26 See above, 4.3.

27 39 of the 48 occurrences of the notion גלולים in the Hebrew Bible are found in the Book of Ezekiel (the rest appear in the Deuteronomic and Deuteronomistic literature: Deut 29:16; 1Kgs 15:12, 21:26; 2Kgs 17:12, 21:11, 21, 23:24; Jer 50:2. Cf. Lev 26:30). The frequency of the word in the prophecies of Ezekiel and the fact that in Jeremiah and Isaiah the forbidden ritual is mentioned using other terms (except for Jer 50:2), led to the assumption that the term גלולים was coined by and used mainly in the social and religious circles of Ezekiel (see Preuss 1978, 2; Zimmerli 1979, 187).

River and in Egypt..." (Josh 24:14). Whether Ezekiel was familiar with the specific allegation in Joshua 24,[28] or acquainted with an alternative tradition about Israel's past relationship with Egypt,[29] the reference to the Egyptian idols works well in the context of Ezekiel 20. Reviewing the people's conduct back to the time of their formation in Egypt, augments the message about the people's sinful nature and thus explains their later fate.

Sabbath observance is the other principle pointed out in the review as regularly violated in the people's past (Ezek 20:12–13, 16, 20, 21, 24). The centrality of the Sabbath in the people's relationship with God matches the attitude toward the Sabbath elsewhere in Ezekiel. The Sabbath is regarded as among God's "holy things" (קֳדָשַׁי, 22:8) and its violation is considered a "violence to God's teachings" (v. 26), similar to the desecration of the sanctuary (23:38). The Sabbath is also awarded a place of honor in the vision of the people's future, in laying out the role of the priests (44:24), and in the "updated" information about the size of the burnt offering on the Sabbath (46:4. Cf. Num 28:9–10). While it is plausible that Ezekiel's focus on the Sabbath stems from the centrality of the commandment in the priestly circles,[30] it might also reflect the growing status of the custom in Ezekiel's time. The commandment did not demand particular practices, and could be easily observed, unlike the laws of worship.[31] Thus, the review in Ezekiel 20 perceives the breaking of the Sabbath as a direct violation of the relationship with God, similar to the sin of idolatry.[32]

---

28 Thus Eichrodt 1970, 266.

29 I would argue (Kugler, forthcoming) for a remnant of a tradition of "Egypt without slavery" preserved in several prophecies in Ezekiel and elsewhere in the Hebrew Bible, revealing another incentive to take the people out of Egypt.

30 Cf. the correlation between Ezekiel's definition of the Sabbath as a sign between God and the people (Ezek 20:12) and the language of the Sabbath law in the Priestly tradition (Exod 31:12–17). This in contrast to the terminology of the occurrences of the law in the Decalogue (Exod 20:8–11; Deut 5:12–15), and in the book of the Covenant (Exod 23:12. Cf. 34:21).

31 Cf. Greenberg's argument, according to which the law of the Sabbath became more significant during the exile, when it was considered equivalent in importance to all other commandments. Thus, a violation of the Sabbath was perceived by the prophets of the time as the ultimate sin and a fundamental explanation for the destruction (Greenberg 1971, 29–30, 35–36, 1983, 366–367). Similarly, Andreasen points to the increasing importance of "sacred time" after the destruction of the "sacred place" (Andreasen 1972, 235). In contrast, Hoffman argues that a careful observance of the prohibition against work on the Sabbath was applied more strictly after the return to Zion (Hoffman 2001, 403).

32 See Ganzel's suggestion (2005, 168) of a possible causal link between the desecration of the Sabbath and the honoring of the idols, as reflected by the conjunction כי in Ezek 20:16: "...and profaned my sabbaths; **for** (כי) their heart went after their idols".

The review portrays the sinful nature of the people that consistently evoked the danger of annihilation. To convey such a message, the review avoids mentioning specific incidents from the people's biography and rather points to generic and consistent patterns in their behavior. While the writer might have known the stories we know today,[33] he certainly did not see himself as responsible for collecting or reflecting on them, and felt no obligation to introduce them as examples in his references. He was driven by the need to explain the current situation. For this purpose he engaged with the collective memory in a non-historical way, using rhetorical devices and promoting theological ideas. Thus he explained the situation of his days, the exile, as a verdict that was determined in the distant past of the people, but at the same time as a response to the people's ongoing wrong behavior.

Nevertheless, the use of the past in the prophecy aimed not only to justify the situation in the recipients' present days, but also to assure their future. This will be discussed below.

7.5 Moses' absence: A promise of peremptory redemption

The absence of Moses from Ezekiel's review, as well as from the rest of Ezekiel's prophecies, is considered by scholars as an outcome of the prophet's attempt to portray himself as a "second Moses".[34] Thus, like Moses, Ezekiel belongs to a family of priests (Ezek 1:3), like him he announces a forthcoming exodus (20:33–34), and receives new instructions for the people (chs. 40–48) while standing on a high mountain (40:2).

However, the historical review in chapter 20 is less oriented to the prophet's image and more to the portrayal of God. The review shows that the plan to destroy the people was cancelled out of a consideration relating to God, namely, his reputation among the nations. This was the core of God's motivation and concerns: "But I withheld my hand, and acted for the sake of my name, so that it should not be profaned in the sight of the nations, in whose sight I had brought them out" (Ezek 20:22. Cf. vv. 9, 14).[35] This motivation replaced any other possible considerations, such as the commitment to the fathers (cf. Exod 32:13), God's attributes (cf. Num 14:17–20), or God's compassion toward the people (cf. Ps 78:38). None of these factors plays a role, according to Ezekiel, in God's influence in history. The sole motivation is any potential damage to God's dignity, for the protection

---

33 Brin (1975, 127, 147) argues that the author probably knew the "legends of the rebellion in the Torah" but was not obliged to consider them. See a similar deduction in Burrows 1925, 14–15; Greenberg 1983, 383, 1993, 36–37; Hoffman 1983, 58; Fishbane 1985, 365.
34 Cf. Patton 1996, 85–89; Levitt-Kohn 2004, 166–167.
35 For the centrality of this concept in Ezekiel's prophecy see recently Kratz 2015, 64.

of which, apparently, no advocacy is required. Within this theological framework there is no room for any human intervention for the sake of the people.

The narrative of God as the ultimate conductor of the people's destiny explains the silence regarding Moses' role in the events of the past. According to Ezekiel, the people's footsteps in history were determined as a result of the consideration of God's reputation, and only for this reason were they saved, again and again, from the deserved punishment of extermination: "...Then I thought I would pour out my wrath upon them and spend my anger against them in the midst of the land of Egypt. But I acted for the sake of my name, that it should not be profaned in the sight of the nations among whom they lived...in bringing them out of the land of Egypt" (20:8–9). This theocentric principle of concern for the divine reputation, to act "for the sake of my name", has been part of the people's biography from their inception and throughout the ages (vv. 13–14, 21–22).

In fact, the risk of the desecration of God's name also appears to be the incentive for the people's future redemption from the current exile, as stated in the prophecy in the chapter: "...when I deal with you for my name's sake, not according to your evil ways, or corrupt deeds, O house of Israel, says the Lord GOD" (20:44. Cf. v. 39). The vision of the people's future exodus is to be understood within the abiding framework of God's self-concern. As further explained elsewhere in Ezekiel's prophecies, though the exile was an execution of justice and retribution, the gentiles have wrongly perceived it as evidence of God's incapacity to protect his people. This interpretation caused a desecration of God's image and damage to his sanctity: "But when they came to the nations, wherever they came, they profaned my holy name, in that it was said of them, 'These are the people of the LORD, and yet they had to go out of his land'" (Ezek 36:20). This distorted impression of God's people, leading to an erroneous portrayal of God, would encourage God to initiate a removal of the people from the exile in the future, even before the date of repayment has come. As stated:

> 23 I will sanctify my great name, which has been profaned among the nations, and which you have profaned among them; and the nations shall know that I am the LORD, says the Lord GOD, when through you I display my holiness before their eyes. 24 I will take you from the nations, and gather you from all the countries, and bring you into your own land (Ezek 36:23–24)

Indeed, a manifestation of God's act of redemption due to his concern about his image appears in the review in Ezekiel 20 in the verdict against the rebels among the people (המרדים והפשעים, v. 38). With the rest of the community those people are to be taken from "...the land where they reside as aliens..." (Ezek 20:38, cf. v. 34), even though they are not designated to enter the land of Israel (v. 38), and are destined to perish in the demilitarized zone of the "wilderness of the peoples"

(v. 35). Thus, rather than gathering God's people together in their land, it is more important to remove them from exile to protect God's dignity in the sight of others. Moreover, the restoration of the rest of the congregation, according to the prophecy, will not happen because of the people's needs or aspirations, but as a result of the ultimate motivation: to maintain the reputation of God. Thus, the future exodus will not be the result of the people's cry or request (cf. Exod 2:23–25), and will even be performed by force, by means of God's "mighty hand and outstretched arm", accompanied by God's wrath (Ezek 20:33–34).[36]

Ezekiel's retrospective review is therefore understood in the terms of the agenda presented in the prophecy, which places the consideration of the name of God as the basis of the relationship with the people. The writer portrays the verdict against the people as determined solely by God. Accordingly, an external intervention to mediate between God and the people could not affect God's exclusive authority.[37] If indeed the author had in front of him the traditions we know today from the Pentateuch, he would erase the traces of Moses' role in them to present God as both the initiator and the executor of the events.

7.6 Purpose and addressees: Ezekiel 20 in comparison to Nehemiah 9

The prophet Ezekiel regards himself as an inseparable part of the exilic community in Babylon (33:21, 40:1).[38] In his prophecies he approaches the exiles (1:1–3, 3:11, 11:24–25), and promises them a return to the land as the legal heirs of the

---

36 The idea that the people will experience forced redemption may also be reflected in Ezekiel's description of the raising of the bones from the graves in chapter 37, an illustration of the passivity of the people in the process of redemption: "...I am going to open your graves, and bring you up from your graves, O my people; and I will bring you back to the land of Israel... I will put my spirit within you, and you shall live, and I will place you on your own soil; then you shall know that I, the LORD, have spoken and will act..." (37:12–14). As Schwartz points out, the vision of reviving the bones does not indicate God's mercy to the people, but serves as a response to the people's loss of hope, mentioned in the previous verse (37:11). The text conveys that the people's redemption would occur even after the people's death, deriving from God's owns needs and concerns (Schwartz 2000[b], 59, 2008, 312).

37 This message stands in striking contrast to the concept of the major and ongoing effect the nations have on God's actions and decisions. Like many other theological ideas, the nature of God's sovereign performance in history reflects dialectical complexity.

38 In contrast to Torrey's argument (1930, 34–44) that Ezekiel dwelled in Judah, and to Brownlee's theory (1986, xxxii–xxiii) about his residence at Gilgal (גלגל) rather than in the גולה (exile, Ezek 1:1, 3:11, 15, 11:24–25, 12:3–4, 7, 25:3).

nation (11:14–21, 36:24–28, 37:1–14). This fate will stand in contrast to the fate of the remnants in Zion: for them, according to Ezekiel, a complete destruction is expected (9:4–11, 11:1–13, 33:23–29).[39]

This idea differs from the approach reflected in the text we saw in Nehemiah 9, which we regarded as created in Judea in the days before the final exile to Babylon, perhaps following the exile of Jehoiachin and his entourage.[40] Thus, Ezekiel 20 and Nehemiah 9 can be viewed as texts in a similar genre – retrospective review – with specific engagement with the days of the wandering in the desert, as well as a shared date of their composition. Despite the closeness of the texts, however, their disparity is noticeable, indicated by the structure of the historical review, the perception of the relationship between God and the people, the approach to current political issues, and the interpretation of the narrative of the people's danger of annihilation.

As we saw, the author of the prayer in Nehemiah 9 mentions the events of the Golden Calf and the spies from the time in the desert, but keeps the notion of destruction relatively vague (Neh 9:17, 18). In contrast to that text, the author of Ezekiel 20 refrains from explicit details of events, while emphasizing the risk of annihilation that accompanied the people at that period (Ezek 20:8–9, 13–14, 21–22). In addition, while the speaker of Nehemiah 9 points to God's compassion as an explanation for God's readiness to uphold the people, Ezekiel explains the survival of the people throughout history as an outcome of God's own concerns,

---

39 A clear idea of the two parts of the equation according to Ezekiel, namely the redemption of the exiles and the loss of the remnants, is found in the prophecy in chapter 11. While the two parts of the chapter (vv. 1–13; vv. 14–21) might reflect two different stages of writing (see: Zimmerli 1979, 256, 264), the perception about the preference for the exilic community is still obvious (cf. Rom-Shiloni 2005, 8–12, 31–35, 42; Tadmor 2006, 318; Kratz 2015, 62). This approach that favors the community of the exiles over the remaining community is similar to the national-religious strategy that Ezra and Nehemiah would adopt at a later stage. In a sense, Ezekiel is a "pioneer" of this strategy (see Rom-Shiloni 2005, 31). But the view about the revival of the exiles is not exclusive to Ezekiel. Jeremiah delivers a positive message to the group of exiles with Jehoiachin in Babylon (Jer 29:1–14), even though he prophesies from among the "remnant" of Jerusalem. It should be noted, however, that the records of this preference are not monolithic, in contrast to the relatively coherent political view in Ezekiel. Jeremiah's prophecies contain a conflicted pro-Judaic view that sees a future in the population remaining in Judah and a deliberate loss to Jehoiachin (22:24–30). This ideological viewpoint might derive from the prophet/author who remained with the remnant of Jerusalem. A later textual intervention brought in the position that the first exiles to Babylon were the true remnant and that there would be no revival for the survivors in the land, Zedekiah's people (Jer 21:1–7, 29:16–20, 34:8–22). These passages might have been created by the descendants of the Jehoiachin exiles who amended existing sources according to their needs and ideology (see Rofe 1997, 182–183; Rom-Shiloni 2009[b], 17–24).
40 See above, 6.2.4.

deriving first and foremost from considerations about his name and image in the sight of the nations. This disparity is noticeable in the comparison below:

Ezekiel 20	Nehemiah 9
The Context: repeated rebellion through idolatry and violation of the Sabbath	**The Context: Two concrete crimes**
But they rebelled against me and would not listen to me; not one of them cast away the detestable things their eyes feasted on, or did they forsake the idols of Egypt... (Ezek 20:8)	...they stiffened their necks and determined to return to their slavery in Egypt... (Neh 9:17)
But the house of Israel rebelled against me in the wilderness; they did not observe my statutes but rejected my ordinances, by whose observance everyone shall live; and my sabbaths they greatly profaned... (v. 13)	...when they had cast an image of a calf for themselves and said, 'This is your God who brought you up out of Egypt... (v. 18)
But the children rebelled against me; they did not follow my statutes, and were not careful to observe my ordinances, by whose observance everyone shall live; they profaned my sabbaths... (v. 21)	
God does not destroy: for the sake of his name	**God does not forsake: forgiveness and mercy**
...Then I thought I would pour out my wrath upon them and spend my anger against them in the midst of the land of Egypt. But I acted for the sake of my name, that it should not be profaned in the sight of the nations... (Ezek 20:8–9)	...But you are a God ready to forgive, gracious and merciful, slow to anger and abounding in steadfast love, and you did not forsake them (Neh 9:17)
...Then I thought I would pour out my wrath upon them in the wilderness, to make an end of them. But I acted for the sake of my name, so that it should not be profaned in the sight of the nations... (vv. 13–14)	you in your great mercies did not forsake them in the wilderness... (v. 19)
...Then I thought I would pour out my wrath upon them and spend my anger against them in the wilderness. But I withheld my hand, and acted for the sake of my name... (vv. 21–22)	

My suggestion is that the variations between the reviews in Nehemiah 9 and Ezekiel 20 derive from the texts' different speakers and addressees, and from the diverse settings of the work of composition, i.e., the two different and even rival communities of Judah. The review embedded in Nehemiah 9 was created on the eve of the Babylonian exile, by a group of people that would be later considered "the poorest people of the land" (דלת עם הארץ, 2Kgs 24:14). The review in Ezekiel 20 was created among the group of the first exiles to Babylon. Each of these two groups viewed themselves as the chosen heirs of the national entity. Those who remained in Judah spoke about being the rightful heirs of the nation and considered the new exiles as losing possession on the land (Ezek 11:15, 34:24).[41] The exiles in Babylon, on the other hand, who at first feared the loss and danger for them in exile (Jer 22:24–30), received permission to settle there (Jer 29:4–7) until their return to the land, replacing the current remnants in Judah (10–20).

The texts that reached our hands reflect the two communities' fears and hopes, and attest the central place they allocated to the past as part of the attempt to understand their current situation and predict their future. The group that remained in Judah, whose sons were afraid of recurring calamities, such as the one that led to the expulsion of Jehoiachin and his group, employed their literary knowledge to teach that the remnant on the land would continue to exist. This is reflected in the review in Nehemiah 9. The review of Ezekiel 20, on the other hand, addressed to the group of the first exiles in Babylon, used the knowledge of the past to prove that the people were destined to survive and return to the land, not because of their deeds, but for the protection of God's name and reputation.

The sequence in Nehemiah 9 ascribes the past events to God's mercy and compassion towards the people, as a projection of the hope for the speakers' present days. Ezekiel, in contrast, offers events of the past to validate a definite redemption. He attributes the very survival of the people in the past to the needs of God, and learns from it about the people's assured future. For this reason, as noted, Moses' role is absent from the review of the past. Interestingly, Nehemiah 9 does not mention Moses either. But that derives from a different motive – to accentuate God's compassionate attitude to the people. As the protection of the people was made possible due to God's ongoing mercies, there was no need of an external advocate like Moses, to awaken the grace of God.[42]

The comparison of the two reviews may indicate the political and ideological polarization that characterized the people in the days leading up to the Babylonian exile, during which each group was concerned about its future. The speakers

---

41 Tadmor (2006, 315) suggests that this view may rely on previous historical experience that taught that there was no return from exile, and moreover, that as a divine punishment it was destined to be an unchangeable fate.

42 In contrast to the view reflected in Psalm 106 of the crucial impact individuals had on God's decisions, and thus the individuals' potential influence on the nation's fate. See below, 8.3.

in Nehemiah 9 created a precedent for their aspirations by reducing the notion of near destruction in the past. Ezekiel, on the other hand, avoided referring to specific events from the people's biography, and instead presented an ongoing and repetitive pattern to indicate God's exclusive control of his plans. Neither Ezekiel nor Nehemiah committed themselves to the details of the past stories; rather they employed the narratives as platforms for their ideas. It was the fear of the future and the need to plant hope that evoked their contrasting allusions to the past.

8 Past precedents pave the way for current pleas: Psalm 106

8.1 Recalling the past threat of destruction: The psalmist's literary sources

Psalm 106 is the only retrospective review in the Hebrew Bible that mentions a threat of destruction in the desert alongside the two core events of the period, the Golden Calf and the spy incidents. Nonetheless, of the two events, only the Calf incident is connected to the threat of destruction against the people: "They made a calf at Horeb and worshiped a cast image... Therefore, he said he would destroy them..." (Ps 106:19–23).

In recounting the incident of the Calf, the psalm points to חרב ("Horeb", v. 19) as the place where it occurred, and names the idol that has been made מסכה ("cast image", ibid.). While מסכה is mentioned both in the account by the omniscient narrator in Exodus (32:4, 8), and in the retrospective view in Deuteronomy (Deut 9:12, 16), the place name, חרב, appears only in the Deuteronomic account (Deut 9:8).[1] The Deuteronomic account also resonates in the reference to the Calf in the psalm with the use of the roots שמד and שחת for the notion of destruction (Ps 106:23). As opposed to the root כלה in the story in Exodus (ויחר אפי בהם ואכלם, Exod 32:10), the version of the event in Deuteronomy 9 uses both שמד and שחת: להשמיד אתכם ("to destroy you", Deut 9:8. Cf. vv. 14, 19, 20), and השחיתך ("to destroy you", 9:26, 10:10).[2]

The closeness to the Deuteronomic source is further indicated by the use of the adjective בחיר, "chosen one", in the psalm (Ps 106:23): this corresponds with the prominent distribution of the root בחר in Deuteronomy in regard to God's preferences.[3] While the account in Deuteronomy 9 does not make use of the term

---

1 As a rule, the book of Deuteronomy locates the occurrence of the making of the covenant at Horeb (Deut 1:6, 4:10, 15, 5:2, 18:16, 28:69). The name Sinai is not mentioned in the book apart from one occurrence in the poetry section (33:2) which is considered to be from earlier material. This stands in contrast to the predominance of the name Sinai in the context of the story in Exodus: Exod 19:23, 24:16, 31:18, 34:2, 4. Cf. 33:6, חרב.

2 Though the verb שחת echoes the accusation that the people had "acted corruptly", שְׁחֵת, in both accounts (Exod 32:7; Deut 9:12).

3 The preference of God for the nations' fathers and their offspring (Deut 4:27, 10:15), his preference of Israel over the nations (7:6, 7, 14:2), the chosen status of the king (17:15), of the Levites (18:5, 21:25) and most importantly, of the place "...to put his name there..." (12:5. Cf. in chapters: 12, 14, 15, 16, 16, 17, 18, 23, 26, 31). An exception is the statement in Deuteronomy 30, which, for this one and only time, grants the people the opportunity to choose: "I call heaven and earth to

https://doi.org/10.1515/9783110609905-008

בחיר in relation to Moses, it highlights strongly the prophet's uniqueness and exclusiveness in the sight of God.[4]

These details lead to the supposition that the author of the psalm was familiar with the story of the Golden Calf through a literary source such as the one known from Deuteronomy 9–10. While the story of Exodus 32 might have been already in existence,[5] it seems to have not been known to the psalmist, or at least, not to have been used by him. Even though the psalm attests familiarity with a large collection of narratives and literary sources,[6] the Deuteronomic source is noticeably central to the psalm.[7] This familiarity with the Deuteronomic account is also attested in the recounting of the story of the spies.

Though the incident of the spies is mentioned in the psalm, there is no implication that it motivated the threat of the people's extermination. Instead it is considered the cause for the people's death in the desert and for a future dispersal of their offspring among the nations:

24 Then they despised the pleasant land, having no faith in his promise.
25 They grumbled in their tents, and did not obey the voice of the Lord.
26 Therefore he raised his hand and swore to them that he would make them fall in the wilderness,
27 and would disperse their descendants among the nations, scattering them over the lands (Ps 106:24–27)

---

witness against you today that I have set before you life and death, blessings and curses. **Choose** life so that you and your descendants may live" (Deut 30:19).

4 Also indicated by the "forty days and forty nights" motif that stresses the prophet's ability to remain in close proximity to God and communicate with him (Deut 9:9, 11, 18, 25, 10:10). See above, 5.3.2.

5 See above, 5.3.4.

6 The psalm also mentions the accounts about the Red Sea (Ps 106:8–12; cf. Exod 14:22–15:21); the craving in the desert (Ps 106:14; cf. Num 11:4, 34); the test put to God (Ps 106:13–15. Cf. Exod 17:2, 7; Num 14:22; Deut 6:16); the jealousy of Dathan and Abiram (Ps 106:16–18; Deut 11:6 [on the latter reference see below, footnote 7]); the incident with Baal Peor (Ps 106:28–30; Num 25:1–13); and the affair at the waters of Meribah (Ps 106:31–32. Cf. Num 20:1–13). These references reflect familiarity with more than one literary source. For example, the mention of the rescue at the Red Sea resonates with many details in the broader story in Exodus: the rescue "from the hand of the foe" (Ps 106:10; Exod 14:30); the covering of the adversaries by water (Ps 106:11; Exod 14:28, 15:5, 10); the trust in God as a result of the event (Ps 106:12; Exod 14:31); and the praising of the Lord (Ps 106:12; Exod 15:1, 21). For the discussion of the diverse literary sources in the psalm see: Gray 1903, 187–188; Holzinger 1903, 67; Kraus 1989, 317; Boda 1999, 66; Hossfeld and Zenger 2011, 87–91.

7 Further evidence for the prominence of the Deuteronomic source is the correspondence of the reference to Dathan and Abiram in the psalm (v. 17) with the remark in Deut 11:6, which mentions the two men's tragic punishment with no reference to Korah (cf. Numbers 16).

Not only does the allusion to the spy incident lack any notion of near destruction, but there is also no mention of the spies' mission and even the spies themselves. Instead, we hear about the people's rejection of the land – "Then they despised the pleasant land..." (v. 24) – as a demonstration of their lack of faith in God's word: "... having no faith in his promise" (לא האמינו לדברו, ibid.). This is then followed by a description of disobedience and grumbling by the people: "They grumbled (וירגנו) in their tents, and did not obey the voice of the Lord" (v. 25).

A closely similar description of "grumbling in the tent" in regard to the land appears in the retrospective account of the spy story in Deuteronomy 1. There the misconduct of the people is also depicted as a rebellion against God, and attributed to the whole congregation rather than to the spies (Deut 1:26–27). The indictment in Deuteronomy 1 accuses the people of lack of faith "in this matter" (בדבר הזה, v. 32), that is, trust in God's willingness (or ability) to protect the people and fight for them (1:30).[8] Similarly, the psalm uses the word דבר in referring to the people's lack of faith:

> Deut 1:32: But in spite of this, you have no trust in the LORD your God
> **ובדבר הזה אינכם מאמינם ביהוה אלהיכם**
> Ps 106:24: ...having no faith in his promise
> **לא האמינו לדברו**

These details indicate a possible literary reliance of the psalm on the Deuteronomic account, that provides the narrative of the people's lack of faith during the process of possessing the land. The psalm continues the approach found in Deuteronomy 1 of disregarding the part of the spies-representatives.[9] Moreover, it continues the silence of the Deuteronomic account about the stories of near destruction and Moses' intervention on behalf of the people (cf. Num 14:11–25). The absence of these matters from Psalm 106, even though they are alluded to in another context in the psalm (Ps 106:23), raises the possibility that the psalmist was not familiar with the version of the spy story known from Numbers 13–14.[10] As in the case of the calf, the account of the spies in Numbers 13–14 might have already been in existence, at least in part, and in use by the Deuteronomic

---

8 In contrast to the the general accusation against the people in Num 14:11, 22–23, of despising God and disbelieving in him.

9 See the arguments above (5.2.4) about "the contribution of the Deuteronomic rewriter" who *inter alia* reduces the role of the spies in the event.

10 A similar deduction was suggested about the versions of the story in Deuteronomy 9 and Joshua 14, where silence about the near destruction seems to derive from the use of Deuteronomy 1 as their literary source. See above, 5.3.3 and 5.4.2.

author.[11] Nevertheless, the psalmist seems to have worked exclusively with the Deuteronomic version of the tradition.

Nevertheless, the reference to the story of the spies in the psalm is not only a summary of the narrative in Deuteronomy 1. The story is also used to connect the wrongdoing from the past to later stages in the Israelites' life-story.

8.2 The spy episode: Explanation and justification for the exile

While the notion of near destruction is missing from the spy narrative recounted in the psalm, the incident is mentioned in relation to an exile that will occur in the future: "and would disperse their descendants among the nations, scattering them over the lands" (v. 27). This comment goes beyond the retrospective review of the past. It indicates a theodicial effort to explain events both past and future in the people's life.

The argument that sins of the past led to a future national exile does not match the narrative known from Deuteronomy 1. On the contrary, the idea that the descendants will be harmed because of the fathers' sins in the desert stands in contrast to the conclusion of the Deuteronomic story, which points to the children's positive fate: "... they shall enter there; to them I will give it, and they shall take possession of it" (Deut 1:39). Likewise, the narrative in the psalm contradicts the promise found in the Priestly version of the story recounted by the omniscient narrator (Numbers 13–14), according to which the descendants will be saved and allowed to enter the land (Num 14:31).[12] The narrative in the psalm also contradicts the Non-Priestly account of the spy story, according to which the punishment will be enacted only on the current sinful generation, "... who have seen my glory and the signs that I did in Egypt and in the wilderness..." (Num 14:23).

The idea that the exile was already determined in the days in the desert appears elsewhere in the Hebrew Bible only in the retrospective review of Ezekiel 20. The Ezekiel review, as we saw, draws a direct line from the people's past wrongdoing to the behavior of the generation in the time of the prophet (Ezek

---

11 See above, 5.2.3.

12 See Nachmanides' effort to relate the alleged ancient roots of the exile according to the psalm to God's proclamation regarding the children in Num 14:31 ("But your little ones, who you said would become booty..."). To this end he transforms the meaning of the sentence, claiming that God meant to say: "For your little ones – it will be as you said, they will be a prey when the time of their visitation comes, for I shall visit the inquiry of the fathers upon the children" (Nachmanides to Num 14:1. Chavel 1975, 133).

20:7–8, 16, 18, 24, 30–31, 39), and thus relates the fate of the later generation to the conduct in the past.[13] Indeed, the two references about the exile in Ezekiel 20 and Psalm 106 are noticeably similar:[14]

גם אני **נשאתי את ידי** להם במדבר **להפיץ** אתם בגוים ולזרות אותם בארצות: Ezek 20:23

I lifted my hand upon them in the wilderness to scatter them among the nations and disperse them through the countries

וישא ידו להם להפיל אותם **במדבר**: ולהפיל (**ולהפיץ**) זרעם בגוים ולזרותם בארצות: Ps 106:26–27

He lifted his hand upon them to make them fall in the wilderness. And to scatter their descendants among the nations and disperse them through the countries

Even though the sentence in the psalm is expressed in the third person and the one in Ezekiel is in the first person, the similarity between the verses is clear enough to indicate a literary connection between them. What was the direction of influence?

Based on resemblance to numerous elements in Ezekiel's prophecies, the verse in Ezekiel 20 seems original in its context. Thus, the reference to God's oath – "lifted my hand" (נשאתי ידי) – recurs several times in the immediate context in Ezekiel 20 (vv. 5, 6, 15), and the phrase "scattering them among the nations and dispersing them throughout the lands" (להפיץ בגוים ולזרות בארצות), resonates with phrases mentioned elsewhere in Ezekiel's prophecies (Ezek 12:15, 22:15, 29:12, 30:23,26, 36:19). The match of Ezek 20:23 to its literary context is indicated also by the relevance of the phrase to the broader view reflected in the prophecy about the fate of the people as predetermined and dependent. Specifically, just as the "positive" event, the redemption, is to be executed because God has willed it (with God's "...mighty hand and an outstretched arm", Ezek 20:34), the negative event, the exile, was planned years ahead and has been executed by God. This idea, as we saw, derives from Ezekiel's unique approach, which does not seem to echo any other known accounts of the past. Ezekiel expresses either his own outlook, inspired by his lifetime, or an interpretation of ideas such as the ones

---

13 Above, 7.2. And see there the argument about Ezekiel's endeavor to reconcile the idea of the influence of the past on the present generation with his view about God's individual and direct ways of retribution.

14 My translation. The NRSV does not sufficiently preserve the similarities between the verses: "Moreover I swore to them in the wilderness that I would scatter them among the nations and disperse them through the countries" (Ezek 20:23); "Therefore he raised his hand and swore to them that he would make them fall in the wilderness, and would disperse their descendants among the nations, scattering them over the lands" (Ps 106:26–27).

found in the passages of *curses and blessings* in the Pentateuch (Lev 26:33; Deut 28:64. Cf. Deut 4:27; Jer 9:15).

Corresponding to the immediate context in Ezekiel 20 and to other statements and concepts in the book of Ezekiel, the phrase in Ezek 20:23 might be the foundation of the reference in Ps 106:26–27.[15] And indeed, the statement in Psalm 106 seems to articulate and refine the sentence of Ezekiel by adding two clarifying expressions to the formulation: "he would make them fall" (להפיל אותם) in the first part of the phrase, and "their descendants" (זרעם) in the second part:

Ezek 20:23	Ps 106:26–27
גם אני נשאתי את ידי להם	וישא ידו להם
	להפיל אותם
במדבר	במדבר
להפיץ	ולהפיל (להפיץ)
אתם	**זרעם**
בגוים	בגוים
ולזרות אותם בארצות	ולזרותם בארצות

In so doing, the psalm distinguishes between the death sentence that had allegedly been carried out in the desert (להפיל אתם, Ps 106:26), and the sentence of exile, intended for the future offspring (v. 27). This is in contrast to the phrase in Ezekiel that may give the impression that the decree is to be executed while still in the wilderness: "Moreover I swore to them in the wilderness that I would scatter them among the nations and disperse them through the countries" (Ezek 20:23). The psalmist clarifies that only the progeny were meant to be scattered "among the nations" and dispersed "over the lands" (Ps 106:27).[16]

A further difference from Ezekiel, who relates the punishment of exile to a continual violation of the divine laws (Ezek 20:21–25), the psalmist relates the exile to a particular event: the despising of the "pleasant land" and the disobedience to

---

15 See also Cooke 1936, 218; Allen 1990, 11–12. Ezekiel 20 exerts further influence on Psalm 106, as can be discerned from the idea stated in the psalm that the nation was saved at the Red Sea for the sake of God's name, and despite their rebellion (Ps 106:7–8). This reference resonates with the unique narrative about the people's rebellion in their first period as a nation (cf. Ezek 20:8), as well as the idea of the risk of annihilation prevented by the consideration of God's name (vv. 8–9, 14, 22). See also: Kugler 2014, 548–549.

16 As suggested by the Peshitta, we should read להפיץ instead of להפיל. The verb להפיץ ("scatter") fits the poetic context better by corresponding to the verb in the second segment of the parallelism, לזרות ("disperse"). The incorrect verb, להפיל, which differs only by one letter, seems to be a mistaken assimilation to the verb mentioned in the previous verse: "להפיל אותם במדבר". See Kraus 1989, 315; Allen 2002, 65; Haran 2008, 379.

God (Ps 106:24–25). For such conduct – a rejection of the land – the punishment of exile is apparently justifiable, even if the punished ones are the offspring. The incident of the spies, in this way, appears to be a turning point in the people's fate.

Just as Ezekiel, whose engagement with the roots of the exile derives from his exposure to it, so the author of Psalm 106 seems to refer to the exile from personal experience. The circumstances of the exile are indicated by the concluding verses of the psalm, which show the desire of the speakers to be saved from among the nations: "He caused them to be pitied by all who held them captive. Save us, O LORD our God, and gather us from among the nations..." (vv. 46–47).[17] This can attest the *Sitz im Leben* of the psalm and its authors.[18]

With this background, we shall now turn to examine the engagement of the psalm with our other core narrative from the days of the desert – the story of the Calf.

8.3 Moses with the Calf and Phinehas with Baal Peor: Past precedents for present action

When we come to examine the psalmist's goals and intentions we need to pay attention to the opening and closing verses of the psalm (vv. 1–6, 47–48). They contain an appeal to God in the present tense and in the first person, differing from the rest of the psalm, which reports the events in the third person, and as set in the past.

As for the speakers' identity, as we saw, their request mentioned in the final verses of the psalm reflects their state in exile, from whence they plead for salvation: "Save us, O LORD our God, and gather us from among the nations..." (הושיענו יהוה אלהינו וקבצנו מן הגוים, v. 47). A similar request for salvation (ישע) appears in the opening verses of the psalm, but there it is phrased in the singular, asking God to remember the speaker, זכרני, and help him, פקדני (v. 4). The LXX for this verse puts the appeal in plural, "remember us" (μνήσθητι ἡμῶν), help/care for us (ἐπίσκεψαι ἡμᾶς). This corresponds with the plural form used in the other references in the opening verses: הרשענו, חטאנו, אבותינו, העוינו, בחיריך (vv. 5–6). However, a sense

---

17 And see my argument about the correlation of the framework verses (vv. 4–5, 47) with the rest of the psalm: Kugler 2014, 552, following Anderson (1972, 736) and Rom-Shiloni (2009[a], 54–55), who argue for the psalm's structural uniformity. In contrast see: Richardson 1987, 197; Allen 2002, 66; Hossfeld and Zenger 2011, 85.

18 This dating follows Gunkel 1926, 465; Dahood 1968, 67; Anderson 1972, 736; Kraus 1989, 317; Broyles 1989, 95–99; Allen 1990, 11; Frankel 2002, 9; Rom-Shiloni 2009(a), 47, 299. Cf. Hossfeld and Zenger 2011, 86, who consider the psalm as post-exilic.

of a collective or national awareness is also gained from the singular form that appears in the MT: זכרני, פקדני (v. 4). The statement moves on to a request for the benefit of the entire nation: לראות בטובת בחיריך לשמח בשמחת גויך להתהלל עם נחלתך, "that I may see the prosperity of your chosen ones, that I may rejoice in the gladness of your nation, that I may glory in your heritage" (v. 5). The terms of the speakers' request for remembrance and salvation (v. 4) is made on behalf of the whole people, God's "chosen ones" (בחיריך, v. 5). The following confessional statement in verse 6 places the speakers alongside their sinful ancestors, attributing to the latter an extensive list of sins from the past (vv. 7–46).[19]

Framed by the speakers' own appeal to God, the list of past sins in the review mentions two specific occurrences when pleas were made to God on behalf of the people. This was done by Moses in the Calf event (v. 23), and by Phinehas, after the incident at Baal Peor (vv. 28–31). In both cases the Israelites faced a threat of death, either directly at the hands of God ("Therefore he said he would destroy them...", v. 23), or by an intermediary outside cause ("...a plague broke out among them", v. 29), and in both cases the threat was thwarted by a person who "stood" and saved the day.

The first plea was made by the esteemed Moses, "...his chosen one", who "stood in the breach before him to turn away his wrath from destroying them" (v. 23). The metaphor describes Moses as a soldier who undertakes to defend a town at a point of a breach in the wall.[20] Thus Moses engages to close the "breach" in the relationship with God, namely the dangerous rupture in the enclosure of the people's protection. This description differs greatly from the other reference to the incident of the Calf outside the Pentateuch, Nehemiah 9, which we dated close to the time of Ezekiel's review. This text relates the survival of the people to God's mercy alone

---

19 As such we can agree with Anderson that the psalm is a liturgical text of confession and repentance, which was used in public rituals in exile or after the return to Israel (Anderson 1972, 735). And see the discussion above (6.3.1) about the speakers' chary acknowledgement of their own misconduct in Nehemiah 9.

20 The word פרץ ("breach") refers to a break in a wall or in fortification: "and I inspected the walls of Jerusalem that had been broken down (פרוצים) and its gates that had been destroyed by fire" (Neh 2:13. Cf. 4:1, 6:1; Amos 4:3). A breach such as this can be fixed by closing and filling the space: "...built the Millo, and closed up the gap in the wall of the city of his father David (פרץ עיר דוד אביו)" (1Kgs 11:27). Metaphorically, the word is used to describe a devastating action that leaves behind a void or emptiness. Thus, the overwhelming slaughter of the people of Benjamin leaves a "breach in the tribes of Israel" (פרץ בשבטי ישראל, Judg 21:15). The void that opens up may affect the state of the entire nation, as a breach in the wall may bring down the entire wall: "therefore this iniquity shall become for you like a break in a high wall, bulging out, and about to collapse, whose crash comes suddenly, in an instant" (Isa 20:13).

(vv. 18–19).[21] The psalm, in contrast, chooses to emphasize the prophet's role in the event.

While the reference to Moses points to a general action that could halt God's wrath, the second case in the review refers to a specific action performed by Phinehas (Ps 106:30–31). The essence of his action, however, expressed with the term ויפלל (v. 30), is quite enigmatic. On the one hand, the root פלל in *piel* can refer to an act of judgment or incrimination (cf. 1Sam 2:25, ופללו), recalling the story about Phinehas, who picked up a spear (and took the law) "in his hands... pierced... the Israelite and the [Midianite] woman, through the belly" (Num 25:7–8). This is the way Ibn Ezra explains the verse in the psalm (Ps 106:30): "He judged as in a criminal (פלילי) case". But this interpretation is problematic, since the verb would require a following object to indicate who or what has been "incriminated".

Another meaning of the form derives from its closeness to the verb in *hithpael* ויתפלל, indicating prayer. This meaning is known from another use of the root פלל in *piel*, in Gen 48:11 (פללתי), meaning a plea or request. But the narrative that Phinehas saves the people in Numbers 25 does not indicate any prayer that was uttered in the event. Nonetheless, the author of Psalm 106 seems to know the story, or a story, like the one in Numbers 25, while using it to indicate the protagonist's attempt to save the people from great disaster.

The psalmist's familiarity with the story in the Pentateuch can be discerned by the coherent flow of the scene in the psalm, unlike the mismatches in Numbers 25, caused by the integration in the text of two or even three varied threads.[22] Thus, Num 25:1–5 recounts the people's debauchery with the daughters of Moab and their gods on the one hand (Num 25:1–2, 4), and a clinging to Baal Peor on the other (vv. 3, 5). The psalm collocates two matters, i.e., the clinging to Baal Peor (Ps 106:28a), and the eating of "...sacrifices offered to the dead" (v. 28b), to resonate with the affair with the daughters of Moab. The psalm also mentions the plague as punishment (vv. 29–30), forming a link to a possible third narrative thread in Numbers 25 about the Midianite woman (Num 25:6–9). The psalmist therefore uses the details included in the final text of Numbers 25 without distinguishing the derivation of the various strands, neatly creating a new coherent sequence. According to Psalm 106, the people clung to Baal Peor (v. 28) and ate sacrifices to the dead (ibid.), causing a plague to break out (v. 29). At this

---

21 See above, 6.1 and 6.4. Cf. also the silence in Ezekiel 20 about Moses' role in the event, which is especially noticeable in light of the prophet's hopeless search for a person that would "stand in the breach before God" (Ezek 22:30. Cf. 13:5; Jer 15:1).
22 For an introduction to the various sources in Numbers 25 see: Kislev 2011, 388.

moment, Phinehas intervened and stopped the plague (v. 30), an act that won him renown for "...righteousness from generation to generation forever" (v. 31).

Within this description, though, there is no hint of the killing performed by Phinehas. Instead, the psalm mentions the action of פלל as accompanying the position of standing: ויעמד פינחס ויפלל (v. 30). By choosing the same word, עמד, for the two men, Moses and Phinehas (vv. 23, 30), the latter also seems to be described as acting vis-à-vis God. Instead of the aggressive attack on the sinners as depicted in Numbers 25, the psalmist chooses an act directed towards God that aims to stop a catastrophe.[23]

Both Moses and Phinehas, according to the psalm, "stood" in a moment of danger and saved the people. They prevented the coming attack, and reduced the danger that threatened the people. By doing so, however, they also left a legacy about the capacity of individuals to influence God on behalf of the collective. Their appeal could indicate the way for those who want to save the congregation in the future. Indeed, such motivation emerges from the speakers' statements in the framework verses of the psalm:

> Ps 106:4–5: Remember me, O LORD, when you show favor to your people;
>> help me when you deliver them;
> that I may see the prosperity of your chosen ones,
>> that I may rejoice in the gladness of your nation,
>> that I may glory in your heritage.

> Verse 47: Save us, O LORD our God,
>> and gather us from among the nations,
>> that we may give thanks to your holy name
>> and glory in your praise.

While, similar to Ezekiel 20, Psalm 106 presents a historiosophical explanation for the fate of the exile (Ps 106:27; Ezek 20:23), it offers, unlike Ezekiel, an earthly means to summon redemption: through intercession by individuals. For that, events from the days in the desert play a dual role. They explain the reasons for the harsh reality of the current situation, as well as giving hope for salvation. The actions of Moses and Phinehas are a precedent for and a reflection of the efforts of the psalmist himself, as he pleads for a redemption of the people from among the nations. The reference to the past opens a gateway to the current exiles – they can influence their own fate by supplication and an approach to God. In this matter they are privileged to rely on and continue the deeds of the "chosen ones" from the past.

---

23 English translations often interpret the verse in such a way, translating the verb ויפלל as "interceded" (NRSV) or "intervened" (NJPS).

8.4 Appendix: Completing the message to the exiles: Psalms 105 and 106

As noted, the speakers in Psalm 106 see themselves as representatives of the people in their appeal to God. They ask to be remembered when God shows favor to his people, and to be helped when he delivers them (v. 4). In that way they play a similar role to that of the two figures of the past, Moses and Phinehas. Unlike these latter, however, the identity of the speakers in the psalm is anonymous. But like their predecessors, the speakers claim legitimacy for their appeal by virtue of their status as "chosen ones" to whom God is committed (v. 5. Cf. vv. 23, 31).

The idea of God's relationship with his chosen people recurs in the previous chapter of Psalms, Psalm 105, which speaks of the people as זרע אברהם ("offspring of Abraham", Ps 105:6) and the sons of Jacob as בחיריו ("his chosen ones", ibid.), to whom God is committed in an everlasting covenant.

Psalm 105, like Psalm 106, outlines events from the people's past, at the center of which stands the relationship between God and the people. The psalm, however, differs greatly from the one that follows it, Psalm 106, and it is difficult to accept the suggestion that they were both created by the same author.[24] The main gap between the psalms is the variation of their ideology and theological message. Psalm 105 stresses the theme of an everlasting covenant between God and the people:

> 6 O offspring of his servant Abraham,
> children of Jacob, his chosen ones.
> 7 He is the LORD our God;
> his judgments are in all the earth.
> 8 He is mindful of his covenant forever,
> of the word that he commanded, for a thousand generations,
> 9 the covenant that he made with Abraham,
> his sworn promise to Isaac,
> 10 which he confirmed to Jacob as a statute,
> to Israel as an everlasting covenant,
> (Ps 105:6–10)

This conveys a picture different from the description of the troubled relations between God and the people according to Psalm 106, where the desire to destroy the people is manifest (Ps 106:23). The difference also arises from a comparison of the period of the desert in both chapters. Psalm 105 briefly

---

24 As suggested by Kirkpatrick 1903, 624; Passaro 2006, 43–44.

summarizes the period by reflecting on the concern of God for the people, i.e., providing them with light, food and water to nourish them along their journey:

> 39 He spread a cloud for a covering, and fire to give light by night.
> 40 They asked, and he brought quails, and gave them food from heaven in abundance.
> 41 He opened the rock, and water gushed out; it flowed through the desert like a river.
> (Ps 105:29–41)

Not so according to Psalm 106, which recounts the period of the wilderness with an extensive elaboration (in more than twenty verses) that highlights the resistant negativity of the people at that time. To recognize this tendency, it is sufficient to review the verbs that describe the deeds of the people in the wilderness. These are: לא השכילו; לא זכרו; וימרו; שכחו; לא חכו; ויתאוו; וינסו אל; ויקנאו; יעשו עגל; וימירו את כבודם; שכחו אל; וימאסו; לא האמינו; וירגנו; לא שמעו; ויצמדו לבעל פעור; ויאכלו זבחי מתים; ויכעיסו במעלליהם; ויקציפו; המרו (vv. 7–33, equivalent to the English: "did not consider"; "did not remember"; "rebelled"; "forgot"; "did not wait"; "had a wanton craving"; "put God to the test"; "were jealous"; "made a calf at Horeb"; "exchanged the glory of God"; "forgot God"; "despised"; "having no faith"; "grumbled"; "did not obey"; "attached themselves to the Baal of Peor"; "ate sacrifices offered to the dead"; "provoked the LORD to anger with their deeds"; "angered the LORD"; "rebelled").[25]

As well as this gap between the two psalms, there is a notable difference between the celebratory statement in Psalm 105 about the inheritance of the land – "He gave them the lands of the nations, and they took possession of the wealth of the peoples" (Ps 105:44) – and the ten verses in Psalm 106 that point to the many offenses that were committed in the land from the moment the people entered it: לא השמידו; ויתערבו בגוים וילמדו מעשיהם; ויעבדו את עצביהם; ויזבחו את בניהם ואת בנותיהם; וישפכו דם נקי; ויטמאו במעשיהם ויזנו במעלליהם; ימרו בעצתם (vv. 34–43: "did not destroy"; "mingled with the nations and learned to do as they did"; "served their idols"; "sacrificed their sons and their daughters"; "they poured out innocent blood"; "became unclean by their acts, and prostituted themselves in their doings"; "were rebellious in their purposes/counsel"). As above, the list is sealed with the notion of rebellion (מרה).

Another striking disparity between the psalms is the different role ascribed to God in saving the people in the past. Psalm 105 chooses to describe in detail two periods from the people's history: the elevation of Joseph to greatness (vv. 17–22), and the escape from Egypt and the survival in the desert (vv. 26–41). Since other

---

25 The translation "rebelled" for המרו (v. 33) is in contrast to the NRSV's choice to take the verb as from "bitter" (Heb. מר), translating the phrase as "made his spirit bitter".

core manifestations of God's gestures on behalf of the people, such as the crossing of the sea and the giving of the law, are missing from the review in Psalm 105 (cf. Ps 106:10–11, 19), the occurrences mentioned in the review in Psalm 105 might reflect the psalmist's attempt to allude to the audience's current issues.[26] Thus, these events have the potential to recur in a similar configuration in the future. As God protected Joseph and his descendants in Egypt (Ps 105:19–24), so he may protect his chosen people when they are in a foreign land.[27] Likewise, just as God redeemed the people from Egypt (v. 37), and led them safely to another territory (vv. 39–44), thus he might save the people in the future and return them to their land. The stories establish a mindset of liberation and rescue to bring hope to the people in times of distress. As such they illustrate God's "deeds" and "wonderful works" (עלילות; נפלאות, vv. 1–2) for his "chosen ones" (בחיריו, v. 6).

In contrast to that, Psalm 106 surveys the negative deeds of the people and their lack of gratitude and disobedience, and makes no mention of any event of redemption from the past, but rather emphasizes the people's instability and the danger of annihilation that accompanied their life (Ps 106:23, 29). Nonetheless, it contains an explicit appeal for deliverance, based on the inherent characteristic of the nation as an entity chosen by God (Ps 106:4–5, 47).

Despite their great disparity, the two psalms were put together in a way that highlights their similar structure, as well as their shared theme of the people's "chosenness". But alongside these common features I would like to propose another reason for the connection between the psalms.

The review in Psalm 105 delivers an optimistic message by presenting the past salvation by God as evidence of God's everlasting covenant with the people. A person who sits in exile and reads such a text can be encouraged by the idea that he belongs to the group of God's "chosen ones", as was already proved in the past by the group's redemption by God. Nevertheless, such a person can be perplexed by the question as to how in the first place these "chosen ones" found themselves in exile, despite the promise to the forefathers of the nation (Ps 105:6), and the covenant for "a thousand generations" (v. 8). An explanation for this will be found in Psalm 106, which teaches that the exile was a punishment for great failures in the past.

---

26 See in contrast Von Rad's suggestion (1996[b], 11–12) that events such as the crossing of the sea and the law giving were unknown to the psalmist.

27 The story of Joseph offers an affinity with the description of the elevation of King Jehoiachin in exile by Evil-Merodach of Babylon (2Kgs 25:27–30). The same motif can be found in the story of Daniel in Babylon, of Nehemiah in Persia, and even of Mordecai and Esther in the kingdom of Ahasuerus.

Placing the two psalms in sequence gives rise to a new message that people can peacefully live with while in exile: Israel is the chosen people and the object of God's concern, as was demonstrated throughout history (Psalm 105). Yet they are not immune to punishment for improper conduct, as attested by the present exile (Psalm 106). The combination of the two psalms solves the problems that arise from each psalm when considered separately, while it meets the needs of perplexed believers. On the one hand, it presents the powerful ethos of the people's chosenness and their everlasting covenant with God, assuring a future salvation. On the other hand, it explains and justifies the tragedy of the exile while providing a method to enable salvation.

9 Conclusions

9.1 The early annihilation-threat motif

In the year of the establishment of the modern state of Israel, the Zionist thinker Simon Rawidowicz reflected on "A nation [which] is going and dying":

> Go and see: there is almost no generation in our Diaspora who did not see themselves as the last ones – the end of Israel, the final link in a nation's lineage. The heart of every genera- tion was caught in a vise of premature death. Whether awake or dreaming, each generation saw the rod of the end pushing to the edge of an abyss which opened wide to swallow them. Building and destroying, rising and falling, uprooting and replanting, and uprooting again, always fearful, they wondered: is the end of Israel coming, are we condemned to be the last of all generations?[1]

Rawidowicz speaks of a consciousness that accompanied the people of Israel during centuries of diaspora – a mindfulness of a coming disaster, a great maw "open wide to swallow them", as is strongly expressed in the medieval Passover Haggadah: "It is not only one that has risen up against us to destroy us. Rather, in each and every generation they rise up against us to destroy us".[2] But such a continual fear dwelled in the national consciousness in periods earlier than the modern era and the Middle Ages. Moreover, rather than any political entity that intended to "rise up against us [Israel] to destroy us", numerous incarnations of this fear of annihilation associated the "abyss" with none other than the Divine, Israel's creator and patron. Early manifestations of the fear in Israel of collective destruction, initiated and executed by their deity, were traced and demonstrated in this book.

Like Mesopotamian mythologies, biblical narratives, historiography and pro- phetic texts recount the potential and actual destruction of people and nations in the world, caused by the creator deity. The recipients of the biblical texts, the Israelites, are not automatically exempt from such a fate. God's various acts of annihilation throughout history indicate that a similar implementation of total destruction is also likely for the Israelites. Thus, narratives in the Pentateuch and several references elsewhere in the Hebrew bible point out that the Israelites were already at risk of destruction in the first moments of their formation as a nation, immediately after their selection as God's protégés. The threat to their

---

1 Rawidowicz 1948, 135 (my translation. The Hebrew is phrased in a somewhat poetic style). I thank my friend, Misgav Har-Peled, for introducing me to Rawidowicz's work.
2 See above, Introduction, section 1.1.

https://doi.org/10.1515/9783110609905-009

existence derived not from arbitrary natural hazards nor from mundane political enemies, but from internal, domestic causes, related to the intimate relationship with their creator and protector, God.

According to the biblical thinking, both despite and due to their unique status, the Israelites were at constant risk of destruction. God's willingness to destroy them was a plausible consequence of their relationship, the other side of the coin of chosenness, which brought with it the cost of high expectations. While God constantly reevaluated his commitment to the people, the latter had only a one-directional path in the relationship. Their responsibilities were unavoidable and the divine expectations for them were non-negotiable. The authoritarian deity could dissolve the relationship at any time, either by utterly destroying the people, or by forsaking them. Meanwhile, for various considerations, he kept the people alive and close to him, though under the ominous threat.

The books of Exodus and Numbers recount that in the early years of the people of Israel, after being saved from destruction by the Egyptians, and before heading further to destroy other peoples, the Israelites faced near destruction by God. The danger occurs in the liminal area of the desert, in the wake of two events, the fashioning of a Golden Calf (Exodus 32) and the sending of spies to examine the intended land (Numbers 13–14). In these events, however, the threat of destruction is immediately cancelled with the intervention of the prophet and the leader, Moses.

Nevertheless, when reading the stories of the divine near annihilation within their broader narrative contexts in the Pentateuch, the motif of annihilation seems out of place. A historical-literary examination of the stories leads to a conclusion about the secondary nature of the motif within its literary contexts and raises the possibility that it was interwoven into the stories at a later stage of composition.

An investigation of the story of the Golden Calf shows that the segment about near destruction is redundant in the plot, added to further strengthen criticism against the northern calf ritual. In the story of the spies, the motif of near annihilation was attached to a Non-Priestly story that first recounted a less than clearly defined sin by the spies and the people. In both stories, the supplementary units aimed at emphasizing both the danger the people faced at a certain stage, and the decisive role the prophet played in preserving their existence. Nevertheless, despite the similar literary process that occurred with the two stories, that is the integration of the myth at a later compositional stage, the stories do not attest a direct literary reliance between them. The absence of linguistic links between the two stories indicates that the texts were created with no interdependent influence. They presented rather, in parallel and separately, two manifestations of the one narrative that was prevalent in the collective ethos.

The independence of the myth of near destruction from its current literary contexts is further evident from Psalm 78, which alludes to the notion of near destruction in the wilderness period with no reference to the particular events known from the Pentateuch. An investigation of the psalm suggests that the silence about the specific events derived either from the psalmist's ignorance of the specific stories, or from unfamiliarity with the association of the stories with the notion of near destruction. Instead, the psalm presents the idea of near destruction alongside a general criticism of the people's rebelliousness and their testing of God during the wandering in the desert.

The psalm's messages and its assumed setting lead to the assumption that the idea of near destruction was part of the consciousness of the ancient scribes even before the kingdoms went into exile. Thus, the myth does not seem to be necessarily rooted in a collective experience of destruction. It is more likely that the Israelites' fear of loss and destruction at the hands of God emerged together with the formation of the concepts of the people's chosenness and uniqueness. This preceded the composition of political accounts such as the story of the Calf and the episode of the spies. Thus, prior to being a political ethos, the narrative of near destruction manifests an engagement with the mythological portrayal of the Divine.

Surprisingly, the addition of the ancient tradition of near destruction to the two specific literary settings in the Pentateuch has limited the portrayal of the people's God as a furious mythological deity, as well as the characterization of the nation as fragile. From a general threat that accompanied the people's life, the image of a deadly end has been reduced to a threat that occurred on specific occasions, when God was not only dangerous and unpredictable but also compassionate because of changes in his expectations.

9.2 A motif evolution

The danger of annihilation in the days of the desert is mentioned throughout the Hebrew Bible several times, both explicitly and implicitly. As in the case of Psalm 78, the retrospective review in Ezekiel 20 recounts the motif with no reference to the two incidents known from the Pentateuch, even though it provides a chronicle of the people's life in the desert. But while the silence about the Calf and the spies in Psalm 78 may be an outcome of the composition stage which presumably preceded the creation of the two stories in the Pentateuch, the absence of the incidents in Ezekiel 20 does not necessarily indicate a lack of familiarity with the stories. Rather it might stem from the author's attempt to portray the people's unstable relationship with God as a repetitive pattern in history, one which does not derive from a particular event or events. In contrast to this portrayal, in another text, Nehemiah 9, which we dated close to the time of Ezekiel's review, we find an attempt to obscure the danger of annihilation. The text paints an optimistic picture about God's commitment to the people in the past, despite their ongoing misconduct. This affirms an expectation of divine protection and national immunity in the scribes' experience of current events.

References to the threat of destruction in the context of the days in the desert reappears in the Pentateuch in Moses' speech in Deuteronomy 9. The speech, however, links the danger of destruction to the incident of the Calf alone, without attributing it to the incident at Kadesh-barnea, even though the place is listed among locations of the people's rebellion in the past. The retrospective description in Deuteronomy 9 points to Moses' decisive role in ensuring the people's survival in the event, though it places his intervention at a stage different from the one mentioned by the omniscient narrator in Exodus 32. By doing so the Deuteronomic text corrects problematic details in the version in use. A similar tendency appears in Psalm 106. The psalm alludes to the events of the Calf and the spies as part of a sequence of rebellious incidents in the past. Nevertheless, the text associates the danger of annihilation and Moses' protection and care for the people only with the narrative of the Calf.

The story of the spies included in the words of Caleb in Joshua 14 also lacks the narrative of the threat of death pronounced against the people at the event. Generally speaking, outside the story told by the omniscient narrator in Numbers 13–14, we no longer find the danger of annihilation associated with the event involving the spies. This phenomenon may derive from the dominant literary use of the version of the spy story reflected in Deuteronomy 1, where the writer deliberately removed the notion of extermination. Similarly, the textual occurrence in Numbers 32 keeps silent about the motif of near destruction in reference to the story of the spies, even though, in this case, it follows the complete version of Numbers 13–14. This has been explained as required to convey the message of the interpolator in Numbers 32.

The above investigation suggests a chronological order for the development of the texts that explicitly or implicitly mention the stories of the Calf and the spies:

1. A myth about a divine willingness to destroy the chosen people preceded the composition of the narratives of the Calf and the spies known in the Pentateuch, as attested in Psalm 78.
2. The myth was interpolated into Non-Priestly (and pre-Deuteronomistic) narratives (in parallel and at independent stages) as reflected in Exodus 32 and Numbers 14.

3. With the old-new addition of the motif of near destruction (without the Priestly version of the story of the spies), the narratives were rewritten into a retrospective text by a Deuteronomic/ Deuteronomist writer as reflected in Deuteronomy 1 and 9.

4. The version of the spy story in Deuteronomy 1 was employed as a foundation for further rewritings of the story (this occured at the expense of the narrative in Numbers 13–14). Thus, the myth of near destruction was excised from the story of the spies, as indicated in Deuteronomy 9:23, Joshua 14 and Psalms 106.

5. The complete story of the spies from Numbers 13–14, along with its later Priestly version, was "found" and reused by a priestly writer who wanted to strengthen Moses' rebuke against the tribes of the Transjordan, as appears in Numbers 32. The motif of a threat of destruction was not at the core of the message and thus was not employed for the rewritten version.

6. The two stories from the Pentateuch – the Calf and the spies – that absorbed the myth of extermination were known in their final form, or in a certain version of it, on the eve of the Babylonian exile, as learned from Ezekiel 20 and Nehemiah 9.

The biblical literature recalls a danger of death that had been invoked on the people by God. It often uses these descriptions as part of an acknowledgment by the people of their own conduct. This attests the ability of the scribes and the audience to reflect on their lives, and to attribute to themselves accountability for their fate. In addition, many occurrences use these narratives as precedents for and support in distresses of the present days. Surprisingly, the harsh stories that the people recount about themselves appear to be part of the mechanism for surviving and coping in times of crisis. With this deduction we can refer again to Rawidowicz's words about "A nation [which] is going and dying":

> ...Sometimes it seems to me as if the sense of the coming end is an essential protection, a feeling that turns into a notion and becomes one of the basic ideas that serves as a shield for the people. It is an encouragement of their ability to defeat the annihilation that accompanied them from the beginning, in their periods of wanderings and kingdoms, which did not fill their hearts with much of a sense of security. Israel indeed kept meditating on their potential annihilation, imagining their coming end. But these reflections and imaginings were their tools to overcome their destruction, to withstand every crisis and extinction, when those [fates] have indeed lurked for them. And thus, the people of destruction turned to be the people of beginning, and their end altered to an endless end...[3]

---

3 Rawidowicz 1948, 144 (my translation).

With the turn from the potential "end" to an "endless end" we can now complete our task. The book traced the ancient myth of the threat of annihilation in its evolving manifestations in various literary and historical contexts in the Hebrew Bible. By looking at the fear of the ancients through an external and critical lens we tried to understand the ideological, religious and socio-political concepts that accompanied the people's life. This enabled us to move to further examination of phenomena such as collective memory, political agendas and national self-conceptions. With this in hand, the engagement with "the coming end" might now clear space for dealing with the continuity of past and present, the "here and now". Nevertheless, there should be acknowledgment of the virtue that accompanied these fears of the ancients: the ability for self-reflection and self-examination, that has the potential to improve the imprint on history and on the future.

List of abbreviations

AB	The Anchor Bible
BZ	Biblische Zeitschrift
BZAW	Beihefte zur Zeitschrift für die alttestamentliche Wissenschaft
CahRB	Cahiers de la Revue Biblique
CBQ	The Catholic Biblical Quarterly
CBSC	The Cambridge Bible for Schools and Colleges
FAT	Forschungen zum Alten Testament
FOTL	The Forms of the Old Testament Literature
HAR	Hebrew Annual Review
HAT	Handbuch zum Alten Testament
HeBAI	Hebrew Bible and Ancient Israel
HKAT	Handkommentar zum Alten Testament
HUCA	Hebrew Union College Annual
ICC	The International Critical Commentary
JANES	Journal of the Ancient Near Eastern Society
JBL	Journal of Biblical Literature
JPS	Jewish Publication Society
JQR	Jewish Quarterly Review
JSOT	Journal for the Study of the Old Testament
JSOTS	Journal for the Study of the Old Testament Supplement Series
KeH	Kurzgefasstes exegetische Handbuch
KHC	Kurzer Hand-Commentar zum Alten Testament
KJV	King James Version
NCBC	The New Century Bible Commentary
NICOT	The New International Commentary on the Old Testament
NRSV	New Revised Standard Version
OTL	The Old Testament Library
SBLDS	Society of Biblical Literature Dissertation Series
TDOT	Theological Dictionary of the Old Testament, I-XV, 1980-2006
TZ	Theologische Zeitschrift
VT	Vetus Testamentum
VTSup	Supplements to Vetus Testamentum
WBC	Word Biblical Commentary
ZAW	Zeitschrift für die Alttestamentliche Wissenschaft

https://doi.org/10.1515/9783110609905-010

Bibliography

Aberbach, Moses and Smolar, Leivy. 1967. "Aaron, Jeroboam and the Golden Calves." *JBL* 86:129–140.

Aberbach, Moses and Smolar, Leivy. 1968. "The Golden Calf Episode in Postbiblical Literature." *HUCA* 39:91–116.

Achenbach, Reinhard. 2003. "Die Erzahlung von der gescheiterten Landnahme von Kadesch Barnea [Numeri 13–14] als Schlusseltext der Redaktionsgeschichte des Pentateuch." *ZABR* 9:56–123.

Aḥituv, Shmuel. 1995. *Joshua—Introduction and Commentary* (Mikra L'Yisrael 6). Tel Aviv: Am Oved (Heb.).

Aḥituv, Shmuel. 2012. *HaKetav VeHmiḵatav*: handbook of ancient inscriptions from the land of Israel and the kingdoms beyond the Jordan from the period of the first Commonwealth. Jerusalem: Mosad Bialik (Heb.).

Albertz, Rainer (1994). *A history of Israelite religion in the Old Testament period* (Vol. 1). London: SCM Press.

Albright, William F. 1968. *Yahweh and the Gods of Canaan*. London: University of London.

Allen, Leslie C. 1990. *Ezekiel 20–48* (WBC 29). Dallas: Word Books.

Allen, Leslie C. 2002. *Psalms 101–150* (WBC 21). Nashville: T. Nelson.

Alt, Albrecht. 1925. "Judas Gaue unter Josia", *Palästina Jahrboch* 21:100–116.

Amit, Yaira. 2000. *Hidden Polemic in Biblical Narrative*. Leiden: Brill.

Anderson, Arnold A. 1972. *Psalms* (NCBC). London: Oliphants.

Andreasený, Niels-Erik A. 1972. *The Old Testament Sabbath:ý a tradition-historical investigation* (SBLDS 7), Missoula: Society of Biblical Literature for the Form Criticism Seminar.

Artus, Olivier. 1997. *Etudes sur le livre des Nombres: Récit, histoire et loi en Nb 13,1–20,13* (Orbis biblicus et orientalis 157). Gottingen: Vandenhoeck & Ruprecht.

Aurelius, Erik. 1988. *Der Fürbitter Israels: eine Studie zum Mosebild im Alten Testament*. Stockholm: Almqvist & Wiksell International.

Bacon, Benjamin W. 1894. *The Triple Tradition of the Exodus*. Hartford: The Student Publishing Company.

Baden, Joel S. 2009. *J, E and the Redaction of the Pentateuch* (FAT 68). Tübingen: Mohr Siebeck.

Baentsch, Bruno. 1903. *Exodus-Leviticus-Numeri*. HKAT ½. Göttingen: Vandenhoeck & Ruprecht.

Balentine, Samuel E. 1985. "Prayer in the Wilderness Traditions: In Pursuit of Divine Justice." *HAR* 9:53–74.

Balentine, Samuel E. 1989. "Prayers for Justice in the Old Testament: Theodicy and Theology." *CBQ* 51:597–616.

Barlett, John R. 1989. *Edom and Edomites*. Sheffield: JSOT Press.

Barnes, William E. 1931. *The Psalms* (vol. 2), London: Methuen & Co., ltd.

Batten, Loring W. 1980 (1913). *Ezra-Nehemiah* (ICC). Edinburgh: T. & T. Clark.

Bedford, Peter R. 2002. "Diaspora: Homeland Relations in Ezra-Nehemiah." *VT* 52:147–165.

Begg, Christopher T. 1985. "The Destruction of the Calf (Exod 32,20 – Deut 9,21)." In: *Das Deuteronomium: Entstehung, Gestalt und Botschaft*, edited by Norbert Lohfink, 208–251. Leuven: Leuven University Press.

Beit-Arieh, Itzhak, and Cresson, B. 1985. "An Edomite Ostracon from Ḥorvat 'Uza." *Journal of the Institute of Tel Aviv* 12:96–101.

https://doi.org/10.1515/9783110609905-011

Beit-Arieh, Itzhak. 2003. "Judean-Edomite Rivalry in the Negev." *Qadmoniot: A Journal for the Antiquities of Eretz-Israel and Bible Lands* 126: 66–76 (Heb.).

Beltz, Walter. 1974. *Die Kaleb-Traditionen im Alten Testament.* Beiträge zur Wissenschaft vom Alten und Neuen Testament 98. Stuttgart: Kohlhammer.

Berlin, Adele and Brettler, Marc Z. 2004. "The Modern Study of the Bible." In The Jewish Study Bible, edited by: Adele Berlin and Marc Z. Brettler, 2084–2096. New York: Oxford University Press.

Berlin, Adele. 2005. "Psalms and the Literature of Exile: Psalms 137, 44, 69, and 78." In *The Book of Psalms: Composition and Reception*, edited by Peter W. Flint and Patrick D. Miller, 75–84. VTSup 99. Leiden: Brill.

Berner, Christoph. 2013. "The Redaction History of the Sinai Pericope (Exod 19–24) and its Continuation in 4Q158." *Dead Sea Discoveries* 20:378–409.

Berner, Christoph. 2017. "'I am YHWH your God, who brought you out of the land of Egypt' (Exod 20:2): Reflections on the Status of the Exodus Creed in the History of Israel and the Literary History of the Hebrew Bible." In *The origins of Yahwism*, edited by Jürgen van Oorschot and Markus Witte, 181–206. Berlin and Boston: De Gruyter.

Bertholet, Alfred. 1899. *Deuteronomium* (KHC 5), Freiburg: Mohr Siebeck.

Bewer, Julius A. 1953. "Textual and Exegetical Notes on the Book of Ezekiel." *JBL* 72:158–168.

Beyerlin, Walter. 1965 (1961). *Origins and history of the oldest Sinaitic traditions*. Oxford: Blackwell.

Blenkinsopp, Joseph. 1996. "An assessment of the Alleged Pre-Exilic Date of the Priestly Material in the Pentateuch." *ZAW* 108:495–518.

Block, Daniel I. 1997. *The Book of Ezekiel 1–24* (NICOT). Grand Rapids: W.B. Eerdmans.

Blum, Erhard. 1990. *Studien zur Komposition des Pentateuch*. BZAW 189. Berlin: W. de Gruyter.

Blum, Erhard. 2002 (1989). "Israel à la montagne de Dieu: Remarques sur Ex. 19–24; 32–34 et sur le contexte littéraire et historique de la Composition." In *Le Pentateuque en question*, edited by Albert de Pury and Thomas Römer, 271–295. Geneva: Labor et Fides.

Blum, Erhard. 2011. "The Decalogue and the Composition History of the Pentateuch." In *The Pentateuch: international perspectives on current research*, edited by Thomas B. Dozeman et al., 289–301. Tübingen: Mohr Siebeck.

Blum, Erhard. 2012. "Der historische Mose und die Frühgeschichte Israels." *HeBAI* 1:37–63.

Boda, Mark J. 1999. *Praying the Tradition: The Origin and Use of Tradition in Nehemiah 9*, BZAW 27. Berlin: W. de Gruyter.

Boda, Mark. J. 2006. "Confession as Theological Expression: Ideological Origins of Penitential Prayer." In *Seeking the Favor of God: The Origins of Penitential Prayer in Second Temple Judaism*, edited by Mark J. Boda et al. (vol. 1), 21–50. Atlanta: Society of Biblical Literature.

Boling Robert G. 1982. *Joshua* (AB), (introduction by Ernest G. Wright). Garden City: Doubleday.

Boorer, Suzanne. 1992. *The Promise of the Land as Oath: A Key to the Formation of the Pentateuch*, BZAW 205. Ann Arbor, Michigan: UMI.

Boorer, Suzanne. 2010. "Source and Redaction Criticism." In *Methods for Exodus*, edited by Thomas B. Dozeman, 95–130. Cambridge: Cambridge University Press.

Brettler, Marc Z. 1995. *The Creation of History in Ancient Israel*. London: Routledge.

Brettler, Marc Z. 1996. "Biblical Literature as Politics: The Case of Samuel." In *Religion and Politics in the Ancient Near East*, edited by Adele Berlin, 71–92. Bethesda, Md: University Press of Maryland.

Brettler, Marc Z. 2005. *How to Read the Bible*. Philadelphia: The Jewish Publication Society.

Brettler, Marc Z. et al. 2012. *The Bible and the Believer – How to Read the Bible Critically and Religiously*. New York: Oxford University Press.

Breuer, Mordechai. 1985. "The division of the Decalogue to verses and commandments." In *The Ten Commandments in history and tradition*, edited by Ben-Zion Segal, 223–253. Jerusalem: Magnes (Heb.).

Briggs, Charles A. and Briggs, Emilie Grace. 1986 (1906). *The Book of Psalms* (vol. 2) (ICC). Edinburgh: T. & T. Clark.

Brin, Gershon. 1975. *Studies in the Book of Ezekiel*. Tel Aviv: Hakibbutz Hameuchad (Heb.).

Brownlee, William H. 1986. *Ezekiel 1–19* (WBC 28). Waco: Word Books.

Broyles, Craig C. 1989. *The Conflict of Faith and Experience in the Psalms: A Form-Critical and Theological Study* (JSOTS 52). Sheffield: JSOT Press.

Budd, Philip J. 1984. *Numbers* (WBC 5). Waco, Tex: Word Books.

Burrows, Millar, 1925. *The Literary Relation of Ezekiel*. Philadelphia: Jewish Publication Society Press.

Butler, Trent C. 1983, *Joshua* (WBC 7). Waco: Word Books.

Butler, Trent C. 2014. *Joshua* 13–24 (WBC 7B). Grand Rapids: Zondervan.

Campbell, Antony F. 1979. "Psalm 78: A Contribution to the Theology of Tenth Century Israel." *CBQ* 41:51–79.

Campbell, Antony F. and O'Brien, Mark A. 1993. *Sources of the Pentateuch: Texts, Introductions, Annotation*. Minneapolis: Fortress Press.

Carmichael, Calum M. 1985. *Law and Narrative in the Bible: The Evidence of the Deuteronomic Laws and the Decalogue*. Ithaca: Cornell University Press, 1985.

Carroll, Robert P. 1971. "Psalm LXXVIII: Vestiges of a Tribal Polemic." *VT* 21:133–150.

Cassuto, Moshe D. 1965. *A commentary on the book of Exodus*. Jerusalem: Magnes (Heb.).

Chavel, Charles B. 1973, *Nachmanides' Commentary in the Torah: Exodus*. New York: Shilo Pub. House.

Chavel, Charles B. 1975, *Nachmanides' Commentary in the Torah: Numbers*. New York: Shilo Pub. House.

Chavel, Charles B. 1976, *Nachmanides' Commentary in the Torah: Deuteronomy*. New York: Shilo Pub. House.

Childs, Brevard S. 1974. *Exodus* (OTL 2). London: S.C.M. Press.

Chrosotowski, Waldemar. 1990. "An Examination of Conscience by God's People as Exemplified in Neh. 9, 6–37." *BZ* 34:253–261.

Clifford, Richard J. 1981. "In Zion and David a new Beginning: An Interpretation of Psalm 78." In *Traditions in Transformation. Turning points in Biblical faith*, edited by Baruch Halpern and Jon D. Levenson, 121–141. Winona Lake: Eisenbrauns.

Coats, George W. 1968. *Rebellion in the Wilderness: The Murmuring Motif in the Wilderness Traditions of the Old Testament*. Nashville: Abingdon Press.

Cogan, Mordechai. 2001. *I Kings: a new translation, with introduction and commentary* (AB 10). New York: Doubleday.

Cooke, George A. 1918. *The Book of Joshua* (The Cambridge Bible for schools and colleges 7). Cambridge: University Press.

Cooke, George A. 1936. The Book of Ezekiel (ICC). Edinburgh:T. & T. Clark.

Dahood, Mitchell S.J. 1968. *Psalms II 51–100* (AB 17). Garden City: Doubleday.

Davis, Ellen F. 1989. *Swallowing the Scroll:ÿ Textuality and the Dynamics of Discourse in Ezekiel's Prophecy* (JSOTS 78). Sheffield: Almond Press.

Day, John. 1986. "Pre-Deuteronomic Allusions to the Covenant in Hosea and Psalms LXXVIII". *VT* 36:1–12.

De Vaux, Roland. 1970. "The Settlement of the Israelites in Southern Palestine and the Origins of the Tribe of Judah". In: *Translating and Understanding the Old* Testament, edited by Harry T. Frank and William L. Reed, 108–134. Nashville: Abingdon Press.

De Wette, Wilhelm M.L. 1806. *Beiträge zur Einleitung in das Alte Testament*. Halle: Schimmelpfennig.

Dentan, Robert C. 1963. "The Literary Affinities of Exodus XXXIV 6f." *VT* 13:34–51.

Dillmann, August. 1880. *Die Bücher Exodus and Leviticus*. Leipzig: S. Hirzel.

Dillmann, August. 1886. *Die Bücher Numeri, Deuteronomium und Josua*. Für die 2. Aufl. neu bearb. Leipzig: S. Hirzel.

Dozeman, Thomas B. 2017. *The Pentateuch: Introducing the Torah*. Minneapolis: Fortress Press.

Driver, Samuel R. 1901. *Deuteronomy* (ICC 5). Edinburgh: T. & T. Clark.

Driver, Samuel R. 1911. *The Book of Exodus* (CBSC 2). Cambridge: Cambridge University Press.

Duggan, Michael W. 2001. *The Covenant Renewal in Ezra-Nehemiah (Neh 7:72b – 10:40) – An Exegetical, Literary and Theological Study* (SBLDS 164). Atlanta: Society of Biblical Literature.

Duggan, Michael W. 2006. "Ezra 9: 6–15: A Penitential Prayer within its Literary Setting." In *Seeking the Favor of God: The Origins of Penitential Prayer in Second Temple Judaism*, edited by Mark J. Boda et al. (vol. 2), 165–180. Atlanta: Society of Biblical Literature.

Durham, John I. 1987. *Exodus* (WBC 3). Waco: Word Books.

Ehrlich, Arnold B. 1969 (1899–1901). Mikra ki-pheshuto: the Bible according to its literal meaning in three volumes. New York: Ktav Pub. House.

Eichrodt, Walther. 1961. *Theology of the Old Testament* (vol. 1). London: SCM Press.

Eichrodt, Walther. 1970 (1965–6). *Ezekiel* (OTL 22). Philadelphia: Westminster.

Eissfeldt, Otto. 1958. *Das Lied Moses Deuteronomium 32: 1–43und das Lehrgedicht Asaphs Psalm 78 samt einer Analyse der Umgebung des Mose-Liedes*. BVASW.PH 104. Broschiert: Berlin.

Ferris, Paul W. 1992. "Hebron." In *The Anchor Bible Dictionary* (vol. 3), edited by David N. Freedman. 107–108. New York: Doubleday.

Fishbane, Michael. 1985. *Biblical Interpretation in Ancient Israel*. Oxford: Clarendon Press.

Fleming, Daniel E. 1999. "If El is a Bull, Who is a Calf? Reflections on Religion in Second-Millennium Syria-Palestine." *Eretz Israel* 26:23–27.

Frankel, David. 2002. *The Murmuring Stories of the Priestly School: A Retrieval of Ancient Sacerdotal Lore*. VTsup 89. Leiden: Brill.

Frankel, David. 2011. *The Land of Canaan and the Destiny of Israel*. Winona Lake: Eisenbrauns.

Friedman, Richard E. 2003. *The Bible with Sources Revealed: A New View into the Five Books of Moses*. San Francisco: Harper San Francisco.

Galil, Gershon. 1983. *The genealogies of the tribe of Judah* (PhD Dissertation). Jerusalem: The Hebrew University of Jerusalem (Heb.).

Ganzel, Tova. 2005. *The concept of holiness in the Book of Ezekiel* (PhD dissertation). Jerusalem: The Hebrew University of Jerusalem (Heb.).

Gärtner, Judith. 2015. "The Historical Psalms: A Study of Psalms 78; 105; 106; 135, and 136 as Key Hermeneutical Texts in the Psalter." *Hebrew Bible and Ancient Israel* 4:373–399.

Gerstenberger, Erhard. 2001. *Psalms and Lamentations* (FOTL). Michigan: Eardmans Publishing.

Gertz, Jan C. at al. (eds.). 2002. *Abschied vom Jahwisten: Die Komposition des Hexateuch in der jüngsten Diskussion*. Berlin: W. de Gruyter.

Gesundheit, Shimon. 2012. *Three Times a Year*. Winona Lake: Eisenbrauns.

Gosling, Frank A. 1999. "Were the Ephraimites to Blame?" *VT* 49:505–513.

Goulder, Michael D. 1995. "Asaph's History of Israel (Elohist Press, Bethel, 725 BC)." *JSOT* 65:71–81.

Graf, Karl H. 1866. *Die geschichtlichen Bücher des Alten Testaments: zwei historisch-kritische Untersuchungen*. Leipzig: T.O. Weigel

Gray, George B. 1903. *A critical and exegetical commentary on Numbers* (ICC 4). Edinburgh: T. & T. Clark.

Gray, John. 1964. *I & II Kings: a commentary* (OTL). Philadelphia: Westminster Press.

Greenberg, Moshe. 1964. "Ezekiel 20 and the Spiritual Exile." *Oz Le'David: Studies in the Bible Presented to David Ben-Gurion on his Seventy-Seven Year Anniversary*, 433–442. Jerusalem: Kiriat-Sefer (Heb.).

Greenberg, Moshe. 1971. "The Shabbat in Jeremiah." Studies in the Book of Jeremiah – The Department of Bible Research at the President's Residence, edited by Benzion Luriah, 27–37. Jerusalem: The compony of the Bible research in Israel (Heb.).

Greenberg, Moshe. 1978. "Moses' Intercessory Prayer (Exod. 32: 11–13,31–32; Deut. 9: 26–29)." In: *Prayer and the Mystery of Salvation*, Tantur Yearbook 1977/78, edited by Walter Harrelson, 21–35. Jerusalem: Ecumenical Institute for Advanced Theological Studies.

Greenberg, Moshe. 1983. *Ezekiel 1–20* (AB 22). Garden City: Doubleday.

Greenberg, Moshe. 1986. "What are Valid Criteria for Determining Inauthentic Matter in Ezekiel." In *Ezekiel and his book: textualand literary criticism and their interrelation*, edited by Johan Lust, 123–135. Leuven: University Press.

Greenberg, Moshe. 1993. "Notes on the influence of tradition on Ezekiel." *JANES* 22:29–37.

Greenstein, Edward L. 1990. "Mixing Memory and Design: Reading Psalm 78." *Prooftexts* 10:197–218.

Gressmann, Hugo. 1913. *Mose und seine Zeit: ein Kommentar zu den Mose-Sagen*. Göttingen: Vandenhoeck & Ruprecht.

Grintz, Yehoshua M. 1976. "The first reform in Israel: the link between the Calf story in the desert and the 'sins' of Jeroboam son of Nebat." *Zion* 41:109–126 (Heb.).

Gruber, Mayer I. 1998. *Rashi Commentary on Psalms 1–89*, Georgia: Scholars Press.

Gunkel, Herman. 1901. *The Legends of Geneis*. Chicago: The Open Court Publishing.

Gunkel, Herman. 1926. *Die Psalmen* (HKAT 2). Göttingen: Vandenhoeck & Ruprecht.

HaCohen, David B.G. 2010. *Kadesh in the Pentateuchal narratives* (PhD dissertation). Jerusalem: The Hebrew University of Jerusalem (Heb.).

Haglund, Erik. 1984. *Historical Motifs in the Psalms*. Stockholm: Cwk Gleerup.

Halevi, Rabbi Judah. 1927 (1139*)*. *Kitab al Khazari*, translated by Hartwig Hirschfeld (Part One). New York: Bernard G. Richards co.

Haran, Menahem. 1981. "Behind the Scenes of History: Determining the Date of the Priestly Source." *JBL* 100:321–333.

Haran, Menahem. 2004. *The Biblical Collection* 2. Jerusalem: Mosad Bialik (Heb.).

Haran, Menahem. 2008. *The Biblical Collection* 3. Jerusalem: Mosad Bialik (Heb.).

Hayes, Christine E. 2004. "Golden Calf Stories: The Relationship of Exodus 32 and Deuteronomy 9–10." In *The Idea of Biblical Interpretation*, edited by Hindy Najman and Judith H. Newman, 45–93. Leiden: Brill.

Heider, George C. 1988. "A Further Turn on Ezekiel's Baroque Twist in Ez. 20:25–26." *JBL* 107:721–724.

Helfmeyer, Franz J. 1995 (1984–1986). "כָּלָה." *TDOT* 7:157–164.

Herrington James P. 1976. *The Caleb Tradition and the Role of the Calebites in the History of Israel* (PhD Dissertation). Atlanta: Emory University.

Hiller, Dov. 1936. "Additions to Daniel." In *Apocrypha. Hebrew-Versions*, edited by Avraham Kahana (vol. 1), 554–575. Tel Aviv: Mekorot (Heb.).

Hoffman, Yair. 1975. "On the question of the structure and significance of Ezekiel 20." *Beit Mikra* 20:473–489 (Heb.).

Hoffman, Yair. 1983. *The doctrine of the Exodus in the Bible*. Tel Aviv: Tel Aviv University (Heb.).

Hoffman, Yair. 2001. Jeremiah 1–24 (Mikra L'Yisrael 11.1). Tel Aviv: Am Oved (Heb.).

Hogewood, Jay C. 2006. "The Speech Act of Confession: Priestly Performative Utterance in Lev.16 and Ezra 9–10." In *Seeking the Favor of God: The Origins of Penitential Prayer in Second Temple Judaism*, edited by Mark J. Boda et al. (vol. 1), 69–82. Atlanta: Society of Biblical Literature.

Holzinger, Heinrich. 1900. *Exodus* (KHC 2). Tübingen: J.C.B. Mohr P. Siebeck.

Holzinger, Heinrich. 1901. *Das Buch Josua* (KHC 6), Tübingen: J.C.B. Mohr P. Siebeck.

Holzinger, Heinrich. 1903. *Numeri* (KHC 4). Tübingen-Leipzig: J.C.B. Mohr P. Siebeck.

Hossfeld, Frank L. and Zenger, Erich. 2011 (2008). *Psalms 101–150* (Hermeneia). Minneapolis: Fortress Press.

Hurvitz, Avi. 1982. *A linguistic study of the relationship between the priestly source and the book of Ezekiel: anew approach to an old problem* (CahRB 20). Paris: J. Gabalda.

Hyatt, James P. 1971. *Commentary on Exodus*. London: Oliphants.

Jacob, Benno. 1992 (1940), *The second book of the Bible, Exodus*, Hoboken, N.J.: Ktav Pub. House.

Jacobs, H.E. 1989. "Confess; Confession." In *The International Standard Bible Encyclopedia*, edited by Geoffrey W. Bromiley (vol. 1), 759. Grand Rapids:W.B. Eerdmans.

Japhet, Sara. 1994. "Composition and Chronology in the book of Ezra-Nehemiah." Eretz Israel 24: 111–121 (Heb.).

Jeremias, Jörg. 2017. "Three theses on the early history of Israel." In *The origins of Yahwism*, edited by Jürgen van Oorschot and Markus Witte, 145–156. Berlin and Boston: De Gruyter.

Johnstone, William. 2014. "Reading Exodus in Tetrateuch and Pentateuch." In *The Book of Exodus: Composition, Reception, and Interpretation*, edited by Thomas B. Dozeman et al., 3–26. Boston: Brill.

Joosten, Jan. 2006. "The disappearance of iterative WEQATAL in the Biblical Hebrew verbal system." In *Biblical Hebrew in Its Northwest Semitic Setting: typological and historical perspectives*, edited by Steven E. Fassberg and Avi Hurvitz, 135–147. Jerusalem: Magnes; Winona Lake: Eisenbrauns.

Joosten, Jan. 2012. *The Verbal System of Biblical Hebrew – A New Synthesis Elaborated on the Basis of Classical Prose*, Jerusalem: Simor.

Joyce, Paul M. 2006. "Ezek. 20.32–38: a problem text for the theology of Ezekiel." In *Stimulation from Leiden: collected communications to the XVIIIth Congress of the International Organization for the Study of the Old Testament*, edited by Hermann M. Niemann and Matthias Augustin, 119–123. Frankfurt am Main: P. Lang.

Kara-Ivanov Kaniel, Ruth. 2014. "Consumed by Love: The Death of Nadav and Avihu as a Ritual of Erotic Mystical Union." In *Myth, Ritual and Mysticism*, edited by Gideon Bohak et al., 585–653. Tel Aviv: Tel Aviv University (Heb.).

Kasher, Rimon. 2004. *Ezekiel 1–24: Introduction and Commentary* (Mikra L'Yisrael 12). Tel Aviv: Am Oved (Heb.).

Keunen, Abraham. 1886 (1865). *An Historico-Critical Enquiry into the Origin and Composition of the Hexateuch*. London: Macmillan.

Kirkpatrick, Alexander F. 1898. *The Book of Psalms XLII–LXXXIX*. The Cambridge Bible for schools and colleges. Cambridge: University Press.

Kirkpatrick, Alexander F. 1903. *The Book of Psalms XC–CL*. The Cambridge Bible for schools and colleges. Cambridge: University Press.

Kislev, Itamar. 2011. "P, source or redaction: the evidence of Numbers 25." In *The Pentateuch: international perspectives on current research*, edited by Thomas B. Dozeman et al., 387–400. Tübingen: Mohr Siebeck.

Kislev, Itamar. 2017. "Joshua (and Caleb) in the Priestly Spies Story and Joshua's Initial Appearance in the Priestly Source: A Contribution to an Assessment of the Pentateuchal Priestly Material." *JBL* 136:39–55.

Klein, Daniel A. 2015. *Shadal on Exodus: Samuel David Luzzatto's interpretation of the Book of Shemot*. New York: Kodesh Press.

Knierim, Rolf P. and Coats, George W. 2005. *Numbers* (FOTL 5). Grand Rapids: W.B. Eerdmans.

Kratz, Reinhard G. 1994. "Der Dekalog im Exodusbuch." *VT* 44:205–238.

Kratz, Reinhard G. 2000. *Die Komposition der erzählenden Bücher des Alten Testaments*. Göttingen: Vandenhoeck & Ruprecht.

Kratz, Reinhard G. 2005. *The Composition of the Narrative Books of the Old Testament*. London: T. & T. Clark.

Kratz, Reinhard G. 2015. *The prophets of Israel*. inona Lake, Indiana: Eisenbrauns.

Kraus, Hans J. 1989 (1978). *Psalms 60–150*. Minneapolis: Augsburg Pub. House.

Krüger, Thomas. 2010. "Transformation of History in Ezekiel 20." In *Transforming Visions: Transformations of Text, Traditions and Theology in Ezekiel*, edited by William A. Tooman and Michael A. Lyons, 159–186. Oregon: Pickwick.

Kugler, Gili. 2006. *Leviticus 26: The Destiny of the People – Predetermined or to be Determined?* (MA Thesis). Jerusalem: The Hebrew University of Jerusalem (Heb.).

Kugler, Gili. 2013. "Present Affliction Affects the Representation of the Past: An Alternative Dating of the Levites' Prayer in Nehemiah 9," *VT* 63:605–626.

Kugler, Gili. 2014. "The Dual Role of Historiography in Psalm 106: Justifying the Present Distress and Demonstrating the Individual's Potential Contribution." *ZAW* 126:546–553.

Kugler, Gili. 2016. "The Threat of Annihilation of Israel in the Desert: An Independent Tradition within Two Stories", *CBQ* 78:632–647.

Kugler, Gili. 2017. "The Cruel Theology of Ezekiel 20." *ZAW* 129:47–58.

Kugler, Gili. 2017. "Who Conquered Hebron? – Apologetics and Polemical Tendencies in the Story of Caleb in Josh 14." *VT* 67:570–580.

Kugler, Gili. 2018. "Moses died and the people moved on: A hidden narrative in Deuteronomy." *JSOT* 43:191–204.

Kugler, Gili. Forthcoming. "Rescued from the sinful pattern of the ancestors – the role of David's kingship in the people's chronicle according to Psalm 78."

Kugler, Gili. Forthcoming. "Egypt without slavery: alternative traditions of Israel in Egypt in Ezekiel and other biblical accounts."

Kuhl, Curt. 1952. "Die Wiederaufnahme – Ein Literarkritisches Prinzip?", *ZAW* 64:1–11.

Leick, Gwendolyn. 1991. *A Dictionary of Ancient Near Eastern Mythology*. London: Routledge.

Lemaire, André. 2006. "New Aramaic Ostraca from Idumea and Their Historical Interpretation." In *Judah and the Judeans in the Persian Period*, edited by Oded Lipschits and Manfred Oeming,413–456. Winona Lake: Eisenbrauns.

Leonard, Jeffery M. 2006. *Historical Traditions in Psalm 78* (PhD dissertation). Brandeis University.

Leonard, Jeffery M. 2008. "Identifying Inner-Biblical Allusions: Psalm 78 as a Test Case." *JBL* 127:241–265.

Levin, Christoph. 1993. *Der Jahwist*. Orschungen zur Religion und Literatur des Alten und Neuen Testaments 157. Göttingen:Vandenhoeck & Ruprecht.

Levine, Baruch A. 1993. *Numbers 1–20* (AB 4). New York: Doubleday.

Levitt-Kohn, Risa. 2004. "'With a mighty hand and an outstretched arm': the prophet and the Torah in Ezekiel 20." In: *Ezekiel's Hierarchical World*, edited by Stephen L. Cook and Corrine L. Patton, 159–168. Leiden/Boston: Brill.

Levy, D. and Milgrom, Jacob. 1999 (1986). "עדה", *TDOT* 10, 468–480.

Lewy, Immanuel E. 1959. "The Story of the Golden Calf Reanalysed." VT 9:318–322.

Licht, Yaacov. 1991. Commentary on the book of Numbers. Jerusalem: Magnes (Heb.).

Loewenstamm, Samuel E. 1969. "The formula 'At that time' in the introductory speech of the book of Deuteronomy." *Tarbitz* 38:99–104 (Heb.).

Loewenstamm, Samuel E. 1973. "The Story of the Settlement Tradition of Gad and Reuven." *Tarbitz* 42:12–26 (Heb.).

Loewenstamm, Samuel E. 1992(a) (1958). "The Death of Moses." *From Babylon to Canaan*. 136–166. Jerusalem: Magnes.

Loewenstamm, Samuel E. 1992(b) (1965). *The Evolution of the Exodus Tradition*. Jerusalem: Magnes.

Lohfink, Norbert. 1963. *Das Haupgebot: Eine Untersuchung Literarischer Einleitungs-fragen zu Dtn 5–11* (Analecta Biblica 20). Roma: Pontificio istituto biblico.

Malbim (Rabbi Meir Leibush ben Yehiel Michel Wisser). 1891. *Mikra'i Kodesh: The Five Books of Moses (with Targum Onkelos, Rashi and the Sages and Ba'al Haturim) with commentary [in the name of the Torah and the Mitzvah] of Rabbi Meir Leibush Malbim*. Vilnius: Raam.

Mann, Thomas W. 1979. "Theological Reflections on the Denial of Moses." *JBL* 98:481–494.

Margaliot, Moshe. 1983. "The Transgression of Moses and Aaron – Num. 20:1–13." *JQR* 74:196–228.

Mayes, Andrew D.H. 1981. *Deuteronomy* (NCBC). Grand Rapids: Eerdmans; London: Marshall, Morgan & Sco.

McConville, Gordon J. 1986. "Ezra-Nehemiah and the Fulfilment of Prophecy." *VT* 36:205–224.

McEvenue, Sean E. 1971. *The Narrative Style of the Priestly Writer*. Rome: Biblical Institute Press.

McNeile, Alan H. 1911. *The book of Numbers*. Cambridge: Cambridge University press.

Milgrom, Jacob. 1983. "Magic, Monotheism, and the sin of Moses." In *The Quest for the Kingdom of God: Studies in Honor of George E. Mendenhal*, edited by Herbert B. Huffmon et al., 251–265. Winona Lake: Eisenbrauns.

Milgrom, Jacob. 1990. *Numbers*. The JPS Torah commentary. Philadelphia: Jewish Publication Society.

Milgrom, Jacob. 1991. *Leviticus 1–16* (AB 3). New York: Doubleday.

Milgrom, Jacob. 1999. "The Antiquity of the Priestly Source: A Reply to Joseph Blenkinsopp." *ZAW* 111:10–22.

Moberly, Walter R.L. 1983. *At the Mountain of God: Story and Theology of Exodus 32–34* (JSOTS 22). Sheffield: JSOT press.

Moore, George F. 1895. *Judges* (ICC). Edinburgh: T. & T. Clark.

Muffs, Yochanan. 1984. "Between judgment and compassion: Prophets' prayers", In *Torah Nidresheth: essays on fundamental questions in the Bible world*, edited by Moshe Greenberg, 39–87. Tel Aviv: Am Oved (Heb.).

Muffs. Yochanan. 2005. *The personhood of God: Biblical theology, human faith and the divine image*. Woodstock, Vt.: Jewish Lights Pub.

Myers, Jacob M. 1965. *Ezra, Nehemiah* (AB 14). Garden City: Doubleday.

Na'aman, Nadav. 2005. *Canaan in the Second Millennium B.C.E.* Winona Lake: Eisenbrauns.

Nelson, Richard D. 1997. *Joshua* (OTL). Louisville: Westminster John Knox Press.

Nelson, Richard D. 2002. *Deuteronomy* (OTL). Louisville: Westminster John Knox Press.

Nicholson, Ernest W. 2002. *The Pentateuch in the Twentieth Century: the legacy of Julius Wellhausen*. Oxford: Clarendon Press.

Niehr, Herbert. 1999 (1986). "נשיא", *TDOT* 10. Grand Rapids: William B. Eerdmans Pub. Co. 44–53.

Niesiołowski-Spanò, Łukasz. 2009. "The Broken Structure of the Moses Story: Or, Moses and the Jerusalem Temple." *SJOT* 23:23–37.

Noth, Martin. 1953. *Das Boch Joshua* (HAT 7). Tübingen: J.C. B. Mohr.

Noth, Martin. 1962 (1959). *Exodus* (OTL 2). London: SCM Press.

Noth, Martin. 1963 (1950). *Geschichte Israels*. Göttingen: Vandenhoeck & Ruprecht.

Noth, Martin. 1968 (1966). *Numbers* (OTL). London: SCM Press.

Noth, Marin. 1972 (1948). *A History of Pentateuchal Traditions*. Englewood Cliffs, N.J: Prentice-Hall.

Noth, Martin. 1981 (1957). *The Deuteronomistic history* (JSOTS 15). Sheffield: JSOT.

Osborne, Rusty. 2011. "Elements of Irony: History and Rhetoric in Ezekiel 20:1–44." *CTR* 9:3–15.

Oswald, Wolfgang. 2014. "Lawgiving at the Mountain of God (Exodus 19–24)." In *The Book of Exodus: Composition, Reception, and Interpretation*, edited by Thomas B. Dozeman et al., 169–192. Boston: Brill.

Paran, Meir. 1989. *Forms of the Priestly Style in the Pentateuch: Patterns, Linguistic Usages, Syntactic Structures*. Jerusalem: Magnes (Heb.).

Passaro, Angelo. 2006. "Theological Hermeneutics and Historical Motifs in Ps 105–106." In *History and Identity: How Israel's later Authors Viewed its Earlier History* (Deuterocanonical and Cognate Literature), edited by Nuria Calduch-Benages and Jan Liesen, 43–55. Berlin: W. de Gruyter.

Patton, Corrine L. 1996. "'I myself gave them laws that were not good': Ezekiel 20 and the exodus traditions." *JSOT* 69:85–89.

Preuss, Horst D. 1978 (1974–1975). "גלולים", *TDOT* 3, 1–5. Grand Rapids: William B. Eerdmans Pub. Co.

Propp, William H. 1988. "The Rod of Aaron and the Sin of Moses." *JBL* 107:19–26.

Propp, William H. 1999. *Exodus 1–18* (AB 2, vol. 1). New York: Doubleday.

Propp, William H. 2006. *Exodus 19–40* (AB 2, vol. 2). New York: Doubleday.

Pryke, Louise. 2016. "Religion and Humanity in Mesopotamian Myth and Epic." In *Oxford Research Encyclopedia of Religion*. 15 Oct. 2018. http://religion.oxfordre.com/view/10.1093/acrefore/9780199340378.001.0001/acrefore-9780199340378-e-247.

Quanbeck, Warren A. 1962. "Confession." in *The Interpreter's Dictionary of the Bible*, edited by George A. Buttrick, 667–668. Nashville: Abingdon Press.

Rawidowicz, Simon. 1948. "A nation is going and dying" (part of "To destruction or to resurrection.") *Metsuda* 5–6:134–148.

Rendsburg, Gary. 1991. "The Northern Origin of Nehemiah 9." *Biblica* 72:348–366.

Rendtorff, Rolf. 1990 (1977). *The Problem of the Process of Transmission in the Pentateuch*. Sheffield: JSOT Press.

Rendtorff, Rolf. 1997. "Nehemiah 9 – An Important Witness of Theological Reflection." In *Tehillah le-Moshe: Biblical and Judaic Studies in Honor of Moshe Greenberg*, edited by Mordechai Cogan et al. 111–117. Winona Lake: Eisenbrauns.

Richardson, Neil. H. 1987. "Psalm 106: Yahweh's Succoring Love Saves from the Death of a Broken Covenant." In *Love & death in the ancient Near East: essays in honor of Marvin H. Pope*, edited by John H. Marks and Robert M. Good, 191–203. Guilford: Four Quarters.

Rofe, Alexander. 1997. "Not exile but destruction to the people of Zedekiah – the message of Jeremiah 52 according to the Septuagint." In *A light for Jacob: Studies in the Bible and the Dead Sea Scrolls in Memory of Yaacov Licht*, edited by Yair Hoffman and Frank Polak, 180–184. Jerusalem: Mosad Bialik (Heb.).

Rofe, Alexander. 2006. Introduction to the literature of Hebrew Bible. Jerusalem: Carmel (Heb.).

Rofe, Alexander. 2014. "Redressing the Calamity in the Transmission of the Bible." *Tarbitz* 82:221–229 (Heb.).

Römer, Thomas. 2004. "Hauptprobleme der gegenwärtigen Pentateuchforschung." *TZ* 60:289–307.

Rom-Shiloni, Dalit. 2005. "Ezekiel as the Voice of the Exile and Constructor of Exilic Ideology." *HUCA* 76:1–45.

Rom-Shiloni, Dalit. 2006. "Socio-Ideological Setting or *Settings* for Penitential Prayer?" In *Seeking the Favor of God: The Origins of Penitential Prayer in Second Temple Judaism*, edited by Mark J. Boda et al. (vol. 1), 51–68. Atlanta: Society of Biblical Literature.

Rom-Shiloni, Dalit. 2009(a). *God in Times of Destruction and Exiles: Tanakh Theology*. Jerusalem: Magnes (Heb.).

Rom-Shiloni, Dalit. 2009(b). "Group-Identities in Jeremiah: is it the Persian period conflict?" In *A Palimpsest: Rhetoric, Stylistics, and Language in Biblical Texts from the Persian and Hellenistic Periods*, edited by Ehud Ben Zvi at al., 11–46. Piscataway: Gorgias.

Rooker, Mark F. 1990. *Biblical Hebrew in Transition – The Language of the Book of Ezekiel* (JSOTS 90). Sheffield: JSOT Press.

Rosenbaum, Morris and Silbermann, Abraham M. 1930. *Pentateuch with Targum Onkelos, Haphtaroth and Rashi's Commentary*. London: Shapiro, Vallentine & co.

Rudolph, Wilhelm. 1949. *Esra und Nehemia* (HAT 20). Tübingen: J. C. B. Mohr P. Siebeck.

Sakenfeld, Katharine D. 1975. "The Problem of Divine Forgiveness in Numbers 14." *CBQ* 37:317–330.

Sakenfeld, Katharine D. 1985. *Faithfulness in Action: Loyalty in Biblical Perspective*, Philadelphia: Fortress Press.

Schart, Aaron. 2013. "The spy story and the final redaction of the Hexateuch." In *Torah and the Book of Numbers*. Edited by Christian Frevel et al. Tübingen: Mohr Siebeck, 164–200.

Schmid, Konrad. 2006. "The so-called Yahwist and the Literary Gap between Genesis and Exodus." In *A Farewell to the Yahwist? The Composition of the Pentateuch in Recent European Interpretation*, edited by Thomas B. Dozeman and Konrad Schmid, 29–50. Leiden: Brill.

Schuller, Eileen. 1996. "Confession." In *Dictionary of Judaism in the Biblical Period*, edited by Jacob Neusner and William S. Green (vol. 1), 129–130. New York: Macmillan Library Reference.

Schuller, Eileen. 2007. "Penitential Prayer in Second Temple Judaism: A Research Survey." In *Seeking the Favor of God: The Origins of Penitential Prayer in Second Temple Judaism*, edited by Mark J. Boda et al. (vol. 2), 1–16. Atlanta: Society of Biblical Literature.

Schwartz, Baruch, J. 1996. "The Priestly Account of the Theophany and Lawgiving at Sinai." In *Temples, Texts and Traditions: A Tribute to Menahem Haran*, edited by Michael V. Fox et al., 103–134. Winona Lake: Eisenbrauns.

Schwartz, Baruch, J. 2000(a). "The question of the commandments validity: 'the basic norm' in the Torah traditions." *Annual of the Institution for Research in Jewish Law* 20:241–265 (Heb.).

Schwartz, Baruch, J. 2000(b). "Ezekiel's dim view of Israel's restoration." In *The Book of Ezekiel: Theological and Anthropological Perspectives*, edited by Margaret S. Odell and John T. Strong, 43–67. Atlanta: Society of Biblical Literature.

Schwartz, Baruch, J. 2008. "The ultimate aim of Israel's restoration in Ezekiel." *Birkat Shalom: Studies in the Bible, ancient Near Eastern literature, and postbiblical Judaism presented to Shalom M. Paul on the occasion of his seventieth birthday* (vol. 1), edited by Chaim Choen, 305–319. Winona Lake: Eisenbrauns.

Schwemer, Daniel. 2007. "The Storm-Gods of the Ancient Near East: Summary, Synthesis, Recent Studies – Part 1." *Journal of Ancient Near Eastern Religions* 7:121–168.

Seebass, Horst. 1962. *Mose und Aaron, Sinai und Gottesberg*. Bonn: H. Bouvier.

Seebass, Horst. 1995. *Numeri*. Biblischer Kommentar; Altes Testament 4/1. Neukirchen-Vluyn: Neukirchener Verlag.

Shalom-Guy, Hava. 1996. "The description of Jeroboam's reform and the Golden Calf episode." *An Annual for Biblical and Ancient Near Eastern Studies* 16:15–27 (Heb.).

Shenan, Avigdor. 1979. "The sin of Nadab and Abihu in the Sages' *Aggada*." *Tarbitz* 48:201–214 (Heb.).

Shiloah, Moshe. 1964. "And he said... And he said." *Korngreen Book*, edited by Asher Weiser and Ben-Zion Luria, 251–267. Tel Aviv: The Bible Research Society (Heb.).

Ska, Jean L. 2006. *Introduction to Reading the Pentateuch*. Indiana: Eisenbrauns.

Skehan, Patrick. 1955. "Exodus in the Samaritan Recension from Qumran." *JBL* 74:182–187.

Sommer, Benjamin D. 1998. *A Prophet reads scripture: Allusion in Isaiah 40–66*. Stanford: Stanford University Press.

Sommer, Benjamin D. 2000. "Translation as commentary: the case of the Septuagint to Exodus 32–33." *Textus* 20:43–60.

Sommer, Benjamin D. 2004. "Inner-biblical Interpretation." In: *The Jewish Study Bible*, edited by Adele Berlin and M.Z Brettler, 1829–1835. New York: Oxford University Press.

Sommer, Benjamin D. 2011. "Dating Pentateuchal Texts and the Perils of Pseudo-Historicism." In *The Pentateuch: international perspectives on current research*, edited by Thomas B. Dozeman et al., 85–108. Tübingen: Mohr Siebeck.

Strickman, Norman H. and Silver, Arthur M. 1996. *Ibn Ezra's Commentary on the Pentateuch: Exodus*. New York: Menorah Pub. Company.

Strickman, Norman H. and Silver, Arthur M. 2001. *Ibn Ezra's Commentary on the Pentateuch: Deuteronomy*. New York: Menorah Pub. Company.

Tadmor, Haim. 1999. "The Appointed Time Has Not Yet Arrived: The Historical Background of Haggai 1:2." In *Ki Baruch Hu: Ancient Near Eastern Biblical Studies in Honor of Baruch A. Levin*, edited by Robert Chazan at al., 401–408. Winona Lake: Eisenbrauns.

Tadmor, Haim. 2006. *Assyria, Babylonia and Judah: studies in the history of the ancient Near East*. Jerusalem: Mosad Bialik (Heb.).

Talmon, Shemaryahu. 1987. "Ezra and Nehemiah." In *The Literary Guide to the Bible*, edited by Robert Alter and Frank Kermode, 357–364. London: Fontana.

Tate, Marvin E. 1990. *Psalms 51–100* (WBC 20). Dallas: Word Books.

Torrey, Charles C. 1896. *The Composition and Historical Value of Ezra-Nehemiah*, BZAW 2. Giessen: J. Ricker.

Torrey, Charles C. 1930. *Pseudo-Ezekiel and the original prophecy*. New Haven: Yale University Press; London: H. Milford, Oxford university press.

Tov, Emanuel. 1985. "The Nature and Background of Harmonizations in Biblical Manuscripts." *JSOT* 31:3–29.

Tweig, Arie. 1977. *Matan Torah at Sinai: The traditions on the giving of the Torah at Sinai, their formation in Exodus 19–24 and their Evolution in the Pentateuch.* Jerusalem: Magnes (Heb.).

Van der Horst, Pieter W. 1994. "'I Gave them Laws that were not Good': Ezekiel 20:25 in Ancient Judaism and Early Christianity." In *Hellenism – Judaism – Christianity: Essays on their Interaction*, edited by Pieter W. van der Horst, 122–145. Kampen: Kok Pharos.

Van der Lingen, Anton. 1992. "BW'-YŞ ("To Go out and to Come in") as a Military Term." *VT* 42:59–66.

Van Seters, John. 1994. *The Life of Moses: The Yahwist as Historian in Exodus-Numbers.* Philadelphia: Westminster/John Knox.

Van Seters, John. 1999. *The Pentateuch: a social-science commentary.* Sheffield: Sheffield Academic Press.

Vervenne, Marc. 1994. "The Question of 'Deuteronomic' Elements in Genesis to Numbers." In *Studies in Deuteronomy*, edited by García F. Martinez et al., 243–268. Leiden: E.J. Brill.

Von Rad, Gerhard. 1966(a) (1948). *Deuteronomy* (OTL 5). London: S.C.M. Press.

Von Rad, Gerhard. 1966(b) (1958). *The problem of the Hexateuch and other essays.* New York: McGraw-Hil.

Wagner, Thomas. 2014. "Recounting מני־קדם חידות in Psalm 78: what are the 'riddles' about?." *JHS* 14:1–21.

Wazana, Nili. 2011. "Joshua." In *The Oxford Encyclopedia of the Books of the Bible* (vol. 1), edited by Michael D. Coogan, 485–500. New York: Oxford University Press.

Wazana, Nili. 2013. *All the boundaries of the land: the Promised Land in biblical thought in light of the ancient Near East.* Winona Lake: Eisenbrauns.

Weinfeld, Moshe. 1972. *Deuteronomy* and the Deuteronomic school. Oxford: Clarendon Press.

Weinfeld, Moshe. 1991. *Deuteronomy 1–11* (AB 5). New York: Doubleday.

Weinfeld, Moshe. 1992. *From Joshua to Josiah.* Jerusalem: Magnes (Heb.).

Weinfeld, Moshe. 1995 (1982–1984). "כבוד Kabod." *TDOT* 7:22–38. Grand Rapids: William B. Eerdmans Pub. Co.

Weinfeld, Moshe. 2004. *Early Jewish liturgy: from Psalms to the prayers in Qumran and Rabbinic literature.* Jerusalem: Magnes (Heb.).

Weiser, Artur. 1962 (1959). *The Psalms.* London: SCM Press.

Welch, A. C. 1929. "The Source of Nehemiah IX." *ZAW* 47:130–137.

Wellhausen, Julius. 1886. *Prolegomena zur Geschichte Israels.* Berlin: G. Reimer.

Wellhausen, Julius. 1899 (3rd edition). *Die Composition des Hexateuchs und der historichen Bücher des Alten Testaments.* Berlin: G. Reimer.

Wenham, Gordon J. 1981. *Numbers: An Introduction and Commentary.* Leicester: Inter-Varsity Press.

Wenham, Gordon J. 1997. *Numbers.* Sheffield: Sheffield Academic Press.

Werline, Rodeny A. 1998. *Penitential Prayer in Second Temple Judaism: The Development of a Religious Institution.* Atlanta: Scholars Press.

Wevers, John W. 1969. *Ezekiel* (The Century Bible New Series). London: Nelson.

Wevers, John W. 1990. *Notes on the Greek Text of Exodus.* Atlanta: Scholars Press.

Widmer, Michael. 2004. *Moses, God and the Dynamics of Intercessory Prayer: A Study of Exodus 32–34 and Numbers 13–14.* Forschungen zum Alten Testament 2. Reihe; 8. Tübingen: Mohr Siebeck.

Williamson, Hugh G.M. 1985(a). *Ezra, Nehemiah* (WBC 16). Waco: Word Books.

Williamson, Hugh G.M. 1985(b). "Structure and Historiography in Nehemiah." *Proceeding of the Ninth World Congress of Jewish Studies* 9:117–131.

Williamson, Hugh G.M. 2004. *Studies in Persian Period History and Historiography* (FAT 38). Tübingen: Mohr Siebeck.

Williamson, Hugh G.M. 2007. "The Torah and history in presentations of restoration in Ezra-Nehemiah." In *Reading the Law*, edited by Gordon J. McConville and Karl Möller, 156–170 (JSOTS 461). New York: T. & T. Clark.

Witte, Markus. 2006. "From Exodus to David – Historiography in Psalm 78." In: *History and Identity: How Israel's later Authors Viewed its Earlier History*, edited by Nuria Calduch-Benages and Jan Liesen, 21–42. Berlin: W. de Gruyter.

Woudstra, Marten H. 1981. *The Book of Joshua* (NICOT). Grand Rapids: W.B. Eerdmans.

Wright, Jacob L. 2014. *David, King of Israel and Caleb in Biblical Memory*. New York: Cambridge University press.

Zakovitch, Yair. 1978. *The pattern of the numerical sequence three-four in the Bible* (PhD dissertation). Jerusalem: The Hebrew University of Jerusalem (Heb.).

Zakovitch, Yair. 1991. *"AND YOU SHALL TELL YOUR SON"*: The Concept of the Exodus in the Bible. Jerusalem: Magnes.

Zakovitch, Yair. 1992. *An introduction to inner-biblical exegesis*. Eben Yehudah: Reches (Heb.).

Zakovitch, Yair. 1997. "Psalm 78: sources, structure, meaning and tendency." In *David, king of Israel, lives and endures?*, edited by Yair Zakovitch at al., 117–194. Jerusalem: Simmor 1997 (Heb.).

Zakovitch 1991 is a book. The quotation is a verse cited in the title. Is there a way to clarify it?

Zakovitch, Yair. 2003. "From Secular to Sacred and Sacred to Secular." In *Borders of Sanctit*, Edited by Emily Bilski and Avigdor Shinan, 56–68. Jerusalem: Keter (Heb.).

Zakovitch, Yair. 2008. *Tongs made with tongs: between an intra-biblical Midrash and an external-biblical Midrash*. Tel Aviv: Am-Oved (Heb.).

Zimmerli, Walther. 1950. "Das zweite Gebot." In *Festschrift für Alfred Bertholet*, edited by Walter Baumgarten, 550–563. Tübingen: J. C. B. Mohr.

Zimmerli, Walther. 1979 (1969). *Ezechiel 1–24* (Hermeneia). Philadelphia: Fortress Press.

Subject index

https://doi.org/10.1515/9783110609905-012

Ancient sources index

Hebrew Bible

Genesis

Post-Biblical literature

Author index